Crossroads: Performance Studies and Irish Culture

Crossroads: Performance Studies and Irish Culture

Edited by Sara Brady and Fintan Walsh

First published in hardback 2009
Published in paperback 2014 by
PALGRAVE MACMILLAN

Palgrave Macmillan in the UK is an imprint of Macmillan Publishers Limited,
registered in England, company number 785998, of Houndmills, Basingstoke,
Hampshire RG21 6XS.

Palgrave Macmillan in the US is a division of St Martin's Press LLC,
175 Fifth Avenue, New York, NY 10010.

Palgrave Macmillan is the global academic imprint of the above companies
and has companies and representatives throughout the world.

Palgrave® and Macmillan® are registered trademarks in the United States,
the United Kingdom, Europe and other countries

ISBN 978-0-230-21998-4   hardback
ISBN 978-1-137-42571-3   paperback

This book is printed on paper suitable for recycling and made from fully
managed and sustained forest sources. Logging, pulping and manufacturing
processes are expected to conform to the environmental regulations of the
country of origin.

A catalogue record for this book is available from the British Library.

A catalog record for this book is available from the Library of Congress.

Contents

List of Figures

Preface to the Paperback Edition: Roots and Routes

When this book was first published in 2009, we were just beginning to register the global financial collapse that was beginning to take place at the time, the implosion of the Irish economy, and its numerous social, cultural, and political side-effects. Although many of the essays gathered here are keenly aware of the sharp distinction between lived experience and national ambition, reading these analyses now packs a different kind of punch. Not only have many of the fault lines traced in these chapters expanded and deepened, but we find ourselves grappling with a different set of circumstances too. No longer just dealing with the pressures of conforming to certain cultural roles and expectations, as so many of the essays astutely bring to light, we are now confronted by the challenge of finding ourselves with few certainties at all.

Performance is the object of study we foreground to think about the many enactments of Irish culture, from sites as diverse as Gaelic games, beauty pageants, and pilgrimage to protest, live art, and contemporary theatre. While these remain rich contexts for the study of Irish culture, we hope that this new paperback edition might prompt further reflection on other sites of inquiry too.

Instead of introducing new case studies, with this preface we take the opportunity to encourage reflection on how performance studies might help us understand not only dynamic processes of cultural production, but also those of its deceleration or unravelling. We question how the study of performance might allow us to consider the various ways in which Ireland's sullied reputation (notably as a result of economic mismanagement and the exposure of Church/State institutional abuse) has altered how the country and its cultural practices and products are received and perceived, processed and performed abroad. We wonder how those prevalent affects of shame, anger and fear performatively circulate, and how they are policed or relieved. We query how the past might be appropriately marked through performance modes as we look to the future. We ask how performance might assist us in formulating and interpreting new modes of sociality, culture, civic participation and political engagement. We find ourselves newly faced with these issues and questions, and we hope that readers and researchers will be provoked to pursue them further.

Since this volume was first published, the term 'Irish performance studies' has developed currency and importance. We have witnessed an increased interest in the subject, not only evidenced by a swell of scholarly publication, but by its enthusiastic academic study in universities across the world, including our own departments. As Ireland turns to face yet another direction, we hope that this book will remain a useful companion, and contribute to conversations along the way.

Fintan and Sara
December 2013

Acknowledgements

This book would not have been possible without the generosity, talent, and hard work of many people. First and foremost, we are grateful to all of our contributors for their diligence and patience throughout the editing process. Thanks to all our colleagues at the Department of Drama, Trinity College, Dublin, and to those mentors whose teaching and research led us in various ways to develop this project. We are sincerely grateful to Christabel Scaife, Paula Kennedy, and Steven Hall at Palgrave Macmillan. Thanks also to those who have allowed us to reproduce material in the book, in particular Bisi Adigun, Amanda Coogan, Willie Doherty, Alastair MacLennan, and the Hugh Lane Gallery. Finally, thanks to our friends and families. In particular, Sara would like to thank Kevin Wilson for his tireless support, Mary Brady for stepping in just when her help was needed most, and Finn Brady-Wilson for arriving just in time. Fintan would like to thank Aileen, Áine, Brian, David, and Laurence with whom so many ventures begin, and Jack for an especially memorable one.

Notes on the Contributors

Sara Brady is Lecturer in Drama Studies at Trinity College Dublin. She is former Managing Editor of *TDR: The Drama Review* and founding editor of the interdisciplinary Irish studies journal *Foilsiú*. Her writing has appeared in *American Theatre* magazine, *TDR*, *New York Irish History*, and *New Hibernia Review*.

Matthew Causey is Senior Lecturer and Director of Postgraduate Teaching and Learning in the School of Drama, Film, and Music at Trinity College Dublin. He is the author of *Theatre and Performance in Digital Culture: From Simulation to Embeddedness* (Routledge 2006).

David Cregan is Assistant Professor of Theatre at Villanova University where he also teaches in the Irish Studies Program. He received his PhD from Trinity College Dublin. His articles have appeared in *Modern Drama*, the *Australasian Journal of Dramatic Studies,* and *New Voices in Irish Studies*.

Emily Mark-FitzGerald is Lecturer in the School of Art History and Cultural Policy at University College Dublin. Her PhD thesis (2007) involved the first large-scale documentation and analysis of commemorative monuments erected to the Famine since 1990 in Ireland, Northern Ireland, the UK, Canada, Australia, and the US.

Holly Maples is Lecturer in Drama at the University of East Anglia. Her research interests are collective memory and commemoration, contemporary Irish theatre, and performance studies. She is also a professional actress and director and has performed in theatre and film in Ireland, the UK, and the United States.

Charlotte McIvor is a PhD student in performance studies at the University of California, Berkeley, where she received the 2007 Mark S. Goodson Prize for Distinguished Theatre Talent. Her research focuses on Irish and Bengali modern drama and their colonial contexts as well as transnational and gendered contexts of production.

J'aime Morrison is a performer and scholar whose work focuses on the intersections between Irish studies, performance studies, and dance history. Her research has been published in *Film Ireland, Eire/Ireland, Yale Journal of Criticism*, and *Inbhear*. She is currently Head of Performance at California State University, Northridge.

Gabriella Calchi Novati is a PhD candidate in Drama at Trinity College Dublin. Her dissertation investigates 'public intimacy' in the works of the Italian company Teatro del Lemming and the French conceptual artist Sophie Calle. Her article 'Language Under Attack: The Iconoclastic Theatre of Societas Raffaello Sanzio' is forthcoming in *Theatre Research International*.

Anne Pulju conducts research in Irish theatre, performance, and politics, with interests ranging from community performance to the relationship between postcolonialism and modernism in the culture of the Irish Free State. She received a PhD from Northwestern University's Interdisciplinary Program in Theatre and Drama in 2007.

E. Moore Quinn is Associate Professor of Anthropology at the College of Charleston. She has written on the oral traditions and verbal art of the Higaonon of the Philippines, the Gullah/Geechee of South Carolina, the Irish in both the Republic of Ireland and Northern Ireland, and Irish Americans.

Jack Santino has been President of the American Folklore Society (2001–2002) and Editor of the *Journal of American Folklore* (1996–2000). His two most recent books are *Spontaneous Shrines and the Public Memorialization of Death*, an edited volume (2006), and *Signs of War and Peace: Social Conflict and the Uses of Symbols in Public in Northern Ireland* (2000).

Matthew Spangler is Assistant Professor of Performance Studies in the Department of Communication Studies at San José State University. His articles on Irish and performance studies have appeared in the *James Joyce Quarterly*, *New Hibernia Review*, *Siar*, the *South Atlantic Review*, *Theatre Journal*, and *Text and Performance Quarterly*.

Scott Spencer is a PhD candidate in Ethnomusicology at New York University. His dissertation investigates the changing lines of transmission in the recent revival of Irish uilleann bagpiping. His work has appeared in the *Journal of Media Ecology* and conference proceedings published by the University of South Carolina Press.

Bernadette Sweeney lectures in drama and theatre studies at University College Cork. She is the author of *Performing the Body in Irish Theatre* published by Palgrave Macmillan in 2008. She is currently editing a collection on Tom Mac Intyre for Carysfort Press with Marie Kelly.

Carmen Szabó is Lecturer in Drama and Theatre Studies at University College Dublin. Her current research focuses on performance studies, science, technology, and applied mathematics in the theatre. She serves on the History and Philosophy of Science committee at University College Dublin.

Fintan Walsh is a graduate of Samuel Beckett Centre, Trinity College Dublin where he also teaches. His research interests include Irish studies, performance studies, and queer theory. He is a critic for *Irish Theatre Magazine* and his writing on performance has appeared in *Contemporary Theatre Review* and *Irish Theatre International*. He is co-editor of this collection.

Eric Weitz is Lecturer in Theatre Studies at Trinity College Dublin. He edited and contributed to *The Power of Laughter: Comedy and Contemporary Irish Theatre* (2004).

Mike Wilson is Professor of Drama and Co-Director of the George Ewart Evans Centre for Storytelling at the University of Glamorgan in Wales. Formerly a professional storyteller and community theater worker, he has published widely on storytelling and popular theatre. His latest book is *Storytelling and Theatre* (2006).

Introduction: Performance Studies and Irish Culture

Fintan Walsh with Sara Brady

That Ireland we dreamed of would be joyous … with the laughter of comely maidens dancing at the crossroads.

Eamon de Valera, reputed address 1943[1]

This crossroads, where foreign cultures, unfamiliar discourses and the myriad artistic effects of estrangement are jumbled together, is hard to define but it could assert itself, in years to come, as that of a theatre of culture(s).

Patrice Pavice[2]

Our radical move is to turn, and return, insistently, to the crossroads.

Dwight Conquergood[3]

I

In the expansive and expanding field of Irish studies, performance has typically featured as drama, theater, dance, and music. Recent changes in Irish society, the arts industry, and modes of critical inquiry have all prompted the need to think further about the complex and under-researched area of performance in and of Irish culture. It is increasingly well recognized that the categories of 'Irish culture' and 'Irishness' are highly performative, effected through a multitude of social practices, cultural formations, and discursive utterances, and in timely need of critical address.

The purpose of this collection of essays is to broach this task by considering Irish culture through some of the methodologies offered by performance studies. In this, we appeal to performance studies'

1

paradigmatic way of thinking about performance as culture in action, while also deploying its vocabularies to analyze a range of specific performance practices and performative subjects. As the title of this book makes clear, we return to the evocative metaphor of crossroads. We do so not simply to recount the historical practice of dancing as other studies have done,[4] or to question the veracity of the statement attributed to Eamon de Valera (a statement now known to be misreported, although significantly resonant within popular cultural memory), but by way of signaling the manifold ways in which Irish culture has been performed in past, present, and likely future tenses at local, national, and international domains. These roads do not respect the static symmetry indexed by a figural cross; rather, the trajectories mapped here are suggestive, multiple, and mobile. Practices, epistemologies, temporalities, geographies, and identities splinter in their wake, clearing the ground for the emergence of nuanced understandings of performance and cultural politics.

In addition to signposting alternative critical directions of interest to Irish studies, *Crossroads* embraces the phenomenological value of being between states that is of special interest to performance studies. We encourage readers and culture-makers to feel the queer disorientation of being at crossroads,[5] of taking up unmarked roads with no predetermined direction or obvious destination as they encounter this collection, if only to think about their own areas of disciplinary interest and points of worldly engagement with renewed intensity. Indeed, it is from the editors' individual experiences of methodological, intellectual, and affective reeling at this disciplinary juncture that this book emerges. In more ways than one, *Crossroads* is the product of strained inquiry along borderlines. But beyond disorientation's initial confusion, the book also embraces the friction, tension, and risk inherent in the process of crossing, where established routes are disturbed as new paths appear and invite us on journeys to unknown territories that might lead to nowhere in particular (as perhaps all anti-teleological trips should), but open up new vistas and horizons of understanding.

II

Drawing on a range of approaches to history, anthropology, sociology, ethnography, psychoanalysis, gender, sexuality, and critical race theory, performance studies is already a well-established interdisciplinary field which accounts for such varied expressive forms as live performance, photography, ritual, play, spectacle, politics, geography, landscape, and architecture among its objects of study. Given this breadth of interest, it is perhaps no surprise that the paradigm has been accused of sacrificing creativity, criticism, and activism in the service of generalization and abstraction. As in the work of Dwight Conquergood, however, where the triangulation of artistic accomplishment, critical analysis, and political articulation is celebrated, we emphasize performance studies' braided and stratified ways of 'knowing': 'This epistemological connection between creativity, critique, and civic engagement is mutually replenishing, and pedagogically powerful.'[6] Far from being evasive or lofty, the book appeals to a performance studies methodology in a bid to unearth what Michel Foucault referred to as those 'subjugated knowledges'[7] either ignored or rendered invisible by more established modes of disciplinary organization, analysis, and documentation. To this end, we have made every effort to include essays that draw attention to 'embodied, tacit, intoned, gestured, improvised, coexperienced, covert' aspects of Irish culture, while implicitly (in so far as a book allows) challenging the hegemony of the word.[8]

While it remains true that much scholarship in the field of Irish studies has focused on issues of language, textuality, and narrativity, these disciplinary boundaries are increasingly being permeated, eroded, and cross-fertilized. In Ireland, many of the earliest calls to engage critically with performance came from individuals affiliated with drama and theater studies, sensitive to developments in the independent theater sector throughout the 1990s. Writing in 1996, for example, Anna McMullan linked the elevation of the word and the suppression of performance to Ireland's colonial history, while also discerning that 'performance is making a comeback.'[9] Focusing specifically on theater, McMullan observed the emergence of practices that foregrounded 'the visual, kinesic and the corporeal as major means of expression and signification,'[10] while urging that these modes of expression be given due critical attention. Other voices followed, with publications such as *Theatre Stuff: Critical Essays on Contemporary Irish Theatre* (edited by Eamonn Jordan, 2000), *Theatre Talk: Voices of Irish Theatre Practitioners* (edited by Lilian Chambers, Ger Fitzgibbon, and Eamonn Jordan, 2001), and *Druids, Dudes, and Beauty Queens* (edited by Dermot Bolger, 2001) steering attention away from the dramatic text alone to centralize performance practice as an area in need of academic attention.

The mounting international interest in Irish performance was foregrounded when the *Australasian Drama Studies* journal published a special issue entitled *Performing Ireland* in 2003 in which editors Anna McMullan and Brian Singleton emphasized that Irish identity and Irishness should be understood as 'historically constructed roles to be played or wrestled with.'[11] In a similar spirit, *Modern Drama* dedicated a volume to *Irish Theatre: Conditions of Criticism* in 2004. While the journal focused on theater in particular, editors Karen Fricker and Brian Singleton emphasized a heightened interest in theater as performance rather than drama, while maintaining that 'it is artificial and unhelpful to assert a divide between critical and cultural practice. Cultural practice is itself critical.'[12] Following on, the editors of this collection believe that performance studies is particularly well equipped to challenge such distinctions by considering performance not only as something that happens in theater spaces, but as the life of culture in action.

In that we, the editors of *Crossroads*, are both currently affiliated with a drama department in Ireland, and presume that many of our readers will share a similar combination of disciplinary if not geographic attachment, it is worth mentioning how a number of recent academic studies have been particularly successful in reinvigorating the analysis of Irish drama, theater, and cultural politics by thinking through a performance studies prism. Addressing a complex dynamic of social process, Joan FitzPatrick Dean's *Riot and Great Anger: Twentieth Century Stage Censorship in Ireland* (2004) illuminates links between the staging of Ireland throughout the twentieth century and upheavals on the wings and in the streets. To similar effect, Paige Reynolds' *Modernism, Drama, and the Audience of Irish Spectacle* (2007) reconstructs and critiques five large-scale public 'events' in the early twentieth century, in a manner that emphasizes the performative tenor to the occasions: the *Playboy* riots in 1907; the events of Dublin Suffrage Week in 1913; the funeral processions of Terence MacSwiney in 1920; the Tailteann Games in 1924; and the organized protests accompanying the premiere of Seán O'Casey's *The Plough and the Stars* in 1926. Recently, *Performing the Body in Irish Theatre* (2008) by Bernadette Sweeney (who also contributes a chapter to this volume) interprets contemporary Irish theater history (1980–) through a performance-conscious lens, mapping connections between embodiment, theatrical form, and cultural politics. Collectively, though not exclusively, these studies have drawn the disciplines of performance and Irish studies into closer, productive proximity.

While theater-as-performance gained more attention in Ireland from the mid- to late 1990s, in the United States, where performance studies departments developed from the 1980s onwards, the parameters of study were more broadly defined. With a background in folklore and ethnography, Jack Santino's (who contributes a chapter to this study) research on the performative dimensions to Irish custom, festival culture, and memorialization in books such as *The Hallowed Eve: Dimensions of Culture in a Calendar Festival in Northern Ireland* (1998), *Signs of War and Peace: Social Conflict and the Uses of Symbols in Public in Northern Ireland* (2004), and *Spontaneous Shrines and the Public Memorialization of Death* (2006) has been especially influential for linking performance and Irish studies. Similarly, John P. Harrington and Elizabeth J. Mitchell's edited volume *Politics and Performance in Contemporary Northern Ireland* (1999) examines performance and the performative power of culture by thinking through notions of policing, governmentality, music, and theater. Finally, two recent collections consider how Irishness is performed in contemporary popular culture, given postmodern representation's tendency to play endlessly, and often irreverently, with signification: *Irish Postmodernisms and Popular Culture* (Palgrave Macmillan, 2007), edited by Wanda Balzano, Anne Mulhall and Moynagh Sullivan, and *The Irish in US: Irishness, Performativity and Popular Culture* (Duke University Press, 2006), edited by Diane Negra.

III

Crossroads attempts to dialogue with these studies and promote further exploration into the performative aspects of Irish culture. To that end, we have divided the chapters into five parts, organized according to key areas of interest. Works included in Part I: Tradition, Ritual and Play emphasize the performativity of Irish culture by focusing on ancient folkloric practices and communicative gestures. Jack Santino opens by surveying a range of traditional performative acts to suggest that a performance-centered approach to Irish culture asks us to consider certain ethnographic questions about a variety of events, the answers to which are not normally made available by established approaches. Deploying folkloristic and anthropological methodologies that differ substantially from dominant models of Irish cultural criticism, Santino centralizes observations and conversations in his commentary.

Bernadette Sweeney considers how folk rituals such as mumming and keening, in addition to the activities of Strawboys and Wrenboys, have been invoked in contemporary Irish theater productions. While these practices have been long ignored by established scholarship, Sweeney reveals how a number of staged performances have worked to recuperate these traditions.

In her analysis of the Gaelic games, Sara Brady outlines the crucial role sport played in Irish nation-making and argues for the potential of such performative acts to continue to redefine and reimagine twenty-first-century Irish identities. Mike Wilson's essay analyzes the relationship between orality and performance in the figure of the story-teller. Reading the playful personae of Jack Lynch against the theoretical writings of Walter Benjamin, Wilson considers how the storyteller manages to subvert national stereotypes, in particular the figure of the stage Irishman.

Finally, with an ear to music, and an eye on formal and informal performance settings, Scott Spencer explores how traditional Irish music negotiates concepts of authenticity and tradition in a postmodern, technological age.

The place of performance and the performance of place concerns authors in Part II: Place, Landscape, and Commemoration. J'aime Morrison takes up the book's leading metaphor and, working with a performative writing style, considers roads as material and conceptual paths of movement and memory in Irish culture. With reference to a wide repertoire of cultural practices, visual depictions, and textual configurations, Morrison challenges the perception of roads as merely static cultural tracts, to posit them 'as conduits for movement and memory operating within the larger spatial history of Ireland and in conjunction with a repertoire of cultural practices.'

Emily Mark-FitzGerald's study of commemorations of the Great Famine examines the way in which the construction of monuments is a deeply performative act which brings the commemorative object into being while inviting modes of physical recognition, such as witnessing and walking, that give the original event significance and sustain its memory. In the course of her essay, FitzGerald seeks to reveal how these 'monumental performances of memory betray conflicting views on what the memory of Famine means in contemporary Ireland, what value the past holds in a post-poverty and newly globalized society, and how political instrumentalization has structured the manner in which such projects have been conceived.'

Matthew Spangler sheds light on the relationship between trauma, heritage, and tourism in his investigation of Free Derry Corner, arguing that the theatricality of commemoration, sacralization, and public display creates highly visible performances of identity and memory.

Drawing on the ritual studies of Edith and Victor Turner, David Cregan looks to Saint Patrick's Purgatory, an archaic site of worship at Lough Derg, Co. Donegal, to consider how many Irish people, despite having turned away from organized religion, continue to perform 'sacred desire' through the arduous bodily work of pilgrimage.

Part III: Political Performances concerns highly charged political moments in historical and contemporary periods. Anne Pulju revisits events surrounding de Valera's signing of the Oath of Allegiance in 1927. Drawing on J. L. Austin's notion of 'unhappy' or 'infelicitous' performatives, Pulju argues that 'de Valera's words and actions on this occasion can be understood within the context of performance studies as an attempt to ensure that his encounter with the Oath was not seen as a binding performative statement or gesture.' Interpreted in this way, Pulju exposes how the Fianna Fáil leader subverted his ostensible commitment to the Crown.

Carmen Szabó discusses the symbolic importance of space to Northern Irish culture and evaluates the achievement of Alastair MacLennan's actuations and installations in the negotiation of memory, history and place.

Matthew Causey offers a unique analysis of three 'unsettling performances of Irishness' – the 2006 Love Ulster march, which ended in violence in city center Dublin; the Beckett centenary events held throughout 2006; and the 2004 citizenship referendum. Drawing on the philosophy of Giorgio Agamben, Causey traces a shift in Irish culture toward biopolitical systems of control.

Contributors to Part IV: Gender, Feminism, and Queer Performance probe the relationship between performance and identity politics. Charlotte McIvor traces the fatal burning of the suspected witch Bridgie Cleary in 1895 through the event's contemporary representation in literature, television, and theater. McIvor interprets the multiple revisions of Cleary's murder as enactments that highlight the shifting concerns of Irish culture: 'The retellings of the story of Bridget Cleary should not be understood merely as attempts to set the record straight about her life and death, but also occasions to perform constantly revised versions of Ireland's own history at the *fin-de-siècle* through her shadowy figure.' Ultimately, McIvor argues that Tom Mac Intyre's *What Happened Bridgie Cleary* restores voice, corporeality, and agency to the ghostly figure.

In her chapter on Amanda Coogan, Gabriella Calchi Novati considers how the Irish performance artist dialogues with Irish patriarchy through a variety of visual and corporeal gestures that center on abjection.

Fintan Walsh's chapter analyzes the relationship between sexuality and eroticism in the public sphere by examining a variety of mainstream and queer beauty pageants, and contests the popular notion that dominant Irish culture has long repressed sexuality by revealing how it has been carefully harnessed, tempered, and produced in the service of national interest. Walsh coins the term 'homelysexuality' to denote the domesticated, marketable, and commercially profitable sexual accent he sees characterizing normative expressions of female sexuality.

Finally, in Part V: Diaspora, Migration, Globalization, contributors investigate the concepts of ethnicity and national identity. Anthropologist E. Moore Quinn reads the display of Northern Irish culture at Washington, DC's 2007 Smithsonian Folk Life Festival as an act of cultural narration in the context of theories of ambivalent selfhood, timeless presence, and entextualization. Quinn qualifies the event as a site in which 'narrators with a stake in the "master narrative" of Northern Ireland found a suitable venue within which to rehearse and perform a new identity.'

Drawing on social phenomenology, Eric Weitz takes on the place of laughter in audience responses to the work of Dublin-based African theater company Arambe, arguing for the pedagogical and intercultural benefit of this kind of somatic engagement to a multicultural society.

Writing as an academic and a participating artist, Holly Maples documents the fraught task of performing cultural diversity in the 2007 St Patrick's Day parade in the context of Dublin City Council's programmed intention to showcase a 'New Ireland'.

IV

Despite the number and variety of essays gathered here, this volume aims to be representative and suggestive rather than encyclopedic or exhaustive. Performance studies is a growing paradigm as well as an emergent approach to the study of Irish culture, and this volume strives to give this development a shape and sure footing that might inform further discovery. Nonetheless, we impress the need for performance as a paradigm and as an object of study to be considered in greater depth in the context of Irish culture. Richard Schechner, one of the original proponents of performance studies, feared that if the study of performance did not 'expand and deepen ... the whole academic performing arts enterprise constructed over the past half-century or so will collapse.' To protect against this, he argued for the need 'to expand our vision of what performance is, to study it not only as art but as a means of understanding historical, social, and cultural processes.'[13] Schechner argues for an understanding of performance beyond 'theatre', one with potential application in a variety of disciplines and contexts. In the case of Irish culture, in which orality has played a far greater historical and sociocultural role than 'text,' Schechner's broad-spectrum approach to the study of expressive behavior has particular relevance.

In addition to enriching Irish cultural process and analysis, the book also aspires to be of interest to performance studies researchers who do not typically share an interest in Irish cultural politics by presenting disparate systems of inquiry and an eclectic range of cultural practices. As Patrice Pavice suggests, to position oneself at the crossroads of culture is to implicate oneself in an unlearned dance of alienation and intimacy.[14] Rather than walk away from the peculiarity of this encounter, we prefer to echo Conquergood's insistence on turning and returning to the crossroads: to those intersecting and intersectional sites of difference, potentiality, and radicalism.

Notes

1 Eamon de Valera served as the first Taoiseach (prime minister) of Ireland, returning for several subsequent terms during the twentieth century. The precise content of his public address (reported in the *Irish Press*, 18 March 1943) is a matter of ongoing debate. While popular memory holds it that the Free State leader referenced 'crossroads' and 'comely' maidens, recent objections have suggested that he never discussed crossroads and spoke of maidens as 'happy' rather than 'comely.' In an audio-recording of the speech, it is clear that he refers to 'happy maidens' but not crossroads. See RTÉ Libraries and Archives, http://www.rte.ie/laweb/ll/ll_t09b.html (accessed 7 July 2008). The exact details of this address were hotly contested in the Letters to the Editor section of the *Irish Times*, 21 June 2008. Nonetheless, we appeal to this particular confusion engendered by the intersection of orality with text–popular memory with established narratives–to set the tone for considering a wide network of performative utterances, (counter-) cultural performances, and their effects.

2 Patrice Pavis, *Theatre at the Crossroads of Culture*, trans. Loren Kruger (London: Routledge, 1992), 1.

3 Dwight Conquergood, 'Performance Studies: Interventions and Radical Research,' *The Drama Review* 46 (2) (T174) (Summer 2002): 145–56, 154.

4 For contextualizing dance against this particular history, see Helena Wulff, *Dancing at the Crossroads: Memory and Mobility in Ireland* (Oxford: Berghahn Books, 2007); and Catherine E. Foley, ed., *At the Crossroads? Dance and Irish Culture* (Limerick: Dance Research Forum Ireland, 2007).

5 In *Queer Phenomenology: Orientations, Objects, Others* (Durham, NC: Duke University Press, 2006), Sara Ahmed foregrounds the queerness of all phenomenological discourse. She suggests that disorientation occurs when the easy extension of bodies into space fails (11). Moreover, Ahmed emphasizes the political ramifications of this uncanny perception arguing that 'to live out a politics of disorientation might be to sustain wonder about the very forms of social gathering' (24).

6 Conquergood, 2002, 153.

7   Michel Foucault, *Power/Knowledge*, ed. Colin Gordon, trans. Colin Gordon, Leo Marshall, John Mepham, and Kate Soper (New York: Pantheon, 1980), 81–4.

8   Conquergood, 2002, 146.

9   Anna McMullan, 'Reclaiming Performance: The Contemporary Irish Independent Theatre Sector,' in *The State of Play: Irish Theatre in the Nineties,* ed. Ebergard Bolt (Trier: WVT, 1996), 29–38, 29.

10   *Ibid.*, 30.

11   Anna McMullan and Brian Singleton, eds., 'Performing Ireland: New Perspectives on Contemporary Irish Theatre,' special issue of *Australasian Drama Studies* 43 (October 2003): 3–15, 3.

12   Karen Fricker and Brian Singleton, eds., 'Irish Theatre: Conditions of Criticism,' *Modern Drama*, XLVII, 4 (2004): 561–71, 562.

13   Richard Schechner, 'Performance Studies: The Broad Spectrum Approach,' in *The Performance Studies Reader* ed. Henry Bial, second edition (London and New York: Routledge, 2007), 7–9, 9.

14   Pavis writes: 'cultures meet either by passing close by one another or by reproducing thanks to crossbreeding.' See *Theatre at the Crossroads of Culture*, 6–7.

Part I
Tradition, Ritual, and Play

1
Performing Ireland: A Performative Approach to the Study of Irish Culture

Jack Santino

Ireland is known for its performances: its storytelling, its music-making, its celebrations. Scholars who have researched these performative genres in the past have largely been concerned with their verbal aspects and have documented them as texts, although the sense of performance was always present in the work of such giants as folklorist Seán O Súilleabháin and others. In the 1970s, folklore as a scholarly discipline engaged the performance qualities of folklore directly, recognizing that stories are told, songs are sung, and celebrations and rituals are enacted.[1] Still, Ireland remains stereotyped as a verbal culture, despite the obvious nonverbal components of music and dance, for instance. In contrast, in the six counties of Northern Ireland, life takes a more obviously visual turn: Belfast and Derry are known for the murals that adorn countless gable-end walls; thousands of parades a year punctuate everyday life, and public displays of flags have been highly contested. In total, traditional culture all across the island of Ireland (including the more emergent events mentioned above) shares qualities of performance that serve to put on display issues to do with politics and society, including gender, modernization, globalization, colonialism, and history, among others.

A performance-centered approach to Ireland asks us to consider ethnographic questions concerning these traditional events. Storytelling, for instance, or a music session, does not exist outside of history. Cultural events are born of the historical moment and shape it as well. Who is present? Where does the occasion occur? What genres are chosen for performance? What texts? Are there any 'hidden transcripts' to be identified?[2] In Northern Ireland, for instance, informal music sessions in pubs may be termed traditional, and local in terms of repertoire, but some of the participants will insist that the Ulster Scots population has no right to call its music traditional. A session in Portrush, Country Antrim, on the other hand, presents itself as Ulster Scots traditional culture in action. To the extent that repertoire may overlap in both cases, participants are eager to insist that 'it's all the same.' But they still insist on the primacy of their own cultural history.

Northern Ireland is riddled with such contested displays, some more obvious than others, such as whether 'God Save the Queen' should be sung at commencement exercises at Queen's University, Belfast. The multiplicity of parades in the North, for instance, is heavily weighted in favor of the majority Protestant population. Of the purported 3,600 parades held annually, 3,000 are 'Orange' and Unionist – held by the Orange Order or similar groups, such as the Apprentice Boys, who favor the ongoing status of Northern Ireland as part of the United Kingdom. Many of the bands in these parades are closely associated with Loyalist paramilitary organizations, which seek to retain that union, through armed conflict if necessary. The major celebration of the year is the 12th of July, which celebrates the victory of William of Orange over the Catholic King James of England and Scotland, and is marked by a large parade in each of the six counties as well as downtown Belfast. These are all-day affairs, with midday trips to a field, picnics, speeches, and sermons. On the other hand, St Patrick's Day parades were only allowed in the small neighborhood enclaves of Roman Catholics and banned from the city center, until a protest march led by Gerry Adams of Sinn Féin (a Republican political party) marched into Belfast, planted an Irish Tricolor flag at City Hall and declared it liberated.[3]

The point here is that not all parades are created equal. Who is allowed to take the streets? Who is forbidden to do so? What is displayed in these events? Is the status quo upheld or challenged? Where do people march and how? The so-called 'blood-and-thunder' bands of the Orange parades are also known as 'kick-the-pope' bands, and are known for their 'swagger' as they process. Some observers see the swagger as arrogance; the band members say it is merely performance style. Likewise, a tourist who encounters a group of musicians playing in a pub in Belfast might not realize that the participants are consciously creating an ethnic identity that they perceive as underappreciated and unrecognized. I would suggest that similar sessions in Dublin and throughout the rest of the Republic of Ireland always include a sense of identity construction – in this case, of native, indigenous Celtic identity – at some level. Further, some sessions in the North intentionally involve members of 'both communities' in an effort to redress the deep social divisions of that state.

There are, in fact, many ways of being Irish – and British – and many different performances to express these identities. Researchers have paid a great deal of attention to mumming, for instance,[4] and the 'mummers' rule' that a troupe must visit every home in the district, regardless of the resident's religion. Often the folk play performed by mummers will reflect that difference in the audience – will St Patrick slay St George, or will St George slay the Turkish Knight? Like all living folk traditions, the plays that are performed are protean. For instance, the figure of the paramilitary soldier has entered the plays in lieu of the medieval knight.[5] Given the severity of the violence that Ireland has suffered over years, decades, and centuries, and perhaps the lack of sense of humor among these paramilitaries, this is quite an extraordinary development. Here we see not only the ability of folk tradition to adapt to contemporary events, but also the power of the people to use their own cultural forms to parody and mock threatening forces that may take themselves too seriously. These folk dramas – and the parades as well – can be viewed as texts that can be read to shed light on society and culture, as Clifford Geertz has famously suggested.[6] More precisely, they are portals into that society and culture, a means of entry, through which we learn to explore the myriad associations and connections and disconnections that are the stuff of everyday social life.

Still, as important as these performances are, for both their participants and researchers, we can see that there is more to performativity than just performance. The linguist J. L. Austin has suggested that speech that accomplishes a certain kind of social change – that which it describes – may be termed 'performative utterances.'[7] Statements such as 'I now pronounce you husband and wife,' 'I do solemnly swear,' or 'I name this ship' are examples of performative utterances. The speech acts often occur in ritual contexts and have a ritual function themselves – that of status transformation. They occur during rites of passage, or are themselves abbreviated forms of such. I have suggested that the concept of performativity be extended beyond simply that of enactment or performance to include a concept of social transformation. I also want to extend this Austinian idea beyond speech utterances to include those enacted events that are intended to effect social change and transformation. When citizens of Derry City hold their Bloody Sunday commemoration event, images of those slain on that occasion are displayed and paraded. This is an act of commemoration and mourning, but the entire event can be seen as an attempt to see to it that justice is done; to influence the minds and hearts of onlookers, spectators, and participants. That is, the event is a large public gathering of people engaged in symbolic actions and bearing highly charged images and icons. They are doing this, not for festive communality or carnivalesque excess,[8] but in order to effect social change. Although it is a regularly occurring symbolic action, it is not a ritual as we generally understand the term: a fully ceremonial event which causes transformation. Instead, it is an event that intends social change as well as personal transformation (one hostile to the message may have her mind changed). I term this type of social event 'ritualesque.'

Having mentioned the carnivalesque, I must add that these two terms are not antithetical. Indeed, carnivalesque events are often also ritualesque. For instance, Gay Pride Day celebrations are often marked by carnivalesque excess, such as public nudity, representations of exaggerated genitalia, and public behavior usually kept private. In these cases the Pride Day participants are using the carnivalesque to say, essentially, 'We're here and we're not going anywhere.' In one way or another, these events are attempts to change social attitudes and, in doing so, to change society. I believe this aspect of public events has not been identified and as a result, public performances have remained less than fully comprehended.

Performances in Northern Ireland

Studies of Irish folklore have often implicitly and explicitly involved the study of performance. Music-making, singing, dancing, and storytelling are almost stereotypically associated with the study of Irish culture, and all of these are performed genres. However, folklore studies tended toward a textual approach to documentation until the 1970s, when the paradigm shifted to a performance-centered approach. Folklorists recognized that texts are fluid and context-dependent. Henry Glassie's *Passing the Time in Ballymenone* (1982) epitomized this approach in the study and documentation of narrative performance. As performance studies has developed as a distinct field, the traditional folkloristic areas of seasonal custom, including folk drama, processions, and bonfires,[9] as well as life-cycle rituals,[10] provide a rich source of scholarship and areas of research. Generally perceived and described as 'calendar customs' and 'life-cycle rites,' important folkloristic studies have been done on Christmas mumming, Halloween, St Brigid's Day, and the festival of Lugh.[11] More recently, anthropologists and social historians have turned their attention to the street theatre of politics and identity, focusing on the parades in the North.[12] Taken together, these approaches proceed from Victor Turner's assertion that rituals (and, I would add, ritualesque events) put on display the values and central symbols of the group responsible for generating the event.[13] Ethnography demands we ask who is involved; what they say they are doing; what they seem to actually be doing, when, where, and how? A performative approach will examine a particular event at a particular point in history: Are participants subverting the official 'message?' Are they doing so consciously? Moreover, a performative approach to Irish culture and society is free to include all types of performances, traditional, emergent, small community, or international; religious, political, or economic. Green beer has started to flow in Dublin during a week-long 'Patrickfest,' while Polish immigrants to Ireland celebrate Polish Independence Day. This is beyond cultural tourism in the former case and ethnic identity politics in the latter. Ireland's entry into the European Union and its resultant prosperity, along with the globalized flow of national groups to economic oases, have resulted in these emergent, hybridized, and spectacular performances, such as the infamous *Riverdance*.

Performativity involves performance in the sense of social action, along with intention and social consequence. Northern Ireland is home to many performative events, including parades, murals, bonfires for anniversaries and calendar events, and other examples of expressive acts that are marked as political and sometimes sectarian in the North. A specifically performative approach will view these acts, and others, as social actions in which participants intend an effect, and observers and others will perceive their own motivations, which may or may not be consonant with those of the participants. These actions will have social effects and consequences which may or may not match the intentions and understandings of the participants. In societies that have been home to a great deal of internal conflict, a performative study is particularly productive.

The public memorialization of death often is staged to bring about social change or to intensify social categories. Paramilitary murals in Belfast portray death as military martyrdom, while the spontaneous shrines communally created in neighborhoods to victims of military violence question these categories by insisting on the personal and familial identities of these victims. Notes displayed publicly are written to 'Daddy,' or 'Grampa.' These shrines undermine the rhetoric of both the state and the paramilitary commanders who want to control the discourse surrounding the Troubles. The shrines are not merely commemorations of certain deceased individuals. Like the Bloody Sunday commemorations, they are performed publicly in order to address public issues. They are not merely commemoratives, but rather, performative commemoratives.[14]

The performances and genres of performance we have considered, such as calendrical customs, can be viewed as historical artifacts and as texts that reflect gender, politics, or identity. Other performances include responses to oppression (murals, parades, demonstrations, Bloody Sunday commemorations). All these events not only reflect the social situations in which they are generated; they simultaneously create these identities and realities. In Northern Ireland, Nationalists claim that Orange parades are triumphalist – that by sweeping through the streets in quasi-military formation, those represented in a parade are laying claim to the territory. Certainly, the parades are at the very least normative; in certain neighborhoods, residents insist that the parades are sectarian and demand that they be rerouted.

Roman Catholic citizens of Derry often complain that the city is trashed during the annual celebrations in the summer Apprentice Boys parades and in the December parades and effigy-burning, which commemorate the relief of the city from the siege of King James by the forces of William of Orange. During the winter events, Robert Lundy (who attempted to come to terms, or surrender, before the arrival of William's army) is burned in effigy. I have been to both events, and they do get rowdy. Inebriated participants can be seen urinating and sometimes vomiting. After the events, there is a great deal of trash and litter to be removed. Organizers of the Apprentice Boys chafe at these accusations, saying that they cannot be responsible for every single participant, but that they certainly do not allow such behavior if they can prevent it. As with so many events in Northern Ireland, we have a sharp contradiction between intention and perception. With all the events of the Loyal Orange Order and the Apprentice Boys, both Protestant fraternal organizations, participants insist that they are merely celebrating their traditions – celebrating themselves and their culture. As stated above, a great many Roman Catholics see the parades and other activities as a public staking of territory and manifestation of power. A Roman Catholic friend once told me that the behavior of the participants at the August Apprentice Boys parades was not without purpose: Derry, he explained, is a majority Catholic city, and the Apprentice Boys' attitude – and actions – are to be taken literally. They were pissing on it.

One can see here the ways in which the concepts of the carnivalesque and the ritualesque come into play – the strategy of the Orangemen is to define what they do as harmless, done for its own sake without social consequence. The Catholic population argues that the parades are performed to make something happen socially – to reinforce and even create an uneven power relationship between the two communities. As in the case of the Pride Day event, both aspects are present. Certainly, intentions vary among participants. Moreover, at any given moment, events of the most serious kind may include the ludic, and moments of fun.

I would suggest that large-scale public events be measured on a continuum from the more festive, inversive, and carnivalesque to the more specifically ritualesque. The Bloody Sunday commemorations are clearly not intended to be festive, though they may be quite convivial. They are meant to be commemorative of deaths that were unjust and unnecessary, deaths that remain unpunished. Individuals are being publicly remembered for a social purpose: to call attention to this (perceived) injustice and to marshal people to do something about it. They are, again, public events that employ many symbolic media–procession, chanting, iconography, and imagery–but they are not rituals in the strict sense of a religious ceremony or a political rite of passage such as an inauguration. For this reason, I suggest we adopt the term 'ritualesque' into our research vocabulary.

Notes

1 Americo Paredes and Richard Bauman, *Toward New Perspectives in Folklore* (Austin: University of Texas Press, 1972).
2 James C. Scott, *Domination and the Arts of Resistance: Hidden Transcripts* (New Haven, CT: Yale University Press, 1992).
3 See Neil Jarman, *Material Conflicts: Parades and Visual Displays in Northern Ireland* (New York: Berg, 1997).
4 Alan Gailey, 'The Bonfore in North Irish Tradition,' *Folklore* 88 (1977): 3–28; Henry Glassie, *Passing the Time in Ballymenone: Culture and History of an Ulster Community* (Bloomington: Indiana University Press, 1982); Séamus Ó Catháin, Críostóir Mac Cárthaigh, Anthony D. Buckley, and Séamus Mac Máthuna, *Mumming in Cross-Border and Cross-Community Contexts* (Derry: University of Ulster Press, 2007); for more on mumming, see Bernadette Sweeney's essay in this volume.
5 Ó Catháin et al., 2007; see also Henry Glassie, *All Silver and No Brass: An Irish Christmas Mumming* (Philadelphia: University of Pennsylvania Press, 1975).
6 Clifford Geertz, 'Deep Play: Notes on a Balinese Cockfight,' in *Myth, Symbol, and Culture*, ed. Clifford Geertz (New York: W.W. Norton, 1971), 412–50.

7   J. L. Austin, *How To Do Things With Words* (Oxford: Oxford University Press, 1962).

8   Mikhail Bakhtin, *Rabelais and His World*, trans. Helene Iswolsky (Cambridge, MA: MIT Press, 1968).

9   Gailey, 1977.

10 Seán Ó Súilleabháin, *Irish Wake Amusements* (Dublin: Mercer Press, 1979 [1961]); Linda May Ballard, *Forgetting Frolic: Marriage Traditions in Ireland* (Chester Springs, PA: Dufour Editions, 1998).

11 Glassie, 1975; Seamus Ó Catháin, *The Festival of Brigit: Celtic Goddess and Holy Woman* (Dublin: DBA Press, 1995); Jack Santino, *The Hallowed Eve: Dimensions of Culture in a Calendrical Festival in Northern Ireland* (Knoxville: University Press of Kentucky, 1997).

12 Jarman, 1997; Dominic Bryan, *Orange Parades: The Politics of Ritual, Tradition, and Control* (London: Pluto Press, 2000); T. G. Fraser, *The Irish Parading Tradition: Following the Drum* (New York: St. Martin's Press, 2000).

13 Victor Turner, *Celebrations: A World of Art and Ritual*, 16 mm film (Washington, DC: Smithsonian Institution Office of Folklife Programs, 1983).

14 Jack Santino, *Signs of War and Peace: Social Conflict and the Uses of Symbols in Public* (New York: Palgrave Macmillan, 2000).

2
Performing Tradition[1]

Bernadette Sweeney

Ireland's performative culture is rich in folk rituals that give the country an arts heritage based not only in text, but also in gesture and embodied, participatory traditions. This fact of our performance history has only recently earned the recognition it deserves among Irish theater scholars. In *Performing the Body in Irish Theatre* I consider how the use of traditions such as mumming, waking, Wrenboys, Strawboys, and Patterns affect notions of performance and mark a theatrical history often overlooked in established histories of Irish theater. Mark Phelan, in 'Modernity, Geography and Historiography: (Re)-Mapping Irish Theatre History in the Nineteenth Century,' notes that archival research reveals

> a wealth of material available, whether related to local commercial theatres, stock companies, national touring circuits, or the virtually unexplored world of music halls, 'free and easies,' singing saloons, variety theatres and vaudeville. Beyond this is the hybrid, heteroglossic plenitude of theatrical activity outside of the urban, institutional and professional sphere in the diversity of popular traditions, forms and practices.[2]

Although often neglected in formal studies, such performance traditions have an embodied influence on evolving performance style and idiom.

Many folk rituals, superstitions, and traditions are inherently performative, and these practices have often featured in canonical Irish dramas by J. M. Synge, Brian Friel, and Marina Carr, among others. Staged Irish rituals and traditions include the funeral rites of keening (*caoineadh*, literally 'crying') and waking (keeping a vigil over the dead), Celtic calendar festivals, religious ceremonies, storytelling, traditional music, and dance. The reduction of folk traditions to 'a set of automatic habits, some traditions of dress and a few broken-down institutions,'[3] in the words of Franz Fanon, was perhaps inevitable as the population became a less rural one. By reclaiming performance traditions theater practitioners have embarked on a powerful and emotive journey. This can be seen clearly observed in the case of mumming,[4] especially when the practice is associated with the assumption of otherness, as in Vincent Woods' *At the Black Pig's Dyke* (first produced by Druid Theatre Company in 1992). Calendar festivals feature in *Dancing at Lughnasa* by Brian Friel (Abbey Theatre, 1990), *The Great Hunger* (Abbey/Peacock, 1983), and the aforementioned *At the Black Pig's Dyke*, while Catholic Church ritual is invoked by many Irish dramatists. Some playwrights have staged folk ritual in a way that, ironically, echoes church appropriation of pre-Christian ritual and representation. However, such stagings have perhaps also secured and restored these traditions in a way that formal histories of performance have not – in a way, performance has historicized itself.

Synge twinned a creative use of language with the dramatization of ritual funeral rites and keening in *Riders to the Sea* (1904). The tradition of waking the dead was treated ironically in *The Playboy of the Western World* (1907) when Pegeen Mike's father sees it as an opportunity to get a free drink, while in *The Shadow of The Glen* (1903), Dan Burke stages his own wake to confirm his suspicions of his young wife's infidelities. This was a darker application of an almost melodramatic device as used by Dion Boucicault in *The Shaughraun*, first produced in 1874, when Conn the Shaughraun also staged his own death. Here Boucicault included a version of keening verse as used by the mourners in the funeral ritual. Traditional music, ballads, and dance have appeared in Woods' *At the Black Pig's Dyke* and Friel's *Dancing at Lughnasa*, for example, as has the oral tradition of storytelling, as in Marina Carr's *Low in the Dark* (1989). Tom Murphy constructed *Bailegangaire* (1985) around the central image of the *seanchaí* (storyteller) in the powerful figure of Mommo. The rhythmic and repetitious nature of Mommo's story recalls the nature of the tradition itself, with the play's added urgency for the story to reach a resolution. The purpose of this chapter is to consider further the invocation and recuperation of traditional performance practices by some key Irish play texts and productions.

Caoineadh/keening

One of Synge's great achievements in *Riders to the Sea* is his placing of Christian burial ritual alongside a pagan tradition of keening or caoineadh. In his book *The Aran Islands*, published in 1907, Synge wrote:

> The women sat down among the flat tombstones, bordered with a pale fringe of early bracken, and began the wild keen, or crying for the dead. Each old woman, as she took her turn in the leading recitative, seemed possessed for the moment with a profound ecstasy of grief, swaying to and fro, and bending her forehead to the stone before her, while she called out to the dead with a perpetually recurring chant of sobs. All round the graveyard other wrinkled women, looking out from under the deep red petticoats that cloaked them, rocked themselves the same rhythm, and intoned the inarticulate chant that is sustained by all as an accompaniment. ... There is an irony in these words of atonement and Catholic belief spoken by voices that were still hoarse with the cries of pagan desperation.[5]

Riders to the Sea, one of the first plays produced by the Abbey Theatre in 1904, is rich in ritual and poetry, and evokes a frugal and elemental lifestyle. Set on one of the Aran Islands (presumed to be Inis Meáin) off the west coast of Ireland, it is a play about loss. The mother, Maurya, has lost four of her six sons at sea. Her fifth son, Michael, is missing, feared drowned, and, in the course of the action, her sixth son, Bartley, prepares to cross to the mainland, leaving Maurya and her two daughters, Cathleen and Nora, behind. At the end of play, as the drowned Bartley is brought back from the sea to be waked and buried, the keening begins.

Synge also wrote on the expressiveness of islanders in *The Aran Islands*: 'I seem to look again into the strangely reticent temperament of the islanders, and to feel the passionate spirit that expresses itself, at odd moments only, with magnificent words and gestures.'[6] Synge saw a performativity of gesture in the rituals of the island and immortalized it in *Riders to the Sea*.

Mumming

The tradition of mumming was a central image in *At the Black Pig's Dyke* by Vincent Woods, as staged by Druid Theatre in 1992. Kevin Danaher identifies that an Irish authenticity is difficult to ascribe to the mumming tradition:

> What the origins of Mumming and the Mummers Play may be, we do not know. It is clear that most of the verses and action of Irish

traditional Mumming are so closely related to that of England that the custom must be ascribed to English influence.[7]

Alan Gailey, author of *Irish Folk Drama* (1969), cites documentation that places the mumming tradition in Cork in 1685, pre-dating any English source text:

> In 1685 a group of mummers in the City of Cork was described in clear terms: Last evening there was presented the drollest piece of mummery I ever saw in or out of Ireland. There was St. George and St. Denis and St. Patrick in their buffe coats, and the Turke was there likewise and Oliver Cromwell and a Doctor, and an old woman who made rare sport, till Belzibub came in with a frying pan upon his shoulder and a great flail in his hand thrashing about him on friends and foes, and at last running away with the bold usurper, Cromwell, whom he tweaked by his gilded nose – and there came a little Devil with a broom to gather up the money that was thrown to the Mummers for their sport. It is an ancient pastime, they tell me, of the Citizens.[8]

Characters listed here appear in later mumming plays with a few changes, but there have been regional variations up to the present day. Other, less specific references to mumming activities date as far back as the twelfth century: 'Hamner's Chronicle, describing King Henry's celebration of Christmas in Dublin in 1172, tells of "the pastime, the sport, and the mirth, and the continuall musicke, the masking, mumming and strange shewes."'[9] Here Danaher dates mumming to the twelfth century, but also illustrates the difficulty of finding an 'authentic' source for the tradition. If mumming has been embodied in Ireland as a performance tradition from as far back as 1172, must it still be regarded as inauthentic because of its English, or non-native, associations? Authenticity is a troubled concept at the best of times, but performance is by its nature adaptive, improvisatory, and even culturally parasitic – if mumming cannot be described as an 'authentic' Irish performance tradition by now, perhaps we can celebrate its adaptive and even insidious nature instead.

Gailey credits the form of mumming and other performance traditions as being responsible for their survival: 'it should also be remembered that (mumming) was an oral tradition, dependence on written texts being rare.'[10] The oral tradition of storytelling is an early example of the respect afforded to the imagination. The storyteller and the listener or listeners established the dynamic between performer and audience in Irish homes around the country. Stories were passed on and elaborated as they were transmitted by word of mouth (*béaloideas*). Gailey records both the details of the mummers' plays and the conditions in which local groups around Ireland performed them. When writing on mumming in the North of Ireland he takes care to note that the enactments of the ritual battle between the two heroes in the course of the mummers' play was tailored to the loyalties of each household:

> At a Roman Catholic home St. Patrick was seen to defeat St. George but in a Protestant kitchen, using the same words, King William always defeated King James. This sort of come and go within the acceptable range of characterisations in the folk plays was not uncommon ... Indeed in mid-county Down one mummers' group included people of every shade of political and religious belief, and they visited all the homes known to all their members.[11]

Other characters varied from region to region, and included Miss Funny, a Fool or Clown, a Butcher, Beelzebub and, on occasion, Oliver Cromwell. Traditionally, mummers were believed to bring a blessing to the house, but the introduction of a collection of money at the end of the mummers' play dismayed some commentators:

> The idea that luck is being distributed is actually included in the rhymes of some plays in west county Tyrone 'We come not to your door to beg nor to borrow / We come to your door to drive away all sorrow.' By contrast, the more recent insistence on the collection of money is more like taking the luck of the house away.[12]

Miss Funny was used primarily to collect money (as she does in *At the Black Pig's Dyke*). She seems, in the mumming of County Fermanagh, to have served the function of wit or commentator – a role taken by Johnny Funny in County Derry and Tom Fool in the North Dublin mummers' plays.

In Woods' staging of mumming in *At the Black Pig's Dyke*, the straw masks and costumes of the mummers are invested with a sinister element of terrorism, a reminder of the costumed agitators for land reform of the nineteenth century such as the Whiteboys. Luke Gibbons explains: 'Agrarian protest based its legitimacy on its intricate associations with peasant ritual ... and was interwoven with important seasonal festivals in the cultural calendar such as Mayday, Halloween (*Samhain*) and the aftermath of Christmas.'[13] Gibbons goes on to recognize 'the almost imperceptible shifts between masquerading in the festive costume of mummers and Wrenboys, and dressing up in the menacing garb of Ribbonmen.'[14] Terms such as Ribbonmen or Whiteboys were a direct reference to the nature of the mummer costumes worn by these secret societies whose violent activities were in reaction to forced labor, tithes, and an unjust land system.[15]

Sympathetic readings of the grievances of these secret society members, if not their methods, are contextualized by the tone adopted by some agents of British Rule in Ireland. H. B. C. Pollard documents the history of such groups in *The Secret Societies of Ireland*. The Ribbon Society emerged in 1805 after the suspension of the British forces' night curfew policy in the wake of the 1798 United Irishmen rebellion. Members were described by Pollard – himself 'a member of the Staff of the Chief of Police at Dublin Castle in the latter days of British Rule'[16] – as '*uneducated savages, but a sprinkling of merchants, schoolmasters and priests were a leavening of the whole.*'[17]

Strawboys and Wrenboys

Like Gibbons, playwright Vincent Woods identifies the potential menace of the costumed folk performers:

> There was always that potential for violence in a lot of the folk traditions, like Strawboys who came to weddings, like the mummers who came around Christmas and to a lesser extent the Wrenboys. With the Strawboys, who came to weddings, there was the belief in some areas that they were almost like official folk gatecrashers, they had to be allowed entry. ... There was a belief that if they weren't made welcome, if they weren't given sufficient in the way of reward for whatever they performed that they could bury the wren beside the house and leave bad luck.[18]

Descriptions of the Strawboys in the Irish Folklore Commission manuscripts correlate with Woods' description of them as 'official folk gatecrashers.' The following is a local's recollection of a wedding feast along the Black Pig's Dyke:

> There is a feast held in the bride's house. There are Strawboys who visit the house. They are dressed in comic clothes and their faces are

blackened. They stuff the chimneys and light fires, block up the way, tie the door, do their best to rush to the house and take away the bride's cake.[19]

Other recollections suggest that the Strawboys, known locally as 'fools,' could be quite aggressive. According to Elizabeth Byrne from County Wexford, 'the "fools" would arrive anytime after dark and there might be upwards of three hundred of them. … They entered without any invitation and the people of the house would be afraid to refuse them admittance for fear they would become unruly and do damage, as it was known for them to do. They were always unwelcome.'[20]

Byrne's recollections, as recorded by J. D. Delaney of *Coimisiún Béaloideasa Éireann*, also give an insight into the performance of gender by the Straw*boys*:

> Mrs. Byrne heard a man named Larry Caulfield of Corrigeen, Grange, Rathnure, tell the following story about a marriage in that townland. Four people turned up at this wedding disguised as fools – four among many others, of course. The four kept together all night and did not dance very much. Larry Caulfield was curious to find out who they were. … The four went outside and Larry followed them … but when he saw that *they had to sit down, when they went outside*, he knew they were four girls.[21]

Wrenboys dressed in a similar way to the Strawboys 'in the old fantastic attire of pyjamas, window curtains, straw hats, and antiquated feminine apparel,'[22] but they performed as they moved from house to house on St Stephen's Day (December 26).

In 1987 the Abbey Theatre staged *Strawboys* by Michael Harding at the Peacock, the smaller of its two stages. This play, like Woods' *At the Black Pig's Dyke* in 1992, referenced a performance ritual within a broader narrative. In the program note, Tom Mac Intyre described the characters as 'Three males. A bully. A coward. And an "innocent," already infected. Two women. A strong woman and a child-woman – the ritual victim.' The play is set in a parish hall and the production seemed to borrow much from the 'theater-of-image' developed by Mac Intyre with director Patrick Mason – hardly surprising given that it was directed by Tom Hickey, actor in *The Great Hunger* and the third of the central figures of that Abbey collaboration of the 1980s. This referencing of a traditional performance form may not have been very successful in this production. Critic Sean Moffatt, however, drew a comparison between *Strawboys* and Mac Intyre's *The Great Hunger*, but concluded that *Strawboys* did not generate 'anything like the same excitement' in its 'tame and ineffectual orchestration of chaos.'[23]

Calendar festivals

Calendar festivals are another source of folk tradition and ritual, and have been documented in detail by Kevin Danaher, E. Estyn Evans, Seán Ó Súilleabháin, and Alan Gailey. The Irish calendar festivals, like others, revolved around seasonal events such as harvest time; there is evidence that these were pre-Christian festivals which became key dates in the church calendar. February 1 (Imbolc) became St Brigid's Day; Gailey gives an account of a St Brigid's Day festival in *Irish Folk Drama*:

> In Ireland the traditional onset of spring was 1st February, St. Brigid's Day. In many places the Eve of the saint's day was marked by a processional, luck-bearing ceremony. ... Almost everywhere the performers were called 'biddy-boys' or *brídeogí*, although the latter word could often refer specifically to an effigy that was carried in the procession of performers.[24]

Although Gailey associates the significance of the first day of February with St Brigid, Seán Ó Súilleabháin finds an earlier, pre-Christian aspect to the ritual: 'St Brigid's Feast (1 February) was originally an important pre-Christian festival, occurring as it did at the time of the start of agricultural work.' He goes on to describe a typical effigy: '[y]oung boys (*Brídeoga*: 'Biddies') went from door to door carrying a churndash dressed as a woman and asked for some gift.'[25] May 1 (Bealtaine) was a time to welcome the summer. E. Estyn Evans writes of the May festival in *Irish Folk Ways*: 'there were public ceremonies, the lighting of bonfires and parades of May Babies, of May Boys and the May Queen. ... The May Baby parades link the festival with the fertility of the family as well as the fields.'[26] Flowers and posies are still gathered for May altars in honor of the Virgin Mary.

In the 1983 Abbey production of *The Great Hunger*,[27] the Mother of Kavanagh's original poem was staged as wooden effigy. The image of the Mother in procession is a visual reference to religious processions of Marian devotion, but is also suggestive of folk tradition. Here paganism is suggested as the characters enact a spring fertility rite, carrying the effigy of the Mother in a procession reminiscent of both St Brigid's Day and the May Day or Bealtaine rituals. The staging of ritual is also present in *The Great Hunger* in the use of church ceremony and an implied suppression of exuberance by the representative of the Catholic Church. The spring festival is confronted and controlled by The Priest in a way that suggests the confrontation of paganism and Christianity and the appropriation of rites and festivals by the Church. The ensuing Mass (hilarious in performance) is a mordant portrayal of a Catholic ceremony, which plays on and to the experiences of audience members, secure in the presumption of a common frame of reference. 'Prayers' are intoned by the congregation, but the sing-song rhythms are actually lines from the original poem, such as 'Kate, throw another sod on that fire' or 'Curse o' God where's that dog?'[28] Literary purists could read this use of Kavanagh's poem as sacrilege in more ways than one. Funeral rites are also suggested in scene 18 of *The Great Hunger* by the funeral of the Mother as effigy and in the reaction of her son Maguire, as he observes the ritual and timorously 'Kiss(ed) the Corpse.'[29] August 1 (Lughnasa) was a harvest festival, which has been conflated with Féile Mhuire 'sa bhFómhar, the Feast of the Assumption (August 15), when Patterns are held at local shrines, again to the Virgin Mary. This calendar festival is central to the image and the action in *Dancing at Lughnasa*. November 1 and its eve, a period associated with death and spirits (Samhain), is now All Saints' Day.

The program for the first production of Brian Friel's *Dancing at Lughnasa*[30] included extracts from Máire MacNeill's *The Festival of Lughnasa*, first published in 1962.[31] Here MacNeill details Lughnasa as a harvest festival, in honor of the pagan god Lugh. The festival rituals included a ceremonial cutting of the corn or wheat, which was echoed in the stage design of the first production, by scene designer Joe Vanek's sloping field of golden wheat, which dominated the stage, encroaching on the domestic space. This fertile abundance was such a vibrant image that it appeared to mock the sisters' barren futures. In 1962 MacNeill found evidence of a version of these Lughnasa festivities 'at a hundred and ninety-five sites in Ireland' and noted that 'Lughnasa was celebrated until recently on ninety-five heights and by ten lakes and five riverbanks.'[32] There is also evidence that picking wild bilberries was part of the festivities and that dancing competitions were held at the festival sites. There is a danger with such festivals, however, as they act as catalysts, or releases from everyday behavior. In Friel's *Dancing at Lughnasa*, Kate identifies the pagan practices of Lughnasa as those performed by 'savages,' the fearsome uncivilized savages that she and her sisters might become if they're not careful:

KATE: (*very angry, almost shouting*) And they're savages! I know those people from the back hills! I've taught them! Savages – that's what they are! And what pagan practices they have are no concern of ours – none whatever! It's a sorry day to hear talk like that in a Christian home, a Catholic home! All I can say is that I'm shocked and disappointed to hear you repeating rubbish like that, Rose![33]

Patterns

Patterns, on the brink of extinction like other folk traditions, are religious rituals with pre-Christian associations. A Pattern is a pilgrimage with a set route to and/or from a holy shrine, with particular points along the way where pilgrims kneel or stand to pray or make offerings. According to Mark Phelan, 'Feast days of parish patron saints celebrated at sacred sites connected with the saint and often with the local topography of a more ancient, Gaelic, pagan tradition.'[34] I mention the Pattern here because it is performative: the pilgrims embody their devotion, and it has a set structure, often demanding extreme physical discomfort as a show of devotion. Many local Patterns were discouraged by the clergy as it was difficult to suppress a carnivalesque energy:

> Although it is true that many of these local celebrations had degenerated into debauchery, it is also unfortunately true that in the course of the nineteenth century, when Victorian 'respectability' had for many of both clergy and laity assumed the sanctity of moral law, many quite harmless customs were discouraged or forbidden because they offended the sanctimonious.[35]

Such a journey has been invoked by two relatively recent Cork productions: Meridian Theatre Company's *Croon* (2004) and Corcadorca Theatre Company's *Midsummer Night's Dream* (2005). These productions, most notably *Croon*, were not merely promenade productions; each guided its audience to different geographical sites along a set route around the city, where scenes were enacted. Each site ensured that space was as much an architecture of the piece as text or design. The journey from site to site became as much part of each production as the scenes, and audiences were implicated in the action, to varying extents, by partaking in these journeys. Corcadorca's *Midsummer Night's Dream* was more tightly tied to its Shakespearean text than *Croon*, which was scripted by the production's (and Meridian's) director, Johnny Hanrahan. Each production demanded an embodied engagement from its audience by constructing a performative 'pattern' or set route through Cork city, with sites of performance en route at which audience members had to stop and observe and/or participate.

Conclusion

Irish ritual and performance traditions complement and complicate the literary in Irish theater. The literary has perhaps ensured the safeguarding of certain aspects of Irish culture and has evidenced the effects of a postcolonial condition on a disparate society. Conversely, elements of the literary tradition, such as poetry, survived in ballad form, so performance could also be said to have safeguarded a literary heritage.[36] Elements of this performance tradition, as stated at the outset, may also have been documented and secured by their staging, such as keening in the work of Boucicault and Synge, or, more recently, mumming in the work of Woods. The staging of such rituals and traditions may be seen to educate audiences, to foster an understanding of national expressive practices, and to communicate on a range of levels by drawing on distinctly physical idioms. The performance of ritual and tradition as a theatrical construct ensures a vibrancy of form as such expression takes full advantage of the mutual presences of audience and performers. Staging of Irish performance rituals and traditions brings precedents of corporeal representation before an audience who would recognize written and spoken language as having been the dominant postcolonial discursive tool.

Notes

1 This chapter includes and develops material from Bernadette Sweeney, *Performing the Body in Irish Theatre* (Basingstoke: Palgrave Macmillan, 2008).
2 Mark Phelan, 'Modernity, Geography and Historiography: (Re)-Mapping Irish Theatre History in the Nineteenth Century,' in *The Performing Century: Nineteenth-Century Theatre's History*, eds. Tracy C. Davis and Peter Holland (Basingstoke: Palgrave Macmillan, 2007), 135–58, 136.
3 Franz Fanon, 'On National Culture,' in *Colonial Discourse and Post-Colonial Theory*, eds. Patrick Williams and Laura Chrisman (New York: Harvester Wheatsheaf, 1993), 36–52, 46.
4 Mummers dressed in straw costumes moved from house to house performing a 'battle' between two key figures, such as St George and St Patrick, or King James and King William, and the outcome of the play would be determined by the politics of each household or audience. Characters included a hero, a butcher, and two 'fools' or commentators, among others.
5 John Millington Synge, *The Aran Islands* (London: Allen & Unwin, 1961), 42.
6 *Ibid.*, 60.

7   Kevin Danaher, *The Year in Ireland: Irish Calendar Customs* (Cork: Mercier Press, 1972), 257.

8   Alan Gailey, *Irish Folk Drama* (Cork: Mercier Press, 1969), 8. Cromwell would have featured here as English anti-Royalist invader of Ireland in 1649; this invasion included the infamous sieges of Drogheda and Wexford, said to have resulted in the deaths of thousands of Royalist supporters, Irish natives, and members of Catholic orders. Cromwell is, therefore, a contested figure in British and Irish histories of Ireland.

9   Danaher, 1972, 257.

10   Gailey, 1969, 16

11   *Ibid.*, 10.

12   *Ibid.*, 14.

13   Luke Gibbons, *Transformations in Irish Culture* (Cork: Cork University Press, 1996), 18.

14   *Ibid.*, 18.

15   This historical connection informed Woods' *At the Black Pig's Dyke*, as seen in his portrayal of Frank Beirne (see Sweeney, 2008, 160–7) and could be read as an attempt to lend legitimacy to the violence of the play.

16   H. B. C. Pollard, *The Secret Societies of Ireland* (Kilkenny: The Irish Historical Press, 1998), cover.

17   *Ibid.*, 24–5 (emphasis added).

18   Vincent Woods, personal interview with Bernadette Sweeney.

19   Brian Sherry, ed., *Along the Black Pig's Dyke* (Co. Monaghan: Castleblayney Community Enterprise Ltd, 1993), 53.

20   Irish Folklore Commission, MS 1399, 81.

21   *Ibid.* (emphasis added).

22   This description is from the South Carlow notes of the *Nationalist and Leinster Times*, 2 January 1943.

23   Sean Moffatt, *Theatre Ireland* 13 (1987), 46.

24   Gailey, 1969, 85.

25   Seán Ó Súilleabháin, *Irish Folk Custom and Belief: Nósanna agus Piseoga na nGael* (Dublin: The Three Candles Ltd, for the Cultural Relations Committee, 1967), 6.

26   E. Estyn Evans, *Irish Folk Ways* (New York: Dover Publications, 2000 [1957] [unabridged]), 273.

27   This was a version of Patrick Kavanagh's poem *The Great Hunger*, scripted by playwright Tom Mac Intyre, directed by Patrick Mason, and featuring Tom Hickey in the lead role as Maguire. For full details of this production, see Sweeney, 2008, 50–77.

28   Patrick Kavanagh and Tom Mac Intyre, *The Great Hunger: Poem into Play* (Mullingar, Co. Westmeath: Lilliput Press, 1988), 43–4.

29   *Ibid.*, 65.

30   This 1990 Abbey Theatre production was directed by Patrick Mason and went on to become one of the Abbey's, and Ireland's, most successful national and international productions.

31   Extracts used were taken from the 1982 edition published by Chomhairle Bhéaloideas Éireann, University College Dublin.

32   Máire MacNeill, quoted in *Dancing at Lughnasa* program, Abbey Theatre 1990.

33 Brian Friel, *Dancing at Lughnasa* (London: Faber and Faber, 1990), 17.
34 Phelan, 2007, 154.
35 Danaher, 1972, 184.
36 See Caoímhin Ó Danachair, 'Oral Tradition and the Printed Word,' *Irish University Review* 9 (1) (1979): 31–40; and Joep Leerssen, *Remembrance and Imagination* (Cork: Cork University Press, 1996), 173–7.

3
Sporting 'Irish' Identities: Performance and the Gaelic Games[1]

Sara Brady

Constructing 'Irish' athletic culture

The founding in 1884 of the Gaelic Athletic Association (GAA) attempted to create an autonomous production of Irishness that could be embodied through performance. As with the Gaelic League and the Irish National Theatre, the GAA needed to distinguish Ireland from Britain. The late nineteenth-century project of Irish nationalism required language, literature, drama, and other expressive culture[2] to be de-anglicized and redefined in order to serve cultural and political purposes. For Gaelic games, this meant displacing contemporary rivals such as cricket, polo, tennis, soccer, and rugby. These 'British' activities (themselves recent products of British nineteenth-century sport codification) needed to be taken out of circulation and replaced by the 'ancient' pastimes of hurling and Gaelic football.

Michael Cusack's 'A Word on Irish Athletics,' published on 11 October 1884 in both *United Ireland* and the *Irishman*, served as a call to Irish athletes in preparation for the founding of the GAA:

> No movement having for its object the social and political advancement of a nation from the tyranny of imported and enforced customs and manners can be regarded as perfect if it has not made adequate provision for the preservation and cultivation of the national pastimes of the people. Voluntary neglect of such pastimes is a sure sign of national decay and dissolution.[3]

Cusack's letter foregrounds the importance of leisure to expressive culture and warns of the consequences if the nation-making project disregards such activities. The idea that 'national decay' will follow 'voluntary neglect' of 'national pastimes' implies an understanding that nations are performative entities or, as Benedict Anderson describes, 'imagined communities' constructed as 'both inherently limited and sovereign,' which are only as healthy as their imaginings, or, in this case, their 'pastimes.'[4] Cusack's efforts led to the first official meeting of the GAA at Thurles on 1 November 1884, which no more than a dozen attended. In the wake of that forgettable meeting, Cusack sought and received the patronage of several key nationalists, including Charles Stewart Parnell, Michael Davitt, and Archbishop Thomas W. Croke, whose letter of support in December 1884 echoed Cusack's concerns about British influences:

> One of the most painful ... reflections that, as an Irishman, I am compelled to make ... is derived from the ugly and irritating fact that we are daily importing from England ... her fashions, her accents, her vicious literature, her music, her dances, and her manifold mannerisms, her games also, and her pastimes, to the utter discredit of our own grand national sports, and to the sore humiliation, as I believe, of every *genuine son and daughter* of the old land.

Croke goes on to lament the decline of indigenous games:

> Ball-playing, hurling, football-kicking according to Irish rules ... and all such favorite exercises and amusements amongst *men and boys* may now be said ... in several localities to be entirely forgotten and unknown. And ... in their stead ... [w]e have got such foreign and fantastic field sports as lawn tennis, polo, croquet, cricket, and the like – very excellent, I believe, and health-giving exercises in their way, still not *racy of the soil*, but rather alien, on the contrary, to it, as are indeed, for the most part, *the men and women* who first imported, and still continue to patronize them.[5]

Like Cusack, Croke pays particular attention to and expresses much concern for the nation's leisure. Games, both men agree, need to be national, and the absence of such programs 'humiliate' both 'son and daughter of the old land.' The actual playing of the 'forgotten' pastimes, however, should (or would) be taken up only by 'men and boys.' All of the 'foreign and fantastic' British sport substitutes are not 'racy of the soil', nor are the 'men and women who first imported, and still continue to patronize them.' With the contemporary phrase 'still not racy of the soil,' Croke places the desire for Irish games close to the land, while firmly rejecting the British body (male and female) from that land. By mentioning women twice, Croke's exclusion of women from playing according to 'Irish rules' foregrounds masculinity in the young GAA.

In a sense, the concerns voiced by Cusack and Croke were valid. They were manifested in pressure by the British sports organizing body, the Amateur Athletic Association (AAA), which insisted on British codifying principles as applied to Irish sports. Cusack criticized British rules. In opposition to AAA hegemony, Cusack proposed 'home rule' for Irish athletics:

> We tell the Irish people to take the management of their games into their own hands, to encourage and promote in every way every form of athletics which is peculiarly Irish, and to remove with one sweep everything foreign and iniquitous in the present system.[6]

Cusack even equated athletics to Irish nationalism:

> The vast majority of the best athletes in Ireland are nationalists [who] should take the matter in hands at once ... It is only by such an arrangement that pure Irish athletics will be revived, and the incomparable strength and physique of our race will be preserved.[7]

Ensuring the survival of the Irish 'race,' therefore, relied on the strong athletes who, by nature, held allegiance to the Irish 'nation.'

Of Croke's many 'exercises and amusements,' only a few became essential to the GAA: hurling (and later camogie), Gaelic football, handball, and rounders. Gaelic football and hurling quickly became the most important of the sports. Neither, however, was common or even well known around 1884 when the GAA was founded. A link was needed between 'favorite exercises and amusements' nearly 'forgotten and unknown' and 'every form of athletics which is peculiarly Irish.' Moving from the absence of a particularly Irish sport and the presence of the 'foreign and fantastic,' to the existence of all-sports-Irish required invention. Such practice evokes Eric Hobsbawm's concept of 'invented traditions,' or

> a set of practices, normally governed by overtly or tacitly accepted rules and of a ritual or symbolic nature, which seek to inculcate certain values and norms of behaviour by repetition, which automatically implies continuity with the past.[8]

As in the case of the Irish language, which had fallen out of everyday usage in many areas of the island by the time the Nationalists attempted to 'revive' it, Gaelic games needed to be found by navigating history in order to link past, present, and a sense of the future. 'However, insofar as there is reference to a historic past, the peculiarity of 'invented' traditions is that the continuity with it is largely factitious.'[9] Gaelic games, like the Irish language, were a cultural practice not viable for the country as a whole before the Gaelic renaissance; their prominent reintegration into the culture can never be true to a reality in which no break has occurred in the cultural practice – continuity is 'largely factitious.'

Hurling: the 'most Irish' of games

Hurling is perhaps the 'most' Irish of the Gaelic games, and has enjoyed a nostalgic history as an ancient sport. According to the GAA's website, hurling 'is chronicled as a distinct Irish pastime for at least 2,000 years.'[10] The game is associated with fairies and Celtic mythology: Cúchulainn played at the Ulster royal palace. 'As the uniquely Celtic brand of the ball game played with sticks [hurling] has survived invasions, wars, internal strife, famine and numerous official and semi-official attempts at its suppression.'[11] Despite the pressure to fold, the story goes, hurling has 'survived' suppression and prohibition: it was banned in the fourteenth century in Kilkenny, in the sixteenth century in Galway, and by the Sunday Observance Act of 1695. Alas, '[n]one of these attempts to kill hurling succeeded.'[12] GAA historian Marcus de Búrca positions hurling as disseminated, not destroyed: 'the invaders themselves eventually took to the game.'[13]

The game certainly existed before the 1884 founding of the GAA, but how far back its history stretches has been questioned. Some scholars, such as Mike Cronin, have questioned the willingness of historians to attribute antiquity to the sport. Tracing this pre-1884 history, he explains, is problematic and usually driven by politics; further, the lack of documentation makes research difficult.[14] Taking for granted the antiquity of the Gaelic games allows the 'script' of the sport to become a millennia-old story instead of a conscious adaptation, attributable in great part to the rules drawn up by GAA founder Maurice Davin and later Dick Blake.[15] Relying on the games' 'history' aids in the construction of the 'memory' of 'ancient Irish games,' which feeds the validity inherent in 'historical sources.'

What cannot be denied, however, is the success of the GAA's project of 'reviving' hurling and Gaelic football, creating viable and competitive games for which many athletes have developed impressive expertise. They have become immensely popular, uniquely 'Irish,' and clearly *distinguishable* from British games. This success, however, as

GAA historian W. F. Mandle notes, was in fact achieved through imitation.[16] By responding to a growing British trend of codifying athletics, GAA founders ended up *imitating* the British AAA. Eventually, the GAA's successful dissemination of codified Gaelic rules spread rapidly throughout the country on the parish level and surpassed the popularity of British games. Alternatively, imitation of the 'ancient' Irish sports provided the much-needed connection between past and present. Through such simulation, the GAA could produce a sense of continuity, of sameness, of a re-membered cultural artifact that ultimately gains autonomy.

Maintaining a perception of purity and authenticity in the Gaelic games requires performance. If you can perform hurling, or Gaelic football, you can perform something 'Irish.' The 'purity' of such performance is, of course, a complicated idea: on the one hand, hurling and Gaelic football are uniquely Irish – they are played for the most part in Ireland, and if played outside Ireland, usually by Irish emigrants; on the other hand, the sports are a creation from a mythic past, and their authenticity can easily be challenged. Parameters are therefore needed around the construction of GAA (and, of course, Irish) identities. Perhaps the best example would be the ban on foreign games, or Rule 27, which roped off sports perceived as not conducive to an autonomous Irish sporting industry by disallowing attendance or participation in rugby, soccer, hockey, or cricket. Repealed in 1971, even the ban's replacement, Rule 21, continued to prohibit British armed forces or police from the Association until 2001.

Performing Irishness on the contemporary Gaelic field

In contemporary Ireland, the Gaelic games now provide a space within which new immigrants to Ireland – from Poland, Nigeria, Romania, and other countries – can 'make' their own Irishness. Gaelic games are not only sites of memory, of re-membering what is perceived to be uniquely 'Irish,' if a precolonial ideal; they are sites of identity. In Ireland, the massive socioeconomic and cultural changes of the past two decades and the end of a longstanding trend of emigration producing the first net migration in decades have placed pressure on Irish identity.[17] In addition to a significant percentage of returning emigrants, Ireland has seen an influx of labor from both EU and non-EU nations, Africa, and Asia, as well as a small portion of Europe's overall asylum seeker applications.[18] Irish society has been slow to adjust, and the new arrivals are perceived as threats to what was in the past constructed as a cohesive culture[19] – the 2004 referendum in which Irish voters approved the end of automatic citizenship for children born in Ireland is but one example of what Ronit Lentin and Robbie McVeigh call a racist state with citizenship based on blood,[20] and what Matthew Causey describes as a 'shift to biopolitics.'[21] As a geographic and psychic space in which constructions of 'Irishness' have heretofore been evoked in the absense of a self-reflexive, critical framework, Ireland must now renegotiate relationships among culture, space, and performance.

The Gaelic games provide an example in which expressive culture inhabits 'Irish' spaces to stage 'identity,' 'ethnicity,' and 'place.' The GAA self-consciously maintains close ties to Irish ethnicity. According to the 2007 GAA Official Guide: 'Those who play its games, those who organise its activities and those who control its destinies see in the GAA a means of consolidating our Irish identity.'[22] As constructed by the GAA, this Irish identity is specifically male: 'The primary purpose of the GAA is the organisation of native pastimes and the promotion of athletic fitness as a means to create a disciplined, self-reliant, national-minded manhood.'[23] Despite the use of this outdated and sexist description of the GAA's mission, women's Gaelic football has over 100,000 registered players, and camogie, or the female version of hurling, has been organized for over a century and has clubs throughout the country. Although the GAA is not without its critics, the coexistence of GAA, women's Gaelic, and camogie headquarters under one roof at Croke Park in Dublin exemplifies the ironic and to a great extent uncontested authority held by the 'male' GAA over Ireland's 'native pastimes.'

Today, on the myriad Gaelic fields across Ireland, where young players have for decades learned how to 'be' Irish by performing hurling/camogie and Gaelic football, communities make contact, offering new immigrants and established Irish opportunities to negotiate – through the performance of sport – cultural expression, and to forge 'new' ideas of what it means to be 'Irish' – or, as Christie Fox inquires: 'Who is Irish–now?'[24] Charlie O'Neill's 2003 play *Hurl* uses the representation of the Gaelic games to re-imagine cultural identities in early twenty-first-century Ireland. In *Hurl*, a group of immigrants and asylum seekers form a hurling team in rural Ireland – and they *win*.

Produced by Barabbas, a theater company known for its conscious de-emphasis on text and exploration of an 'Irish' physical theater aesthetic,[25] *Hurl* presents an intensive physical engagement with sport and the 'new' Ireland. The play depicts the rise of a non-traditional club hurling team made up of members originally from Nigeria, Cuba, Argentina, Sierra Leone, Bosnia, Vietnam, and inner-city Dublin: an unexpected picture of rural Ireland and the GAA. The athletes, some of whom played hurling in their home countries ('Pajani PJ Ndingi. From Nigeria. Corner Forward. Taught by the Christian Brothers!'),[26] are led by an alcoholic priest and a washed-up trainer. With impressive optimism, O'Neill imagines a team that – despite discrimination and bureaucratic obstacles – wins through sheer will, determination, and some hard work. In a country such as Ireland in which 'inward migration ... was not anticipated' and where research indicates that 'racist incidents against non-nationals have increased in recent years,'[27] O'Neill challenges audiences to rethink the status quo.

Hurl attempts to create what Jill Dolan calls 'utopian performatives':

> small but profound moments in which performance calls the attention of the audience in a way that lifts everyone slightly above the present, into a hopeful feeling of what the world might be like if every moment of our lives were as emotionally voluminous, generous, aesthetically striking, and intersubjectively intense.[28]

Using storytelling and stylized movement, *Hurl* employs the cultural text of the Gaelic games to respond positively to rapid shifts in the sociocultural makeup of Ireland – a project not without its problems.

The provincial semifinal sequence is arguably the most compelling moment in the play, when one African player, Musa, interrupts the action by addressing his mark:

> MUSA You see Paddy I'm from Sierra Leone in west Africa. I was a child soldier. They would drug us and beat us and force us to do terrible things. In a way, Paddy hurling is like a therapy to help me get over that lost childhood. We used have these long machetes and they would make us do amputations. Sometimes the legs or feet but most often the hands or arms.

Although played in the original production for a more comic than serious effect, Musa's speech potentially works well as a compelling interruption; its force has the ability to break up the lighthearted style and communicate that O'Neill understands the complexities of what his characters represent. Whether the monologue offers what Jill Dolan (2005) calls a 'utopian performative' during which an audience can – in a frozen or slow-motion sequence in the middle of an action-packed game – experience for a moment an Ireland open to asylum seekers instead of a country filled with dread and fear of the 'Other' perpetuated by assumptions about handouts given to asylum seekers and pregnant women poised to give birth on Irish soil – remains to be seen.

Whether *Hurl* resists easy 'Irish' nostalgia in the service of a progressive utopian performative, it still insists on imagining a GAA that agrees to accept a team like the Freetown Slashers. A recent editorial in the *Kingdom*, a County Kerry newspaper, argued: 'After all, sport is one of the main vehicles through which foreign nationals can integrate into its host country. If the GAA take on this new challenge there is every possibility that an African born player will lift the Sam Maguire[29] in the next 30 years.'[30] What potential lies on the real-life performance space of the Gaelic pitch where players and spectators perform cultural memory? Do the Gaelic games provide a bridge between 'Irish' and 'Immigrant' or 'Other'? What opportunities might exist to both inform and transform culture?

A look at the GAA's 2006 annual report remains disappointing in its assumption that incorporating new Irish into the GAA is a future project:

> It is also important that we recognise and understand the needs and challenges of our new immigrant population and that our clubs supplement and support the work of Cumann na mBunscol in tackling this. A sports organisation such as ourselves needs to be ready for this demographic change, which is relatively near in planning terms.[31]

Frank Buckley of SARI (Sports Against Racism Ireland) expressed frustration with the organization: the GAA know that they have to get on board, he believes, and they are starting, but at this point it is still a lot of talk and not much action.[32] Groups like SARI and the Red Card initiative, which works in several countries, including Ireland, work with education and sport in an attempt to eradicate racism on and off the pitch. Both organizations work with other sports, especially soccer and rugby, in addition to the Gaelic games. Much – but certainly not all – of their work concentrates on youths. The GAA also focus heavily on youths:

> Kids from all over the world are brightening up classrooms all over Ireland with their cool cultures and Cumann na mBunscol is delighted that they are really enjoying playing Gaelic games. It's only a matter

of time before a Polish, Lithuanian or Nigerian kid appears on a county minor team and lifts a major trophy in the Hogan Stand.[33]

The Central Council seems satisfied to wait for the 'kids' to come up through the ranks, without paying attention to ways in which adult foreign nationals might get involved. Perhaps even more telling of the organization's distanced approach is the GAA initiative to 'get young people off the sofa and onto the playing fields'—in the *English* Midlands.[34] The program, which began in 2000, now includes 20,000 youths from a variety of ethnic backgrounds. 'The GAA pins great hopes on young women like Becky [Daley, now aged 16], who has won an All-Ireland under-14s skills medal, acting as something of a poster girl for the association.' Although Becky points out that '"It's a sport everyone can play,"' one that is '"easy to pick up and ... doesn't exclude people,"' the Central Council favors a youth-training system rather than adult programs – a strategy that seems strange for an organization which boasts of such an enormous rate of adult participation.

Perhaps the most hopeful example to date is the work of the Ulster GAA. In contrast to the GAA Council's unspecified and unsupported attempts to embrace the realities of the 'new' Ireland, the Ulster Provincial GAA board – an organization well versed in the politics of sport and identity – has already implemented programs in an attempt to open GAA doors to new arrivals. Ulster has held 'Non-National Fun Days,' as well as a round of 'Have a Go' nights – open evenings during which newcomers are invited to watch, learn, and try to play Gaelic games. The 2006 Have a Go night program formed Gaelic football and hurling teams made solely of non-nationals, and culminated in December 2006 with a top-town competition.[35] Although it may be far from a provincial club final, the work of the Ulster board exhibits the deployment of a receptacle of culture. Through the script developed during the turn of the twentieth century with the intent to create a unique form of expressive culture, immigrants *to* Ireland can access through performance – and alongside a diversity of experiences – community, cultural, and sporting identities.

Notes

1 This chapter adapts and develops material from 'Home and Away: The Gaelic Games, Gender, and Migration,' *New Hibernia Review* 11 (3) (2007): 28–43; and 'The Construction of Memory and Identity in the Gaelic Games,' in *Memory Ireland*, ed. Oona Frawley (Syracuse, NY: Syracuse University Press, forthcoming).

2 See, for example, Scott Spencer's chapter on traditional music in this volume.

3 Michael Cusack, 'A Word on Irish Athletics,' *The Irishman*, 11 October 1884.

4 Benedict Anderson, *Imagined Communities: Reflections on the Origins and Spread of Nationalism* (London: Verso, 1991 [1983]), 5.

5 Archbishop Thomas W. Croke, 'The Gaelic Athletic Association,' *The Nation*, 27 December 1884 (emphasis added).

6 Cusack, 1884.

7 *Ibid.*

8 Eric Hobsbawm, 'Introduction: Inventing Traditions,' in *The Invention of Tradition*, eds. Eric Hobsbawm and Terence Ranger (Cambridge: Cambridge University Press, 1983), 1.

9 *Ibid.*, 2.

10 Gaelic Athletic Association, 'History.' http://www.gaa.ie/index_history.html (accessed 20 January 2004); see also A. Ó Maolfabhail, *Camán: Two Thousand Years of Hurling in Ireland* (Dundalk: Dundalgan Press, 1973).

11 Marcus de Búrca, *The GAA: A History* (Dublin: Gill & Macmillan, 2000 [1980]), 1.

12 *Ibid.*, 2.

13 *Ibid.*

14 Mike Cronin, *Sport and Nationalism in Ireland: Gaelic Games, Soccer and Irish Identity Since 1884* (Dublin: Four Courts, 1999), 73.

15 W. F. Mandle, *The Gaelic Athletic Association and Irish Nationalist Politics 1884–1924* (Dublin: Gill & Macmillan, 1987), 107.

16 *Ibid.*, 14–15.

17 In 2006, the Central Statistics Office (CSO) reported a 2 percent annual population growth rate for the years 2002–6 – the highest on record. The 2006 population figure of 4.23 million is the highest since the 1861 census (4.4 million). See Central Statistics Office, 'Census 2006 Preliminary Report' (Dublin: Stationary Office, 2006).

18 Asylum applications to Ireland between 2001 and 2005 made up 2 percent of Europe's overall applications of nearly 2 million. These applications have steadily decreased over the past several years, with 2006 being the lowest, with 300,000 asylum seekers worldwide and Ireland receiving less than 1.5 percent of applications (4,314). Countries with the most applications to Ireland in recent years include Nigeria, Romania, and Somalia. Irish Refugee Council, 'Irish Asylum Statistics,' 23 March 2007, http://www.irishrefugeecouncil.ie/stats.html (accessed 9 June 2007).

19 In addition, the Immigrant Council of Ireland, formed in 2002, released a report in 2003 calling for 'a more strategic, long-term approach to immigration and integration policy' that is 'rights-based and should proceed from a fair and transparent immigration and reception system to a comprehensive approach to integration which recognizes that Ireland will remain an intercultural society, one that respects diversity within a framework of shared core values.' See Piaras MacÉinrí and Paddy Walley, 'Labour Migration into Ireland' (Dublin: Immigrant Council of Ireland, 2003), ix.

20 See Ronit Lentin and Robbie McVeigh, *After Optimism? Ireland, Racism and Globalisation* (Dublin: Metro Éireann Publications, 2006).

21 See Matthew Causey's chapter in this volume.

22   Gaelic Athletic Association, 'Official Guide, Part 1' (Dublin: Central Council of the GAA, 2007), 3.

23   *Ibid.*

24   Christie Fox, 'The Only Country I Own: Irish Immigration, Sports, and Drama,' paper presented at the American Conference for Irish Studies, St. Louis, 2006, 1.

25   Charlie O'Neill, email to author, 30 May 2007.

26   This and all subsequent quotes are from the unpublished script *Hurl*, courtesy of Charlie O'Neill.

27   MacÉinrí and Walley, 2003, v.

28   Jill Dolan, *Utopia in Performance: Finding Hope at the Theatre* (Ann Arbor: University of Michigan Press, 2005), 5.

29   The Sam Maguire is coveted cup won each year by the winning county of the All-Ireland Gaelic football final.

30   'The GAA Should Open its Doors,' *The Kingdom*, 27 January 2007, http://www.the-kingdom.ie/news/story.asp?j=23033 (accessed 6 April 2007).

31   Gaelic Athletic Association, Annual Report (Dublin: GAA Central Council), 10.

32   Frank Buckley, telephone conversation with author, 5 April 2007.

33   Cúl4kidz: The Official GAA Site for Boys and Girls, 'CúlBytes: News and Events,' http://www.cul4kidz.com/culbytes.htm#ungaa (accessed 7 April 2007).

34   Joe Lynam, 'GAA Takes off in "Most Unlikely Places,"' *BBC News online*, http://news.bbc.co.uk/go/em/fr/-/2/hi/uk_news/northern_ireland/4970248.stm (accessed 7 April 2007).

35   Ulster Council GAA (UCGAA), 'Have a Go Initiative,' Comhairle Uladh CLG – Ulster Council GAA Newsletter (October 2006), http://ulster.gaa.ie/newsletter/october06/october06.htm#4 (accessed 8 April 2007).

4

'It's beyond Candide – it's Švejk': Wise Foolery in the Work of Jack Lynch, Storyteller[1]

Mike Wilson

Introduction: Benjamin's model of the subversive storyteller

In 1936, as fascism advanced across Europe, the German essayist and critic Walter Benjamin penned a short article entitled 'Der Erzähler' ('The Storyteller').[2] Ostensibly it is an essay about the Russian writer Nikolai Lesskov, but running through it is an exploration of the nature of storytelling and the role of the storyteller in society. For Benjamin, 'a great storyteller will always be rooted in the people, primarily in the milieu of craftsmen'[3] and his call is for storyteller-artisans who offer meaningful stories as ways of developing strategies for change. Benjamin's storyteller is a subversive force, disseminating truth and wisdom in otherwise fraudulent times.

It could, of course, be argued that there have never been times that were not fraudulent, although some may be more fraudulent than others and it is these times that particularly require Benjamin's subversive storyteller. In part, Benjamin's essay is a response to the mechanization of society and the commodification of culture. He bemoans the demise of 'genuine storytelling,' as practiced by the farmer (the community-based storyteller, rooted in his/her neighborhood) and the sailor (the traveling storyteller, constantly nourishing communities with stories from afar).[4] Whilst much of what Benjamin feared has not come to pass and storytelling is very much alive and well, his essay has found new life and resonance among the contemporary professional storytelling movement.

In his essay 'How Storytellers Can Change Education in Changing Times: Stealing from the Rich to Build Community Bridges,'[5] American scholar of storytelling and fairy tales Jack Zipes develops Benjamin's idea, calling for storytellers to become cunning, or good thieves, in today's equally fraudulent, or 'impossible,'[6] times, a theme Zipes develops elsewhere in his writings:

> As we all know, we live in a world of lies in which states, business conglomerates, the mass media, educational institutions, and organized religions use story to cloud truths and to devastate the lives of millions of human beings. We live in a world in which truth has been abandoned for the spectacle of cruel and imperious deceit.[7]

For Zipes the current major threat to our communities lies in globalization and the unchallenged power of multinational corporations, against which the storyteller must take a stance. He explains:

> The difference between the good thief and the bad crook is that the good thief admits that we are all obliged to rob in some way and somehow wants to offset injustices and repay his or her crime by helping the disadvantaged and maintaining a subversive tradition of human compassion and responsibility, whereas the bad crook refuses to admit his or her involvement and culpability and continually seeks ways to deceive the majority of people ... [H]e or she uses the forces of the mass media, government, and courts to gain more of a stranglehold over the minds and lives of common people.[8]

In mentioning the model of the good or cunning thief, Zipes is, of course, referring to the folktale commonly known as 'Jack, the Cunning Thief.'[9] In this story, Jack sets out in search of his fortune, but falls in with a gang of ruthless robbers, who threaten to kill him unless he is able to steal the three prize cows from the greedy farmer – a task that even the robbers have been unable to accomplish. Through his own skill and ingenuity, Jack manages to outwit the farmer (greed and brains are, of course, rarely found together) and Jack wins both his freedom and a bag of gold. For Zipes, the good storyteller is one who robs stories from the rich and reinvents them for the poor.[10] But he argues that there is an additional threat that lies within the professionalization of storytelling which has taken place over recent years. On the one hand, it is a phenomenon that is to be welcomed for providing highly skilled, socially motivated storytelling artists, but it has also led to an inevitable commodification of storytelling, where stories can be bought and sold on the open market to the highest bidder, and therein lies the great paradox at the heart of contemporary professional storytelling – a paradox that is best solved by Jack, the cunning thief, himself.

The context of contemporary professional storytelling

In Ireland, as elsewhere, there has been a significant revival of interest in storytelling as a performance and applied art over the past few decades. Whilst retaining its own distinctive character, by drawing on the long traditions of oral storytelling in Ireland as described by Georges Denis Zimmermann, the 'revival'[11] in Ireland is closely related to the revivals in the UK and, less so, in the US. The Irish revival owes much to the work of Liz Weir, a former children's librarian from Northern Ireland, who now works prolifically as a professional storyteller and is a robust advocate for storytelling and organizer of storytelling events. It is also partly as a consequence of Weir's early role in supporting cross-community and cross-border storytelling initiatives that it is possible to talk about a distinctive Irish revival as being an all-Ireland affair.

In spite of an informal network of 'Yarnspinners Clubs' and 'Storytelling Houses,' the storytelling movement in Ireland has resisted too much organization on a national level compared to other countries, and has largely avoided some of the fierce debates around definitions that have taken place in England, Wales, and Scotland. Since 1992 the Society for Storytelling has operated in England and Wales and the Scottish Storytelling Forum was founded in Scotland in the same year. According to a recent survey,[12] there are now almost 400 professional storytellers operating within the UK, although this number no doubt includes many Irish storytellers. In Ireland a similar organization, Storytellers of Ireland, was formed only in 2003 and now advertises the services of over 50 professional storytellers.[13]

The contemporary storytelling movement originally emerged from the countercultural movements of the late 1960s and early 1970s. As Joseph Sobol rightly says in his survey of contemporary storytelling in the US, *The Storytellers' Journey*, in the early days the movement was driven by idealism.[14] In particular, many theater and community arts practitioners were drawn to storytelling because of its inherent democratic nature (in the sense of its being an artistic skill that everybody possesses to a greater or lesser degree) and its ability to subvert the traditional methods of theater production. At a time when theater companies were experimenting with dispensing with the idea of a director in favor of a more collective model, storytellers were dispensing with props, costumes, their fellow actors, and even theater buildings.[15] The utopian ideal of the participatory arts movement, whereby consumers of art also became the producers of art, acquired new resonance with storytelling. Everybody told stories, of course, as storytelling is 'the art form of social interaction,'[16] and so everybody could be a storyteller.

The growth of professional storytelling over the past 30 years is certainly a remarkable success story. Storytelling clubs and festivals attracting thousands of people have sprung up, and increasingly fewer children will go through their education without having a visit from a professional storyteller. The business in storytelling workshops is likewise booming as increasing numbers of people want to acquire the skills with which they too can earn their living from telling stories.

On one level this has all been very encouraging, but there is also a danger of storytelling becoming a victim of its own success. In the US, for example, professionalization has inevitably led to commodification, which in turn has led to a hierarchy and 'star system' emerging amongst storytellers. In his essay 'The Wisdom and Folly of Storytelling,' Zipes declares:

> More and more storytellers have tried to transform themselves into star commodities and advertise their wares as though they were indeed magical. ... The commodification that afflicts so many storytellers has led to a situation where there are two large camps: those commercial storytellers who perform largely for the sake of performance and who have foregone any sense of cultural mission, and those professional storytellers who continue to reflect both on their role as storyteller within the situation into which they insert themselves and on their stories and who question the value of storytelling that they urgently want to pass on to their auditors.[17]

To be this second type of storyteller is not easy. To become a freelance professional storyteller inevitably means subjecting oneself to market forces, so that it is far easier to entertain and please one's audience, the paying customer, than to challenge or provoke them. As Walter Benjamin's friend Bertolt Brecht might have said, 'Food is the first thing – morals follow on.'[18] On the other hand, professionalism brings with it resources (skills and time, for instance) to develop work of the highest quality, yet in a market system, and especially in a globalized world, it is difficult to remain true to those oppositional ideals. Yet it is the second category of storyteller – she/he who has managed to retain a sense of Benjamin's model of the subversive storyteller – that is the real subject of this chapter and, specifically, Jack Lynch, one of the leading 'Wise Fools of Irish Storytelling.'

Jack Lynch: Wise Fool

I am, in this sense, using the oxymoron 'Wise Fool' as an extension of the good thief/cunning thief model proposed by Zipes. It is Jack's (the character's) seeming lack of intelligence, whilst he is able to display feats of wit and ingenuity, that enables him to be the cunning thief he is. For the Wise Fool is ultimately a subversive, what Karl Kerenyi calls 'the spirit of disorder, the enemy of boundaries'[19] and Ruth Stotter 'the father of creativity.'[20] Indeed, theater scholar Joel Schechter, in his fine study of political clowning, *Durov's Pig*, eloquently draws parallels between clowning or fooling, and storytelling. Furthermore, Schechter's own division of clowns into two categories – those who serve the powerful (the court) and those who serve the powerless (the people) – is broadly similar to Zipes's own division of storytellers into the commercially-minded and the community-centered.[21]

Certainly, what might be defined as 'Wise Fool' stories (Jack Tales, Nasruddin Stories, Coyote Tales, or other underdog-wins-the-day-through-his/her-own-ingenuity stories) are popular amongst contemporary storytellers across the board. The sense of anarchy and utopian vision they express are standard fare and may in themselves suggest a subversive stance from the storyteller. But my argument here is that this in itself is not enough for Benjamin, Zipes, Schechter, or even me. What I am interested in here are the storytellers who adopt the persona of the Wise Fool for themselves, who bring the figure of the subversive out of the story and make him/her the storyteller.

Jack Lynch is a Dublin-based storyteller with long experience as a stage and television actor. Having established himself in alternative and political theater in Ireland in the 1970s and 1980s, he gradually moved into storytelling as a way of exploring some of the ideas he wanted to pursue as a solo performer. Influenced more by the work of Brecht and Dario Fo, Lynch discovered that storytelling was a form that allowed him to work directly with audiences in an improvisatory and subversive manner, yet also within his own cultural traditions.

Lynch's material comes from two main sources: traditional (predominantly Irish) folk narrative and a series of riotous stories, redolent of Garrison Keillor's *Lake Wobegon* and Giovanni Guareschi's *Don Camillo* stories, centered on the invented character of P. J. Galligan, a ne'er-do-well trickster, whose 'heart is in the right place, but his head is full of mad-dog shite,'[22] and his sidekick, Quighie 'the Feather.' The material for these stories comes principally from three sources: Michael J. Murphy's collection of tales from County Cavan; certain amounts of local Cavan folklore (the stories are set in Cavan, the home county of Lynch's father); and jokes that Lynch has overheard on his travels.

The personae of the storyteller that Lynch adopts for the telling of these two types of stories are demonstrably different. The Lynch that tells the folktales is presented as the authentic Lynch, whereas the Lynch who narrates the P. J. stories is clearly much more of a stage character, a neighbor of P. J. and Quighie who is telling the stories as firsthand accounts. Nevertheless, there are also important similarities and one might argue that they are, in fact, different versions of the same Wise Fool character.

The P. J. narrator, whose name is never revealed (except that one assumes he is also called Jack) first emerged when Lynch was working with Joe Duffy, a roving reporter on the Gay Byrne radio show. Lynch's brief was to be on hand to provide vox pops, folk knowledge, and general advice of a dubious nature:

Say there was a news story like the 'Floozy in the Jacuzzi'[23] had dried up ... So it was a very warm summer and this dried up and so they had people out on the street and they were just asking locals for their reaction to this and that they had, you know, spot competitions and prizes and all that. But they had my character on talking about a local way of water-divining, say, This would be total nonsense, you know, and he'd be saying, 'Here's something from Quighie "the Feather," who you know, Joe, don't you?'[24]

Duffy would then help break up Lynch's monologue by engaging him in conversation about these imagined characters, before allowing him to proceed with the absurd story:

'Well, Quighie taught me this one. The thing is, you get ... what you need is...you need about two gallons of vinegar and you'd need a fairly robust container. Then you'd get the lead from a vacuum cleaner – the bit that goes from the cleaner to the nozzle, you know, you cut the nozzle off. And you attach this – somehow – you attach this to the container and you hold it at a certain angle and ...' This, that and the other. And 'I have one here and I'm going to try it.'[25]

This whole conversation would be taking place on the Dublin streets and Lynch would find himself performing for both the radio audience and the live audience that began to gather in the street to watch the antics of Duffy and himself:

> So I'm divining for water along Talbot Street or somewhere, you know, and there's a huge crowd watching this and it's all bullshit. … And then Gay Byrne would ask some questions, 'Can *anybody*…?' 'Oh yeah, and it's very handy too, 'cos when you're finished, you can recycle this liquid, you know. It's very good, I'll tell you, Gay, it's very good to cure schizophrenia in greyhounds …'[26]

From these beginnings Lynch developed a whole series of Cavan[27] narratives concerning the exploits of P. J. and Quighie. The neighbor/narrator remains nameless, thus allowing him to keep a distance from his protagonists, but at the same time being a reflection of them – we have no doubt that the neighbor has nothing but admiration for P. J. and sympathy for Quighie, and is effectively the personification of both. In other words, Lynch is P. J./Quighie is Lynch – the narrator is merely a reflection of the characters about whom he is talking. The stories themselves are scurrilous episodes where P. J. gets the better of all manner of authority, convention, and the establishment, in particular politicians, the police, the *nouveau-riche* entrepreneurs of the Celtic Tiger economy, and – especially – the clergy. And if there is any comeback, it always falls on Quighie, not P. J. Yet the pair also display a degree of naivety and are driven by a survival instinct. By adopting the character of the Wise Fool for himself, Lynch is able to show that naivety and simultaneously the semi-hidden subversive ingenuity that suggests he is not so innocent after all.

There are a number of literary progenitors for this narrator-fool, but Lynch is clear that, if anything, it is Švejk, the eponymous hero of Jaroslav Hašek's biting First World War satire, who stands as the best model. Švejk is a born survivor, assumed to be a half-wit by all around him, yet he is far from the idiot he pretends to be. As Cecil Parrott says, Švejk

> is quite capable of making himself *appear* a fool to save a situation … [b]ut the irony underlying his remarks is always perceptible … Švejk is no ignoramus. He is the brother of a schoolmaster and is clearly an educated man. Although he expresses himself in the Prague vernacular he has a rich literary vocabulary combined with an almost encyclopedic knowledge, no doubt derived from considerable reading of newspapers and journals.[28]

Švejk, the Wise Fool, like Lynch's neighbor/narrator, uses his innocence to puncture the pomposity of his so-called superiors by resorting to relating stories about the people in his village. Hašek himself no doubt admired many of the qualities he had given Švejk – he was a political subversive, itinerant writer, humorist, and practical joker – and it is interesting that Lynch has a similar relationship with the neighbor/narrator.

There is much of Lynch in the character, but he also borrows heavily from the character's anti-authoritarianism to create his own story-telling persona when telling traditional folktales. This persona, a hybrid of the 'real' Jack Lynch and the neighbor/narrator, is used to deliver often quite lengthy introductions to the stories and enables Lynch to undercut the seriousness of the scholarship he likes to include in this part of his performance, as well as sometimes allowing him to be more politically daring with an audience.

Performing the footnotes

In a style redolent of Dario Fo's *Mistero Buffo*, Lynch typically introduces what may turn out to be a five-minute story with a contextual framing that may be ten minutes or longer. For Lynch, as with Fo, these introductions are the opportunities to provide the historical, social, and political framing necessary to enable the audience to read the *Gestus* of the piece more effectively. But it goes further than this. What Lynch is doing is not simply providing contextual information. Much of the material used in these introductions is of a very scholarly nature and Lynch is keen to furnish the audience with this information, but, as a performer, is wary of the potential of scholarship to become pompous. The Wise Fool character allows him, therefore, to subvert any pomposity by 'undercutting the seriousness'[29] of the scholarship. He turns himself into an accidental genius, as if he is simply stumbling on the scholarly framing, completely unaware of his own erudition and intellectualism. He is effectively taking what might be the footnotes to the story and turning these into performance material in their own right. This performing of the footnotes Lynch traces back to earlier work in children's television when he 'used to play an Einsteinian character on television and it involved a lot of putting across actual scientific facts in a humorous, or in a daft way.'[30]

The performance of footnotes, however, is not restricted to the introductory material, although that is where it is to be found at its most substantial. Lynch will also step aside from the telling of the story itself to add a footnote. He is able to do this because, as a performer, he is able to remain separate from his material and the characters in the story and move between his roles of footnote performer/narrator/storyteller. It is this separation of performer and role, a defining feature of Brecht's model of epic acting,[31] that allows Lynch to step outside the story in order to comment on it as the Wise Fool.

A story that Lynch calls 'Caoilte the Mighty Runner' is a case in point. In the story the High King requires an athlete to perform a job that requires great swiftness and invites each applicant to describe his quickness. Caoilte is the third, and final, applicant and declares that he could perform the task 'quicker than it takes for a woman to change her mind,' and so he is given the job.[32] At face value this punch-line might appear to be sexist, but Lynch cleverly turns it into a piece of positive political commentary. As soon as he has delivered the punch-line, he steps away from the story into his footnote-performer persona and says, 'Now, I noticed that not all the women were laughing tonight,' thus acknowledging the potential problematic nature of the story and, in doing so, eliciting more laughter. Then, in a manner that is redolent of Brecht's claim for the right 'to rethink everything anew' (*alles neu nachzudenken*),[33] Lynch proceeds to explain that he considers the ability to change one's mind, to adapt one's thinking to suit ever-changing contexts, is not only a virtue, but a necessity if one is going to act with political and social effectiveness. Having made the serious point, however, Lynch then counterbalances it with another self-deprecating joke: 'As long as women have that talent for changing their minds, who knows, some day there may be hope for a wretch like me!' This is followed up with a further comment directed at the audience: 'Do you think I got away with that?' In this way he is constantly playing with the audience and simultaneously drawing their attention to the subversive nature of his performance and also to its primary function of entertainment, inviting them to question and interrogate continually what he is saying and the intention behind it.

Subversiveness and conclusion

During a performance, it is a defining feature of storytelling that the storyteller will be required to manage a series of transitions between different personae, as the performance moves from introduction to story then back to introduction. In Jack Lynch's case, he is managing a particularly complex set of identities, whether that is the Jack Lynch who is mingling with and befriending the audience before the shoe, Jack Lynch, the footnote-performer, Jack Lynch the storyteller of folk-tales, Jack Lynch the neighbor/narrator, or Jack Lynch the neighbor/narrator as storyteller. All these personae are in part reflections of his non-performer self and all are variations on the Wise Fool figure. It is this figure, combined with the ability to move between personae and thus stand apart from the story, that allows Lynch to play the subversive storyteller, challenging hegemony, exposing hypocrisy, and, in Brechtian fashion, drawing 'the audience's attention to everything worth noticing.'[34]

Furthermore, Lynch exemplifies a key feature of effective storytelling, which is the apparent effortlessness of the performance. There is nothing labored about his storytelling work, no open display of artistry, but an informality and lightness of action that appears careless, but is, in fact, most careful. The transitions between personae seem natural, not managed. It is the lightness that is evident in Fo's performances of *Mistero Buffo* or in Ken Campbell's one-man shows,[35] the lightness which Italo Calvino describes as embodied in 'the sudden agile leap of the poet-philosopher who raises himself above the weight of the world.'[36] It was also a quality which Brecht recognized and admired in his poem in praise of Charles Laughton's belly[37] or which he wrote about in his final memo before his death in 1956 to the Berliner Ensemble, as they prepared to tour Britain:

> This is not a question of hurry, but of speed, not simply of quick playing, but of quick thinking. We must keep the tempo of a run-through and infect it with quiet strength, with our own fun. In the dialogue the exchanges must not be offered reluctantly, as when offering somebody one's last pair of boots, but must be tossed like so many balls.[38]

Underpinning Lynch's multiple personae is a subversive critique of the derogatory stereotype of the 'Stage Irishman' as a vulgar, uneducated, and uncultured itinerant. At the same time, he is reinventing the image of the Irish storyteller, away from its various incarnations as 'the solitary bard,'[39] 'the truculent Irish storyteller,'[40] or even D. J. Donoghue's description of the roguish 'Paddy the Sport,' a nineteenth-century storyteller 'much given to lying and tobacco, and an admirable hand at filling a game-bag or emptying a whisky-flask,'[41] and toward a reinterpretation of these images into a figure who is more sophisticated, more worldly, more politically aware, and more socially active. Whilst Lynch may feign foolishness, he is not a gullible greenhorn, but is literate, well read, and able to live on his wits, thus undermining the stereotype and ultimately turning prejudice on its perpetrators. As Lynch himself says, 'It's beyond Candide – it's Švejk.'[42]

So, through his use of the figure of the Wise Fool to inform his multiple performance personae, Lynch is able to maintain his roles of Benjamin's subversive storyteller and Zipes's honest thief. In Lynch's own words:

I bed down with that noble tradition in folklore that mocks the master, the tyrant, the exploiter, the unjust, the cruel, the pompous, the greedy...Jack the Refusenik![43]

Notes

1 Some of the ideas in this chapter were developed out of a conference paper entitled 'The Wise Fools of Contemporary Storytelling,' first delivered to the International Conference on the Wise Fool, Malta, December 2006.
2 See Walter Benjamin, *Illuminations* (London: Fontana/Collins, 1973), 83–109.
3 *Ibid.*, 101.
4 This division of storytellers into two types, the resident and the itinerant, is also noted as a feature of Irish society in the middle of the twentieth century and earlier by Georges Denis Zimmermann in his exhaustive study of representations of the figure of the Irish storyteller, *The Irish Storyteller* (Dublin: Four Courts Press, 2001), 434–5.
5 Jack Zipes, *Speaking Out: Storytelling and Creative Drama for Children* (London and New York: Routledge, 2004), 35-59.
6 See Jack Zipes, 'The Possibility of Storytelling and Theatre in Impossible Times,' preface to Michael Wilson, *Storytelling and Theatre: Contemporary Storytellers and their Art* (Basingstoke: Palgrave Macmillan, 2006), xiv–xviii.
7 Jack Zipes, 'Storytelling as Spectacle in the Globalised World', Unpublished Keynote Lecture to the 'Storytelling in the Globalised World Symposium,' The George Ewart Evans Centre for Storytelling, University of Glamorgan, 13 February 2007.
8 *Ibid.*, 38.
9 In the Aarne-Thompson *Types of the Folktale*, this story is listed as Tale Type 1525. See Antti Aarne, *The Types of the Folktale: A Classification and Bibliography*, trans. and enlarged by Stith Thompson (Helsinki: Suomalainen Tiedeakatemia, Academia Scientiarum Fennica, 1964).
10 Zipes, 2004, 38.
11 I acknowledge that the term 'revival' remains contested within storytelling circles. What has emerged in recent years is primarily a new performance art-form, but one that claims its roots in a pre-industrial folk art. I have continued to use the term because storytelling practitioners do so themselves, whilst recognizing its problematic nature as a term.
12 Ben Haggarty, *Memories and Breath – Professional Storytelling in England and Wales: An Unofficial Report Conducted by E-mail Survey*, 2004, www.sfs.org.uk (accessed 6 February 2005).
13 Storytellers of Ireland/Aos Scéal Éireann website, http://www.storytellersofireland.org (accessed 3 June 2008).

14 Joseph Sobol, *The Storytellers' Journey* (Urbana and Chicago: University of Illinois Press, 1999), 29.

15 Michael Wilson, *Storytelling and Theatre: Contemporary Storytellers and their Art* (Basingstoke: Palgrave Macmillan, 2006), 14–16.

16 Michael Wilson, *Performance and Practice: Oral Narrative Traditions Among Teenagers in Britain and Ireland* (Aldershot: Ashgate, 1997), 25.

17 Zipes, 2004, 27.

18 Bertolt Brecht, *The Threepenny Opera*, trans. Stefan S. Brecht (London: Eyre Methuen, 1973), 46.

19 Quoted in Ruth Stotter, *About Story: Writings on Stories and Storytelling 1980–1994* (Stinson Beach, CA: Stotter Press, 1994), 50.

20 *Ibid.*, 51.

21 Joel Schechter, *Durov's Pig: Clowns, Politics and Theatre* (New York: Theater Communications Group, 1985), 11.

22 Jack Lynch, *The Humours of Breffni: Scurrilous Tales* (audio cassette) (Dublin: Ojious Records, 1999).

23 The nickname given to the Anna Livia statue, representing the spirit of the Liffey, which stood in O'Connell Street until 2001. It featured a bronze figure reclining in a fountain made of granite.

24 Jack Lynch, interview with author, 26 April 2008.

25 *Ibid.*

26 *Ibid.*

27 Lynch's Cavan is an imagined Cavan, rather than an accurate one: 'What I'm doing compared to John Campbell or Eamon (Kelly) is very postmodern, do you know what I mean? I didn't go through those experiences. It's a fictional geography of Cavan' (interview with the author, 26 April 2008).

28 Cecil Parrott, 'Introduction' to Jaroslav Hašek, *The Good Soldier Švejk*, trans. Cecil Parrott (Harmondsworth: Penguin, 1973), xv-xvi.

29 Lynch, 26 April 2008.

30 *Ibid.*

31 Bertolt Brecht, *The Messingkauf Dialogues*, trans. John Willett (London: Methuen, 1965), 76.

32 Dáithi Ó hÓgáin from University College Dublin has identified the story as a late folktale from County Galway and in a tradition of stories in which Caoilte performs a task by means of his extraordinary skills (Tale Type 513) (email correspondence with Jack Lynch, 4 June 2008).

33 Best represented in the short play *Der Jasager/Der Neinsager* (He Who Said Yes/He Who Said No). (Bertolt Brecht, *Der Jasager und Der Neinsager: Vorlagen, Fassungen und Materialen* [Frankfurt am Main: Suhrkamp Verlag, 1966.])

34 P. W. Thomson, *Brecht: Mother Courage and Her Children* (Cambridge: Cambridge University Press, 1997), 73.

35 Ken Campbell is a British actor and founder of The Ken Campbell Roadshow (with Sylvester McCoy and Bob Hoskins), which performed anarchic comedy in the pubs and clubs of north-west England in the late 1960s/early 1970s. He later went on to found The Science Fiction Theatre of Liverpool and received critical acclaim for his production of *Illuminatus* for the National Theatre.

36 Italo Calvino, *Six Memos for the Next Millennium*, trans. Patrick Creagh (London: Vintage, 1996), 12.

37 Bertolt Brecht, 'Der Bauch Laughtons' ('Laughton's Belly'), *Gesammelte Gedichte, Band 3* (Frankfurt-am-Main: Suhrkamp Verlag, 1976), 875.

38 Bertolt Brecht, *Brecht on Theatre*, trans. John Willett (London: Eyre Methuen, 1978), 283.

39 Zimmermann, 2001, 176.

40 *Ibid.*

41 D. J. Donoghue, *Legends and Stories of Ireland, First Series*, 1899, quoted in Zimmermann, 2001, 194.

42 Lynch, 26 April 2008.

43 Quoted in Wilson, 2006, 165.

5
Traditional Irish Music in the Twenty-first Century: Networks, Technology, and the Negotiation of Authenticity

Scott Spencer

Performance paradigm

A traditional Irish musician prepares for months for the Fleadh Cheoil na hÉireann – an annual music competition sponsored by Comhaltas Ceoltóirí Éireann (the Irish Musicians' Club). The musicians who have made it to this final All-Ireland championship round have been given excellent marks by highly respected traditional musicians at competitions at the county and provincial levels. On the day of the *fleadh*, competitors perform their pieces for an adjudicator who has been carefully picked by Comhaltas for his or her traditionality and high regard within the musical community. Adjudicators in each competition use a strict set of criteria, also developed by Comhaltas. Top honors go to the musician who, according to the panel of adjudicators and set of category-specific criteria, brings to the stage the most perfect performance. One musician in each category is honored with the coveted All-Ireland prize.

The festival atmosphere surrounding these competitions brings together a great many participants and observers, including family, fans of the tradition, and traditional musicians representing a variety of experience levels. Throughout the festival, music is played informally at all hours in impromptu gatherings called sessions (*seisiún* in Irish), which break out at public and private areas in the surrounding town. Immediately after the day's competitions, many involved visit a few of these local sessions where competitors, adjudicators, and others join to play music and discuss the events of the day.

At these sessions, both competitors and adjudicators immediately set aside the strict competition criteria and relax into a much more informal system. At this gathering, the youngster with that day's top honors for a flawless fiddle performance may be playing alongside a senior musician who has difficulty holding the bow and is somewhat out of tune. In this informal system, in which decisions are made communally and through conversation, the same musicians informally assess each other using many of the categories used in the competition arena. Yet, in this forum, the senior musician may be considered the most traditional, historically accurate, and authentic of all the musicians present. More remarkably, the senior musician's playing may be considered by the participants as the best that day. The senior musician would be held in such high regard by the participants because s/he represents an earlier generation of traditional musician who learned his/her repertoire by ear from a lineage of teachers, and embodies the style of the region in which s/he was raised.

Though these two performance arenas are vastly different, the qualities of performance being considered in each space are almost identical. Surprisingly, the determinations of authenticity and traditionality may turn out to be contrary. This duality reflects divergent social situations, or parallel aesthetic systems, and provides a lens through which to view the mechanics of determining authenticity in Irish music.

Framework for thought

In the formal competition setting, musicians are judged through a strict set of criteria developed by Comhaltas Ceoltóirí Éireann, evaluated and numerically ranked by an adjudicator or panel of adjudicators. Scores are publicly posted at the competition and later published in the organization's newsletter, *Treoir*. In the informal setting, the same criteria are discussed obliquely, often through vague questions, careful use of stock phrases, a nod and a knowing glance, or things understood and left unsaid – a subtle game of knowledge-sharing and tacit understanding in which listening and personal interaction are as important as playing music. The competitiveness of the formal setting is dropped for a sense of cooperation – an understanding that the participants are collectively taking part in a tradition much larger than any one player. Despite the public ranking system of the competition, the stakes are much higher at the informal gathering. Top honors come with a medal and last for a year. An informal reputation amongst one's community of musicians for being authentic and at the core of the tradition lasts well beyond one's own life.

These contrasting systems raise a great number of questions: How can authenticity be dependent on situation? What is authenticity if the authentic can change? How is authenticity determined? A few of these questions have been treated to a fierce parsing of words through the fields of musicology, folklore, and anthropology, and yet in many cases, inquiries have mainly been focused on what is 'the authentic' rather than how ideas of authenticity are determined and used by traditional musicians. As folklorist Regina Bendix has written, 'the crucial questions to be answered are not "what is authenticity?" but "who needs authenticity and why?"'[1]

Interestingly, 'authenticity' is not a criterion in Comhaltas competitions, nor is it often openly discussed by musicians. Yet, a traditional performer bases most of his or her artistic decisions in relation to personal ideas of the authentic. Much of the language surrounding traditional Irish music involves this as well – looking for the 'pure drop,' trying to find that 'wild lonesome sound,' hunting down a session that embodies 'great craic,' searching for older musicians who are 'the real thing.' It seems that with most traditional Irish musicians and enthusiasts, the idea of authenticity is so fundamental to the art-form that it is an assumed foundation of every conversation, performance, recording, and publication.[2]

These ideas of traditionality, historic continuity, authenticity, and quality of performance in traditional Irish music are not inherent in the music as performed. Rather, they are dependent on situation and community, and are constantly negotiated and performed by those who play and discuss the music. This chapter explores the reasons why these concepts are engaged by both musicians and those viewing the tradition from the outside. As the music and its proponents have expanded to a global diaspora, these essential negotiations have become reliant on an intricate web of technological communications, strung together by a wide variety of interpersonal, affiliative, and institutional lines of communication and served by a number of core resources.

The various networks through which musicians determine traditionality within this art-form are representative of the ongoing process of change within this oral tradition, and the constant negotiating and reshaping of the corpus of collective memory within such a tradition. Simply put, practitioners within a musical tradition continuously determine what is traditional and authentic through their interactions.

Our inherited theoretical framework

Authors and artists of Ireland's Gaelic Revival sought out as 'Gaelic' those traditions and aspects of culture in Ireland that were distinctive to Ireland before British colonization. In their quest for an authentic Irish culture, they imagined as traditionally Irish that which had remained seemingly unspoiled by continental influence. Areas of the Irish-speaking west were singled out as especially pure and were deemed to hold the highest concentration of aspects of Ireland's Celtic origins – still embraced by what was considered an unmediated oral tradition.

Concepts of traditionality, orality, and authenticity were first applied to traditional Irish music by the Gaelic League, Comhaltas Ceoltóirí Éireann, and other cultural groups, due to a lingering academic engagement with *what* had been passed on in an oral tradition rather than *how* culture is transmitted. The ideas and definitions employed in conceptualizing traditional music mirrored concurrent modernist academic thought on authenticity and oral heritage. The intellectuals of the Gaelic Revival, most of whom were attending continental universities during the formation of the movement, were profoundly exposed to these conceptualizations, especially those developed in the field of folklore by academic disciples of Francis James Child and his ballad collections.[3] In many cases, academic treatments of traditional Irish music–not to mention the entire realm of folk music–still follow this modernist academic model of traditional music, associating exclusive orality with authenticity and purity. Only recently has Comhaltas begun to embrace the idea that change is inherent to Irish music, just as music scholars have embraced this idea among traditional forms of music around the world.

In many cases, academic studies of traditional Irish music have assumed that musical traditions deemed authentic and traditional are a product of an exclusively oral transmission process, despite ample evidence to the contrary.[4] As a result, academics and musicians alike have placed traditional music in an unearned (by their standards) position of purity and authenticity, as they have conveniently ignored the use by traditional musicians of available technologies throughout history.

The fields of folklore and ethnomusicology have traditionally assumed that the effects of mass media on traditional culture are inherently destructive. In *Cassette Culture*, Peter Manuel writes about the role of mass media – especially cassette tapes – in the distribution of popular music in northern India as technology, urbanization, and development spread recorded music throughout the region. 'The expense, of course, is the destruction of insular, cohesive traditional societies.'[5] Though this quote is not representative of Manuel's larger work, such a historically reductive approach toward the role of technology in the transmission of culture suggests that the adaptation of recording technology by a regional oral culture would result in a fundamental corruption of that culture, and the reorganization or destruction of traditional modes of communication.

I would instead argue that in the case of traditional Irish music, the musicians have incorporated all forms of recording technology (transcription, print, analog and digital audio, video) into their traditional modes of communication throughout the history of the art-form, and have used these technologies to preserve and maintain their traditional culture. Though incorporation of technology has in some ways changed regional, and especially local, styles, I argue that new media have enabled Irish musicians to transcend their distinctly regional (Irish) cultural and social networks to communicate among an international (Irish, diasporic, and affiliative) base of practitioners allowing a global negotiation within the strict, self-imposed ideals of regionality, traditionality, and authenticity.[6]

Codification of tradition and competition

In traditional Irish music, another wonderful irony exists: the group charging itself with the preservation of this constantly changing oral art-form and repertoire has taken steps to codify its performance practices. By organizing the annual Fleadh Cheoil, Comhaltas Ceoltóirí Éireann has developed a set of categories and a specific lexicon through which musicians are evaluated. Through these criteria, competitors are judged in a way designed to remove individual preference from the aesthetic system. County Clare-based concertina player and scholar Tim Collins, who has adjudicated at many of these events at every level, explains:

> The adjudication sheets that you get have a series of criteria by which you adjudicate competitors – solely based on the mechanics of the music. So they would say, X amount of marks for Timing; Y amount of marks for Rhythm; Phrasing; Command of Instrument. And the adjudication sheet then varies slightly, depending on what instrument, what competition, or category they are. For instance, for concertina, they are not going to have tuning in it. So you can see that they're really looking at the mechanics and they're trying to get rid of – this is my understanding – they're trying to get rid of this subjectivity of adjudicating. This is the irony of competition.[7]

In Irish music circles, debates have raged about this codification and institutionalization of traditional music and resulting effects upon the fluidity and change inherent in the tradition. Many critics of Comhaltas Ceoltóirí Éireann point to the emphasis on students' preparation for All-Ireland contests and the codification of critical response to the tradition for fleadh adjudicators as factors in the stagnation of a historically oral tradition.[8] Critics of such movements point to the collection of recordings and transcriptions of music as the first step in stifling cultural change. Yet those who have worried about the possibility of traditions becoming extinct have argued that, though facilitating cultural stagnation at some levels, such institutions are important vehicles for the perpetuation of at least a vestige of the tradition.[9] In this regard, a student's preparation for a competition highlights dual aesthetic systems. Preparation for competition requires a static interpretation, though the aim of the competition is to foster interest in an otherwise dynamic living tradition.

Dual aesthetic systems such as this also lead adjudicators into odd dualities. This is especially true if a judge considers one player to be more sophisticated within the larger tradition, yet must award top honors to a musician who has performed in a way understood as 'more traditional' within the terms of the competition.[10] Such predicaments occur quite often, as when a competitor uses innovations generally accepted by the larger community – such as individualized ornamentation techniques or newly composed repertoire – but which are considered outside the bounds of traditionality as conceived by Comhaltas Ceoltóirí Éireann.

It is generally understood by the adjudicators that the criteria by which competitors are judged reflects an aesthetic system developed during the formation of the Gaelic League and Comhaltas Ceoltóirí Éireann in the late nineteenth century – a period just before the widespread impact of the recording age. Yet, these same judges, when the adjudication is over and the informal music session break out in the local pubs, would not play as they adjudicate. As Tim Collins has mentioned, after the fleadh the adjudicators and performers

> leave the competition arena, and go to a different arena of music, and you'd probably revert back to how you'd play yourself, you know? People tend to play a certain way in competition: they play the game, they know how to perform within the competition in contrast to how they would normally play.[11]

The nature of the dual aesthetic systems in play at the fleadh demands that both musician and adjudicator shift back and forth between performance situations and contrasting temporal criteria – they 'play the game' by performing such switches. The formal system of competition functions to evaluate the playing of competitors within a strict set of parameters and an institutionalized understanding of the tradition to create a public record, while the informal system imparts its information to the collective memory through constant discussion.

Recordings, location, tradition

In art-forms like traditional Irish music – where many of the influential players are in the diaspora – distance must be bridged and the tradition must allow vehicles for this to happen, or risk fractioning. Because of this distance, and today's availability of personal recording devices, the culture of recording has permeated traditional Irish music. Musicians have, however, incorporated technology while respecting the tradition. Recording without permission at informal settings is frowned upon,

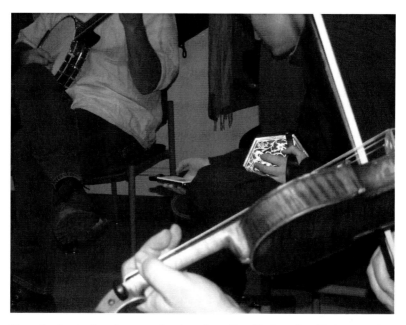

Figure 1   Louisa Bennion records a tune from Dan Neely on her iPod at a session in New York City. Photo by Scott Spencer.

and those recording will usually defer to those musicians being recorded. Tim Collins has observed that the role recording takes in a session is somewhat touchy.

> There's a certain etiquette attached to it. Normally, you'd just ask and listen. Especially younger people would come in and say, 'Listen, I heard you playing a lovely tune recently. I'd love to learn it. Could you record it for me?' With etiquette, you wouldn't really accept them coming in and trying to covertly record anything.[12]

The recordings gleaned from such formal and informal settings are then coveted, learned, and passed from person to person throughout the Irish music scene. Sometimes these recordings have multiple owners or have been reproduced through multiple generations of recording media. These recordings seem to follow established paths between friends, often through mutual interests such as regional repertoire, shared instrumental tradition, or through admiration for the music of particular players.

American fiddle player Cleek Schrey has lived at the heart of this system. As an avid learner of older styles and settings of traditional Irish fiddle tunes, he actively sought out situations in which he could record repertoire and has a voracious appetite for the informal recordings of others:

> When I was learning Irish music as a teenager, I would collect and trade recordings obsessively. These recordings laid the foundation for the bulk of my repertoire. Aran Olwell might come back from Ireland and have two or three killer session tapes that he would copy off for friends, and the process would be repeated over and over. This sort of exchange was typical and reciprocated. These recordings were mostly traded among peers, musicians ranging from their teens to their early 20s. It was one way of keeping up to date with new tunes that were added to a collective repertoire.[13]

These tapes and field recordings have proven to be a major influence on the tradition, especially to the younger players who are quite comfortable with recording technology. As many of these younger players live in the diaspora, their connections to the tradition rely in part upon a constant flow of these tapes.

Where is authenticity?

In the new realm of digital communications, music moves across all borders and media, and a geographic anchor through which to prove authenticity is not necessarily applicable. In his search for the authentic, *Irish Echo* writer Earle Hitchner asked, 'What is authentic Irish music? It's a moving target, hard to hit definitively, and that's not a critical copout. Geography is less significant in this age when a profusion of home recordings and Internet access enables people around the world to develop their avocational or vocational interest in Irish music.'[14]

Iain Chambers has also written on regionality and the authentic in Irish music, arguing that the presence of differing regional styles reflects not an inherent quality of the music, but a system through which musicians can develop and express their identity – simultaneously looking out from the local and in from the global. He states that there can be authenticity in the face of regional variances in Irish music, because there is 'a central distinction between music as the assumed site of "authenticity," with its associated closure of community and ready to wear "identity," and music as a source of difference, where unicity and ethnocentricity are constantly contested and denied.'[15]

So where does authenticity in Irish music reside and how is it passed on? Anthony McCann, a gifted and patient observer of musical conceptualization, reminds us to react to the social situation instead of dictate it:

> We need to be careful not to prescribe cultural activity. We need to assert the contemporary validity of traditional practices as a contemporary response to contemporary conditions ... We need to carefully examine the registers of social interaction within which traditional practices occur, for it is here that the keys to transmission will be found.[16]

In the case of traditional Irish music, especially in the light of the All-Ireland competition, parallel performance paradigms arise. In these parallel situations, traditional Irish musicians must be cognizant of the directions through which they are expressing their art-form. In competition, they must be ready to anchor their music in the past by naming their teachers and repertoire sources – even through the names of the tunes and the versions or variations they play. Adjudicators will interpret these subtleties in performance practice as statements of a player's authenticity.

In the informal session, the player is better able to discuss these aspects of his or her repertoire and engage in dialogue with others on such facets of the tradition. Half the fun of the informal session is that these anchoring details are always open to discussion, elaboration, and contestation. In this way, performances for competition are inherently limited in their scope, in their ability to engage with the tradition, and in their access to the full range of performative and communicative vectors. In a competition, it is the adjudicator's role to rule on such issues – questions are rarely asked of a competitor. With this in mind, competitions are merely an inherently limited expression of ongoing performative behavior – a packaged version of a vibrant, multi-vectored culture presented through the limited vectors of the stage.

Contextualization

Possibly the most important aspect of this personal negotiation of the traditional and authentic resides in the contextualization of the music being played. As musicians perform their tunes formally on the stages of the world, or share their tunes informally in pubs and kitchens throughout the Irish music world, they will constantly contextualize the tunes they are playing. In an informal setting, a tune will always be followed by a discussion of its origins, or a description of where that musician learned it. As Sally K. Sommers-Smith has keenly observed:

> More than just the music is transmitted in this fashion. Often, the people who have played the tune – or, in some cases [the person who has] composed the melody – are recalled in the making and remaking of the music. A portion of the social fabric that bound the tune as it was played in the past is thus transmitted as well in the traditional process.[17]

This contextualization serves three functions. First, it places the musician in the larger tradition, and helps to establish his or her level of engagement with the tradition. Second, it allows the musician to discuss and develop the authenticity of the tune or setting. Third, it allows a communal experience, which helps to maintain and reinforce the collective memory.

The relation of a tune to specific musicians is vital to contextual-ization and authentication, and discussing the players associated with a particular tune is a major part of determining the tune's role in the tradition. Tim Collins explains:

> Associating it with musicians, for me, authenticates music in a very important way. These tunes were composed by somebody. Why did they compose them? Where did they compose them? When did they compose them? What were the influences – what made them compose this tune, you know? And why do people do that? They do that because it is a way that people can express their identity, you know? Through music.[18]

With the current ease of website development and the need for the global musical community to engage with these ideas, this system for contextualization has also spread to the Internet. In much the same ways that lines of communication have formed between musicians with mutual interests, Internet sites have been developed – mostly through the efforts of amateur enthusiasts – through which this contextualization can take place. These websites range from informal chatrooms in which devotees can discuss every aspect of repertoire and the tradition,[19] to formal web presences for the leading institutions in traditional Irish music.[20] Most recently, some of the most influential sites for this exchange of contextualizing information, repertoire, and ideas have sprung up for particular instruments.[21]

Lines of communication

As I have argued above, ideas of authenticity, oral tradition, and continuity with history and traditionality were established as essential aspects of traditional Irish music as early as Irish musicians began to solidify their traditions. Today, these concepts have a constant presence in Irish music and are the basis for many musical interactions. As the local has become the global, and the global has become the 'glocal'[22] thanks to digital technologies – the sites through which these negotiations are conducted have transcended geographic place, allowing practitioners to be at once global *and* local while engaging with the tradition. The informal session is now but one of many realms used for the negotiation of tradition, especially as younger players who have great comfort in conducting their lives through digital technologies lend their passion to traditional music. Their performances transcend classic performance venues, or rather they perform on a variety of tangible and conceptual stages: live, mediated, digital.

I would suggest that the different performance realms explored in this chapter engage this sort of dialogue in divergent ways, and therefore result in contrasting forms of transmission. The competition, with a static and unidirectional reading of performance by adjudicators, results in the transmission of a historical document and functions as a vehicle for the individual in service of the greater tradition. The informal session, with its constant, omni-directional, dynamic give-and-take, helps to form a series of communal experiences which are the basis for developing the collective memory.

Conclusion

In the competition performance paradigm, the performers on stage conform to and compete within one aesthetic system as they develop and negotiate the 'traditional.' Yet the same individuals, in an informal setting, perform the same music for the same people within a different performance paradigm and set of criteria, and achieve many of the same results, though through a much different process. One could argue that the difference is between an organic system of aesthetics – one that incorporates change and is flexible to respond to external influence, and a static and codified system – where the only realm of change is the personal adjudication of the judges. As the performers shift between realms, they are also shifting between artifice and reality: the real world of traditional music – in which all things are negotiated, and the codified recreation of this world – in which this negotiation is discouraged in favor of tangible (and unchallengeable) results. The role of these ongoing negotiations is vital in the determination of authenticity within much of the tradition. These interactions are performative and manifested at the level of the individual through lines of communication between musicians, their interactions with institutions in traditional Irish music, and practitioners of the greater tradition. With this in mind, and with an eye to the events, institutions, resources, and individual interactions within these structures, it is clear that fundamental concepts of authenticity and traditionality within traditional Irish music are performed and negotiated, rather than imbued or inherent.

Notes

1   Regina Bendix, *In Search of Authenticity: The Formation of Folklore Studies* (Madison: University of Wisconsin Press, 1997), 21.

2   See Mary Trachel, 'Oral and Literate Constructs of the "Authentic" in Irish Music,' *Eire-Ireland* 30 (3) (1995): 27–46. See also Earle Hitchner, 'What Exactly is Authentic Irish Music?,' 'Ceol,' *Irish Echo*, 23 August 2006, www.celticcafe.com/celticcafe/EarleHitchner/Columns/Ceol/08_Ceol_ Aug.23.06.html (accessed 23 June 2008).

3   Francis James Child, *The English and Scottish Popular Ballads*, vols. 1–10 (Boston, MA: Houghton Mifflin, 1882–98).

4   See Jimmy O'Brien Moran, 'Paddy Conneely – The Galway Piper: The Legacy of a Pre-Famine Folk Musician,' PhD Thesis, University of Limerick, 2006. See also Scott Spencer, 'Early Traditional Irish-American Recordings and Atlantic Migrations,' in *The Irish in the Atlantic World*, ed. David Gleeson (Charleston: University of South Carolina Press, 2009).

5   Peter Manuel, *Cassette Culture: Popular Music and Technology in North India* (Chicago, IL: University of Chicago Press, 1993), 8.

6   See Spencer, 2009.

7   Tim Collins, telephone interview with author, 12 December 2007.

8   Rachel C. Fleming, 'Resisting Cultural Standardization: Comhaltas Ceoltóirí Éireann and the Revitalization of Traditional Music in Ireland,' *Journal of Folklore Research* 41 (2) (2004): 227–57.

9   Fleischmann suggests transcriptionists capture only 'fossil remains' of musical traditions. See Aloys Fleischmann, ed., *Sources of Irish Traditional Music. 1600-1855* (New York: Garland, 1998), xvii.

10 Though Comhaltas does not define ideas of traditionaliy, the Comhaltas Ceoltóirí Éireann Bunreacht (Constitution) reminds readers that the function of the organization is to promote traditional forms. In the 'Aims and Objectives' section of the Bunreacht, printed in every competitor's rulebook, it states that CCÉ functions '(a) To promote Irish Traditional Music in all its forms ... (c) To promote Irish Traditional Dancing; (d) To promote and foster Traditional singing in both Irish and English.' See 'Comhaltas Constitution (Bunreacht),' 29 November 2006, Comhaltas website, http://comhaltas.ie/press_room/detail/comhaltas_constitution_bunreacht/ (accessed 24 October 2008).

11 Collins, 12 December 2007.

12 *Ibid.*

13 Cleek Schrey, email with author, 7 March 2007.

14 See Hitchner, 2006.

15 Iain Chambers, *Migrancy, Culture, Identity* (London: Routledge, 1994), 83.

16 Anthony McCann, 'All that is not Given is Lost: Irish Traditional Music, Copyright, and Common Property,' *Ethnomusicology* 41 (1) (Winter 2001): 89–106, 98.

17 Sally K. Sommers-Smith, 'Irish Traditional Music in a Modern World,' *New Hibernia Review* 5 (2) (2001): 111–25, 112.

18 Collins, 12 December 2007.

19 See, for example, www.thesession.org.

20 See the Irish Traditional Music Archive's website, www.itma.ie.

21 See the website for Na Píobairí Uilleann, www.pipers.ie; or Pat D'Arcy's www.uilleannobsession.com.

22 See Tony Dundon, María-Alejandra González-Pérez, and Terrence McDonough, 'Bitten by the Celtic Tiger: Immigrant Workers and Industrial Relations in the New "Glocalized" Ireland,' *Economic and Industrial Democracy* 28 (4) (2007): 501–22.

Part II

Place, Landscape, and Commemoration

6

'Tapping Secrecies of Stone': Irish Roads as Performances of Movement, Measurement, and Memory

J'aime Morrison

Oh, my roads and their cadence!

Jean Caubère[1]

... what is your body
now if not a famine road?

Eavan Boland[2]

Roads have always held a particular fascination for me. Perhaps it is because they hold the promise of movement, travel, and escape. Certain roads remain embedded in my memory: the roads to the bluffs of Santa Cruz where I choreographed my first dance; Tioga Road in the Sierra Mountains of California where I drove as a 20 year old and watched shooting stars from my Volkswagen, and the Wicklow mountain roads I explored as a student hoping to commune with the literary spirits of Samuel Beckett, J. M. Synge, and James Joyce. Roads run deep – they inscribe themselves in us. They can suggest motion or enact a boundary, provide a connection between distant places, beckon a journey without end, or disguise a secret route. This chapter considers roads as vital cultural spaces which give rise to scenes of performance and which at times might be seen as performances themselves. Roads direct and redirect our movements and sometimes play with our perceptions of reality and illusion, shifting our perspective when they change direction. Like the 'perils of Dublin pavements' that confronted Bloom as he headed through the city's streets, roads are gestures, intersecting with our bodies and our thoughts as we negotiate the uncertainties of the ground.[3] Rather than view Irish roads as inert or static cultural tracts, I see them as conduits for movement and memory operating within the larger spatial history of Ireland and in conjunction with a repertoire of cultural practices.

Pictures of Irish roads register traces of embodiment (or disembodiment), and so offer routes for accessing those areas of cultural experience that may seem recalcitrant to historical inquiry. When we study bodily or spatial histories, subjects that can elude traditional methods of historical analysis, we must look for traces of the past in images, in words, and in the broader repertoire of embodied culture. Performance theorist Joseph Roach suggests that such a project must attend to 'counter-memories' or 'the disparities between history as it is discursively transmitted and memory as it is publicly enacted by the bodies that bear its consequences.'[4] Roads run at the intersection between history and memory because they offer material evidence of movement: cracked concrete, pot holes, signage, mile markers, lane dividers, and landmarks – while they also reference a wide range of embodied practices and behaviors: road bowling, road racing, cycling, dancing, walking, marching, praying, hitchhiking, smuggling. What do roads tell us about cultural, social, and political conceptions of space – about how space is ordered, controlled, measured, and moved through? What do images of roads reveal about the politics of movement? Perhaps roads make legible what and who has passed by and passed on, referencing bodies that no longer exist. In this sense roads are haunted spaces of memory that bear the traces of many forms of movement – those of exile and homecoming, invasion and insurrection, pilgrimage and performance.

Tim Robinson, mapmaker and geographer of the west of Ireland, begins his study of Inis Mór by describing his own 'circuits' around the island. For Robinson, the Irish landscape is saturated with 'geologies, biologies, myths, histories and politics,' and his steps, which retrace those early pilgrimage circuits, embody a momentary congruence 'between the culture we bear and the ground that bears us.'[5] Robinson lets this movement guide his writing; his narrative wanders between cartographic observation and poetic reverie, imaginative recreation and oral history, in order to evoke the contours of the land. Irish topography has long been associated with historical accretions, the sediment of a culture dispossessed of its land and language. As soil, ground, territory, and landscape, Irish land represents what Australian geographer Paul Carter refers to as a 'folded ground.' Carter invokes the image of fieldwork – the literal unfolding and folding of the earth – and metaphorically refers to the ground of convergences, departures, and coincidences that shape our movements.[6] For Robinson and Carter the ground is not static, but active, producing a resonance between foot and earth that animates the bodies in the landscape.

In *The Lie of the Land* Carter posits a theory of movement within the landscape of colonized territory. He counters Paul Valéry's remark that '[t]he state of mind of a man dancing is not that of a man advancing through difficult country of which he is making a topographical survey' by asserting that because of his leveling and clearing gestures, 'the explorer precedes the pirouetting dancer.'[7] In this statement the dancer occupies the firmer ground, a landscape from which obstacles have been removed. Viewed as 'difficult country' by colonial cartographers and would-be invaders, the topography of Ireland did not yield easily to such leveling operations. As noted by Irish map historiographer J. A. Andrews, '[t]he roughly articulated terrain of Ireland presented numerous obstacles for surveyors as did Ireland's history of rebellion.'[8] Ireland's porous, soggy, and often unchartable landscape invites the challenge of moving (or pirouetting) on an uneven ground. These early descriptions of Irish topography produce a geography of movement that is aligned with the contours of the land.[9]

In Ireland the building of roads often coincided with colonial efforts to assert power and control. In his study of Ireland's first toll roads, David Broderick notes that as early as 1690 those in government were highly aware of the 'most passable roads for the army to march to the siege of any place.'[10] Especially following the rebellion of 1798 Broderick points out that the military road in County Wicklow was built to give the British army access to rebel strongholds. Early Irish roads were quickly expanded and formalized by the Irish Parliament, which made road construction and repair a priority during the eighteenth century in order to facilitate greater communication, increase trade opportunities, and facilitate the collections of rents and tariffs.[11] *An Inquiry into the Effects of the Irish Grand Jury Laws* (1815) is a treatise dealing with the importance of road maintenance within each county. It clearly outlines the importance of roads as instruments of social progress and control in Ireland: 'There are few points in domestic economy, which more powerfully effect, and more exactly measure the improvement of a nation, than the state of the roads and highways.'[12] However, attempts to render Irish land profitable through the construction of roads were met with small acts of resistance. Local roads known as boreens (*bóithrín*) refer to the unsurfaced, narrow lanes and pathways that crisscross the countryside. Such a network of passages could have offered people a means of escape from military forces, access through large private estates, tracks for driving cattle, or conduits for local news and information. From a performance studies perspective, we might consider these roads as subversive gestures that participate in a geography of resistance to official routes.[13]

In 'That the Science of Cartography Is Limited,' poet Eavan Boland aligns maps with authority and with the flattening lines and imposing grid of empire, but the poem also alludes to the palpable, unseen presence of those who disrupted the colonial plot.

[in] 1847, when the crop had failed twice,
Relief Committees gave
The starving Irish such roads to build.

Where they died, there the road ended.[14]

Boland interrogates the colonial map to unfix it so she can view it choreographically as a space for movement's trace. By challenging the authority of the official map she makes visible the lost movements of those who built the roads. In 1831, the Irish Board of Works (established by the British government) sought to promote the economic development of Ireland by providing paid relief work for famine victims through the construction of new roads. Yet these roads often went nowhere. As described in the poem, they end where the bodies of the starving give out. Her poem refigures Ireland as a fragrant wooded grove, a space of contours and curvilinear forms that has been disciplined to fit a topographical grid. Yet the linear outlines of the official road map cannot be read because these roads disappear; unfinished and often without a fixed destination, famine roads function as fragmentary geographies of resistance.

During excavation for the new M3 motorway from Dublin to surrounding communities, workers for the Irish Roads Authority discovered what is believed to be a prehistoric ceremonial site at Lismullen, County Meath, between the ancient hills of Tara and Skryne. In a reversal of Boland's image, in which the straight line of the surveyor obfuscates the contours of the earth, this new highway cannot bury the power of the submerged ritual landscape – the proposed Tara Road will offer residents of the area a more direct and quicker route into the city center – indicating that buried histories do resurface, reminding us of their presence and their enduring influence. Digging is an important motif in Irish cultural narratives. Seamus Heaney recognizes the significance of digging as an embodied practice akin to writing. In his work he unearths mythic, political, and personal histories by 'striking/Inwards and downwards.'[15] When the past rises up, or, as in the case of the Tara Road, is inadvertently dug up, or accidentally on purpose dug up, the absent past becomes present. Roads literally bring to the surface the complexities of Irish identity. Building roads requires digging, does it not? In this sense roads function as double gestures: on the one hand, they are essential to modern life, to commerce, productivity, and transport; yet in order to build a road one must dig, thereby exposing the past, which must be confronted. The multilayered archeology and intricate genealogy of Irish roads advance a critical imperative for movement that cannot be repressed.

Almost 20 years ago American scholar Cheryl Herr wrote 'The Erotics of Irishness,' a provocative essay in which she considered what she saw as an inherited distrust of the body and physical expression in Ireland. Herr concludes her analysis of various forms of bodily censorship with a reference to Irish topography – the mounds, cairns, tumuli, and massive circular field monuments which she sees as bodily 'disruptions' in the landscape which upset traditional notions of geographical fixity, cultural paralysis, and stillness. She writes, 'the cairns might operate as mediators to a register of meaning that accommodates concepts of other symbolic orders, an alternativity, a visual semiotic that could foster new ways of looking and moving.'[16] Representations of Irish land as a body, particularly a female body, persist in both colonial and nationalist discourse. Ireland has been identified visually as mysterious territory or as virgin land in need of protection. In the Victorian journal *Punch*, Ireland was frequently allegorized as a young woman, Hibernia, in need of protection from Irish anarchists, or as a demure young girl who is being seduced by Britain.[17] The image of women in need of rescue from colonial oppression served as a popular nationalist motif in songs and poems. Cultural geographer Catherine Nash has identified the feminization and eroticization of Ireland as an important cultural trope which serves to uphold oppressive gender identifications that align Irish women with passivity, obedience, and ultimately *stillness*.[18] But Herr conceives of the ancient (feminine) geographical forms embodied in the landscape as sites of movement and cultural agency. This feminine (or feminist) geography asserts a vision of the land as body as a powerful force that can reroute roads and thus reveal the past or revivify ancient systems of movement that have been buried. As part of this kinetic geography, roads offer new pathways for thinking about manifold systems of cultural mobility.

'I was off. I was going down the road of my dreams. I wanted as quickly as possible to get on the strange roads where Romance wearing gold earrings was waiting for me.'[19] In his series of autobiographical essays, published as *The Green Fool*, Patrick Kavanagh quite literally sets out on the road to becoming a poet. In 'A Visit to Dublin,' he informs his bemused mother, 'I'm walking to Dublin.' The poet acknowledges his inheritance of 'road-hunger' from his grandfather, who set out on 'the road Queen Maeve took.'[20] Kavanagh's own steps echo with the reverberations of history and myth. His long walk to the door of the poet George Russell becomes a literary pilgrimage to the works of admired writers, but his steps also take him on a journey into himself. When we walk along a road that is dense with personal, mythic, or national memory, we join our steps with those that have gone before. Maybe this is what Kavanagh meant when he wrote that when we walk our feet are 'tapping secrecies of stone':

> Half-past eight and there is not a spot
> Upon a mile of road, no shadow thrown
> That might turn out a man or woman, not
> A footfall tapping secrecies of stone.[21]

Whether divining the secrets of the road or weaving an idea into a larger fabric of story, writers have invoked roads to chronicle the movement of thought. Declan Kiberd ascribes the original impulse for the twinning of words and movements to medieval Irish culture, a time when 'the very rhythms of poetry were linked to the delight which people took in the act of walking or riding, as their bodies moved through the world.'[22] John Millington Synge was an Irish writer who knew intimately the 'secrecies of stone' and in his work paid tribute to the knowledge that could only come from physical movement through space: 'Man is naturally a nomad…and all wanderers have finer intellectual and physical perceptions than men who are condemned to local habitations. But the vagrant, I think, along with perhaps the sailor, has preserved the dignity of motion.'[23] Roads beckon us onward with the promise of companionship – they are witnesses to our innermost thoughts and dreams that offer solace or distraction from what we have left behind. Synge was an avid walker himself and most likely recognized the 'dignity of motion' that a tramp might come to know. Another devoted walker, Samuel Beckett, set his play *Waiting for Godot* – in which two tramps attempt to divert themselves while waiting – on a country road that could be anywhere and nowhere: '*A country road. A tree. Evening.*' This might be a famine road, a traveler road, or an imaginary road, but it is primarily a space that is enlivened by the tramps' performances of everyday existence.

For these writers the act of walking a road – or the movements of the road itself – suggests that a kinetic consciousness rewards those who move. To acknowledge this form of embodied knowledge is not to disregard the importance of language and orality in Irish culture; rather, it allows us to attend to what the body writes in space. Poems, plays, and stories do register movement, but movement also articulates what Michel de Certeau called 'spatial stories,' in which the act of walking becomes as eloquent as a spoken or written narrative. 'Every story is a travel story,' de Certeau observes, referring to the enunciation of physical and spatial stories through narrative structures: 'whether everyday or literary, [stories] serve us as a means of mass transportation.'[24]

In his account of walking the border that divides Northern Ireland from the Republic of Ireland, Colm Tóibín observes the many rituals and ceremonies of the body that define this contested region. In addition to his own ruminations on the legacy of the Troubles made visible on his walk, Tóibín reports on the marches, parades, funerals, and protests that take place along the border roads. With a surveyor's sense of geographical perception he encounters a diverse landscape of historical trauma and geopolitical division, which he records in movement. At the outset Tóibín acknowledges his strategy:

> I went out and stood on the road. I had made certain arrangements with myself about walking. I had made rules. All progress along the border must be on foot, I had agreed ... every move toward my destination, Newry, must be on foot, except if there was danger, and then I would do anything.[25]

During his journey, Tóibín encounters dangerous roads, smuggling roads, prayer roads, abandoned roads, and roads that have become graves. He tries to adhere to the official border, but at times does not know if he is actually in the North or the South – his map does not register the intricacies of the divide as accurately as his own stride. At other times his location is clearly marked by checkpoints, flags, or emblems painted directly on the road. In the North it is not uncommon for inhabitants of a town to paint the roads in sectarian colors as a way of laying claim to certain streets and neighborhoods. When Tóibín stumbles across the word 'Paisley' painted on a road in a predominantly Protestant area, he becomes acutely aware of the unspoken laws of place that govern the roads in the North.[26] To transgress these spatial codes would be to invite suspicion and even violence.

During their annual parade season the Ulster Protestant community maintains cultural legitimacy and asserts geopolitical dominance by invoking the rhetoric of the road. Ulster Protestants frequently refer to the conflict in Northern Ireland by using the image of a road as a material link to their ancestral past. The Unionist parades perform that link through the marchers' bodies. A member of the Orange Order affirms his right to the road:

> If you stepped back to 1848 … you would find my great-great-grandfather walking in a procession on the same country lanes I now walk … My father's father worked these fields, these, roads, marched down this very road. It is in the blood and calls from deep within us.[27]

It is interesting to note the shifting nouns as the speaker describes the parades as 'walking,' then as a 'procession,' and finally as a 'march' as he becomes more passionate about the subject of the parades. When does walking become marching? What are the physical differences, the political differences? Marching bespeaks an authoritative claim to the route, the land, and the country: the parade cannot go down another road – in the name of tradition it is fixed.

The rhetoric of the road has also offered the public, media, and politicians spatial metaphors for political engagement or retreat. In May 2007 Reverend Ian Paisley invoked the metaphor of the road to signal progress made in political negotiations: 'We're on a road, and we're not going to turn back.'[28] Known for his ideological intransigence, Paisley's comment registers a shift from his usual tactic of non-engagement with Republican government officials. His words spatialize the historic moment by referencing opposing factions who occupy the same road, and he brings history into a new spatial dimension by acknowledging the significance of shared political responsibility. In making these hopeful comments, perhaps Paisley was acknowledging that even opponents must share the same battleground. Referring to the concept of a 'rift' such as a stream or a river, Martin Heidegger reminds us that even a divided space 'does not let opponents break apart; it brings the opposition of measure and boundary into their common outline.'[29] Geographic fissures are recognized as both a dividing line of boundary and also a conjoined space that gestures beyond the vicissitudes of nature to refer to the potential for shared economic, political, and social aspirations. The space between becomes a place for engagement, negotiation, and exchange. Crossroads, a familiar image in Irish cultural narratives, also serve as spaces of intersection that demand our acknowledgement of choice and forward an imperative for movement.

Dancing, worshiping, or meeting at a crossroads were popular activities that brought people from neighboring villages or parishes together. If, as Paul Carter alleges, 'Straight lines that form crossroads offer emblems of hope,' the movements of dance performed at the crossing of two roads promise a collective ritual that transfigures the multifaceted metaphor of the road into a figure of embodied joy.[30] No longer imagined as a route for escape, exile, or confrontation, Irish roads that cross mark places of connection, continuity, and celebration. In popular memory Eamon de Valera is reputed to have invoked the image of dancing at the crossroads to express his vision of the new Irish Free State as a stable national entity that was immune to the gathering forces of change. However, it was through bodily and spatial codes that Irish culture would declare its presence and define its cultural and political trajectory: meet, retreat, encounter, engage, depart, circle, reverse. Crossroads are junctures that may imply hesitation or contemplation, conditions associated with stasis, but crossroads also reference the possibility for a new course of action or a change in direction. Because of their double focus, crossroads are important spaces for reconsidering Irish identity. 'Ireland at a crossroads' may now refer to a broad range of issues: the new Northern Ireland Assembly, the need for new policies on drugs and alcohol, the plight of the Irish traveler community, the influx of migrants, or the need for faster routes into the major city centers. The metaphor of the crossroads still holds cultural currency despite the fact that it no longer references a pastoral scene, but instead alludes to the unavoidable impact of globalization.

What do Irish roads perform now, and how are they related to new constructions of identity in contemporary Ireland? Ireland's rapidly expanding transit systems, from the LUAS (Dublin Light Rail Network), to the construction of new motorways, roads, and bridges, offer important sites for conceptualizing movement and space in Ireland. The Irish word 'luas' translates into English as 'pace' or 'rate' and reveals a national preoccupation with speed. Several new construction projects, including the M3 motorway discussed earlier, are underway or in the planning stages in and around Dublin in order to facilitate faster commutes. The underground Dublin Port Tunnel, officially completed in December 2006, was said to be the largest civil engineering project ever undertaken in Ireland and the longest road tunnel in an urban area in Europe.[31] The tunnel was intended to ease Dublin traffic congestion by diverting large trucks and haulage vehicles away from the city center. There are also plans for additional LUAS lines and an expansion of the DART (Dublin Area Rapid Transit) suburban rail system. With so much new construction, much of it underground, what cultural understandings of space, movement, or memory are being newly exposed? It seems that many of the projects have engendered a great deal of public controversy. The debates have focused on safety, the price of tolls, noise from the construction, and damage to the local landscape and habitat, as in the controversy over the M3 motorway through the Tara Valley. These controversies suggest the complexities of re-imagining Ireland in such concrete terms.

Images from the M3 motorway controversy and the Dublin Port Tunnel construction offer two possible directions to pursue toward an understanding of what contemporary Irish roads perform. In March 2008 a young woman named Lisa Feeney buried herself beneath the active construction zone surrounding the Hill of Tara in protest of the destruction of the heritage site. She chained herself to a car jack in a four-foot-wide chamber which she and other protesters had reached by digging a 33-foot tunnel. She strategically positioned herself directly underneath the road being worked on so that her removal posed a danger to workers, emergency crews, and herself. Her underground performance of protest halted construction and drew international attention to the site.[32] The image of a woman submerged in the landscape recalls ancient bog bodies, the mythic cairns of Celtic queens, and the fairy forts of Irish folklore. But in this contemporary rendering of the motif the woman's body becomes her medium, her theater through which she will attempt to reroute history. Feeney is performing what Herr terms a bodily 'disruption' in the landscape that challenges traditional notions of spatial authority while lending the body a critical agency. Her protest embodies Jacques Derrida's conception of stillness as a condition of movement, in which even microscopic shifts and tremors bear cultural significance.[33]

Feeney's underground counterpart in her subterranean endeavor would be Gráinne, the rock-boring machine named after one of Ireland's most notorious mythic queens which was used to excavate the bedrock for the tunnel. 'She' has lasers for eyes and metal limbs to 'walk,' making her look like an action figure or an alien from a science fiction film. Gráinne carved over one million tons of rock and stone from one end of the tunnel to the other and back again – her mechanized movements actually produced the space for the tunnel road. These bodies in the landscape perform a complex cultural choreography that provokes questions about what new kinds of cultural movement will emerge as a result of expanding, burying, or exposing the old pathways. Both Feeney and the robot Gráinne seem related to Heaney's pioneers 'striking/ Inwards and downwards' but their actions are different: no pens or spades, only the body itself as a kind of tool that digs and folds the earth, forging a new relationship to the ground. After all, our bodies are our very own roads and we can take them anywhere.

Notes

1 Quoted in Gaston Bachelard, *The Poetics of Space: A Classic Look at How We Experience Intimate Places* (Boston, MA: Beacon Press, 1994), 11.
2 Eavan Boland, 'The Famine Road,' *Selected Poems* (Manchester: Carcanet Press, 1989), 20.
3 Stuart Gilbert, *James Joyce's* Ulysses (New York: Random House, 1955), 237.
4 Joseph Roach, *Cities of the Dead: Circum-Atlantic Performance* (New York: Columbia University Press, 1996), 26.
5 Tim Robinson, *Stones of Aran: Pilgrimage* (London: Penguin, 1986), 277.
6 Paul Carter, *The Lie of the Land* (London: Faber and Faber, 1996), 4.
7 Paul Valéry quoted in Carter, *ibid.*, 291.
8 Quoted in Thomas A. Boogaart II, review of *Shapes of Ireland: Maps and the Makers, 1564–1839*, by J. A. Andrews, *Annals of the Association of American Geographers* 89 (1) (March 1999): 162–3, 162.
9 In *Seven Versions of an Australian Badland* (St Lucia: University of Queensland Press, 2002), Ross Gibson discusses the origin of the Australian Badlands as a tract of land that was geographically resistant to colonial ambitions.
10 David Broderick, *The First Toll-Roads: Ireland's Turnpike Roads 1729–1858* (Cork: Collins Press, 2002), 26.
11 L. M. Cullen, 'Man, Landscape and Roads: The Changing Eighteenth Century,' in *The Shaping of Ireland: A Geographical Perspective*, ed. William Nolan (Dublin: Mercier Press, 1986), 123–36, 131.
12 Cited in Broderick, 2002, 6.
13 The phrase 'geography of resistance' references Steve Pile and Michael Keith's *Geographies of Resistance* (New York: Routledge, 1997).
14 Eavan Boland, *In a Time of Violence* (New York: W. W. Norton, 1994), 7.
15 Seamus Heaney, 'Bogland,' in *Opened Ground: Poems 1966–1996* (London: Faber and Faber, 1998), 42.
16 Cheryl Herr, 'The Erotics of Irishness,' *Critical Inquiry* 17 (1) (Autumn 1990): 1–34, 32.
17 See L. Perry Curtis Jr., *Apes and Angels: The Irishman in Victorian Caricature* (Washington, DC: Smithsonian Institution Press, 1997), 41, 168.
18 See Catherine Nash, 'Embodied Irishness: Gender Sexuality and Irish Identities,' in *In Search of Ireland: A Cultural Geography*, ed. Brian Graham (London: Routledge, 1997), 108–27.
19 Patrick Kavanagh, *The Green Fool* (London: Penguin Classics, 2001), 223.
20 *Ibid.*, 222.
21 Patrick Kavanagh, 'Inniskeen Road: July Evening,' in *The Complete Poems* (New York: Peter Kavanagh Hand Press, 1972), 18.
22 Declan Kiberd, quoted in Deirdre Mulrooney, *Irish Moves* (Dublin: Liffey Press, 2006), xi.

23 John Millington Synge, Notebook Entries '[People and Places],' *Collected Works II: Prose* (Washington, DC: Catholic University of America Press, 1982), 195–6.

24 Michel de Certeau, *The Practice of Everyday Life* (Los Angeles: University of California Press, 1984), 115.

25 Colm Tóibín, *Bad Blood: A Walk along the Irish Border* (London: Vintage, 1994), 4.

26 This is a reference to the Reverend Ian Paisley, leader of the Democratic Unionist Party (DUC) in Northern Ireland from its founding in 1971 to 2007.

27 Quoted in Ruth Dudley Edwards, *The Faithful Tribe: An Intimate Portrait of the Loyal Institutions* (London: HarperCollins, 1999), 29.

28 Quoted in Frank Millar, 'We're on a Road, and We're not Going to Turn Back,' *Irish Times,* 5 May 2007.

29 Martin Heidegger, *Poetry, Language, Thought,* trans. Albert Hofstrader (New York: Perennial Library, 1971), 63.

30 Paul Carter, *The Road to Botany Bay: An Exploration of Landscape and History* (Chicago, IL: University of Chicago Press, 1989), 222.

31 'Interesting Facts,' Dublin Port Tunnel, http://www.dublinporttunnel.ie/about/interesting_facts (accessed 10 June 2008).

32 See Brenda Heffernan, '"Skweak" Set to Resume her Tara Tunnel Protest,' *Irish Independent,* 7 April 2008. See also www.tarawatch.org for information on the protest and the international response to the M3 motorway controversy.

33 See Jacques Derrida, 'Choreographies' (interview with Christie V. McDonald), *Diacritics* 12 (1982), 66–76.

7
Commemoration and the Performance of Irish Famine Memory

Emily Mark-FitzGerald

What is the relationship between memory, commemoration, monuments, and performance? Superficially, public commemorative monuments might seem antithetical to notions of performativity, as static, material, and permanent insertions into the landscape, usually associated with inscribing a fixed, often one-dimensional, memory of a historical event for the viewer. Their physical form and unity of purpose contrast with what we know to be true of memory itself, its elusive and transitory nature and chimeric manner of expression. Yet in many important ways the construction of monuments is itself a deeply performative act: it is the action of commemorating agents which brings the monument into being in the first place, and their vigilance which sustains it against the forces of time, decay, and forgetting. Following Paul Connerton,[1] Joep Leerssen has observed:

> community remembrance is iterative, predicated on repetition ... the praxis of community remembrancing is a performative one. It does not solidify into objects occupying public space, such as monuments, but it persists by dint of being always performed afresh.[2]

The public monument may constitute the product of performance, but it is the social praxis of iterative remembering that sustains its ongoing significance. In other words, the temporally defined act of creating the monument possesses a value apart from, and often exceeding, that of the physical monument itself.

In another crucial sense monumental commemoration also evokes the notion of 'agency' so central to the sociology of performance: by transforming 'places' into practiced 'spaces' (to borrow Michel de Certeau's term) through the activity of monument-building.[3] The protracted and socially performative processes of development – discussion, planning, tendering, commissioning, and execution of the work – all constitute integral aspects of the finished memorial, just as the continued incorporation of the monument into commemorative ritual will determine its ongoing social significance. By examining the performative processes of creation, adoption of visual strategies, and the 'business' of commemoration, we may observe how (and which) collective values, memories, and meanings are expressed in the act of remembrance and memorialization.

In this chapter I seek to engage with these two dimensions of monumental performance – of commemorative ritual and the social construction of monuments – as manifested during the 150th anniversary of the Irish Famine, marked in the mid-1990s in Ireland. In recent years no other Irish historical experience has attracted such high levels of commemorative attention and widespread memorialization, with over 80 Famine monuments constructed worldwide since the early 1990s.[4] Although space permits only a cursory discussion of a few of these projects, I argue here that these monumental performances of memory betray conflicting views of what the memory of Famine means in contemporary Ireland, what value the past holds in a post-poverty and newly globalized society, and how political instrumentalization has structured the manner in which such projects have been conceived.

Prior to its 150th anniversary during the 1990s, the Irish Famine of 1845–50 had received meager commemorative attention at either local or national level, and its centenary in 1945 likewise occasioned little response from the Irish government or community groups.[5] The scale of commemorative activities launched in the 1990s was therefore unprecedented and remarkable, encompassing a wide array of Famine commemorations in local, national, and international contexts across Ireland, the UK, US, Australia, and Canada. What reasons can be found for this transformation of public attitudes toward Famine memory? Peter Gray has suggested that in Ireland:

> the dislocations produced by rapid economic growth may help explain the recent surge of interest in the traumatic experience of the 1840s famine ... there remains a demand for some historical continuity, a collective identity rooted in a distinctive 'Irish' past; and the Famine appeared to many to offer a focus that was at once catastrophic, local, diasporic and relevant to the modern world.[6]

The anniversary of the Famine formed a 'perfect storm' of a commemorative sort: occurring at a time of relative economic prosperity, widely activated (especially in the diaspora) amongst well-established, funded, and organized social networks, providing an opportunity for the assertion of ethnic identity within a climate of fraught cultural politics, and malleable to familiar modes of commemorating catastrophic social events. In Ireland in particular, the Famine anniversary coincided with a growing cultural confidence, which accompanied the emergent Celtic Tiger economic boom, as well as a period of intense growth in the national tourism and heritage industry. As Cormac Ó Gráda wryly observed, 'the commemorations probably spoke more about Ireland in the 1990s than in the 1840s,'[7] and this projection of present interests onto the Famine past included the marshaling of Famine memory in support of a wide array of contemporary political and social concerns.

One of the most frequently cited motives for the reawakening of Famine memory (as articulated within public discourse of the time) included the 'moral responsibility' of the Irish people toward third world humanitarian action and the alleviation of contemporary famine, as particularly championed by President Mary Robinson. Another involved the reinscription of Irish Famine experience into contemporary narratives of Irish heritage, as dozens of local heritage groups across the island 'reclaimed' what they viewed as a previously lost or marginalized Famine past through acts of community commemoration. Both of these perspectives involved the reinvestment of modern meaning into Ireland's Famine past, suggesting the emergence of a modern Irish cultural identity where Famine memory might inform what Robinson termed 'our self-knowledge as a people,'[8] on a new global and economic stage. By way of example, in this chapter I consider two case studies of Famine projects in Doolough, County Mayo and Skibbereen, County Cork, with particular attention to how their performances of monumental commemoration were circumscribed by the ideologies of humanitarianism and heritage, and the particular ritualistic and commemorative forms which emerged to meet these objectives.

Doolough

The aid organizations Action from Ireland (AfrI) and Concern were among the first to align the memory of the Famine with an agenda of third world relief and social activism in the early 1980s,[9] a theme that would be embraced at large as the 150th Famine anniversary gained prominence in the mid-1990s. Following the 1984 commencement of its 'Great Famine Project,' in 1988 AfrI launched its first 'Famine Walk,' a ten-mile trek between Louisburgh and Doolough, which would become a staple of its Famine fundraising and awareness campaign over the next twenty years.[10] The walk is a re-creation of an incident from March 1849, when a large crowd of the starving poor walked overnight from Louisburgh to Delphi Lodge to seek assistance from the local Board of Guardians. Refused aid, they were forced to return to Louisburgh; weakened and suffering from exposure, many died on the return journey.

These 'Famine walks' received significant coverage in local and national media, including broadcast coverage on several major US networks, and were instrumental in shaping the direction of both national and local efforts to commemorate the 150th anniversary of the Famine. Such Famine walks served as cultural and social performances expressing empathy for the 'unseen victim,' whilst relying on the physical 'performance of opposition' of protest and the 'aesthetics of movement'[11] to attract public and media attention. These strategies ultimately proved successful, as it was during AfrI's seventh annual Famine walk in May 1994 when Fianna Fáil minister Tom Kitt officially announced the establishment of the government's National Famine Commemoration Committee under his own direction.[12] According to AfrI, more than twenty of these walks had taken place by 1995[13] and expanded to other counties as well, although the annual Doolough walk remained the most publicized and well attended. Key figures invited annually to lead the walks helped raise their profile and encourage such publicity; Archbishop Desmond Tutu's participation in 1991 twice made front-page news in the *Irish Independent*.[14]

Nevertheless, the importance of the walk to AfrI's Famine awareness efforts culminated, in 1994, with the erection of a permanent monument in the Doolough Valley. Throughout the 150th commemorative period, the high cross proved one of the most popular forms adopted for local Famine commemorations in both Ireland and the diaspora, building on its long history as a public commemorative symbol used for many diverse kinds of memorial purposes. In place of the more typical insular-form Famine high cross monument, however, the Doolough memorial opts for the enigmatic early Christian cross form, allying the contemporary memorial with a sense of permanence and unbroken lineage with the Irish past, and granting the work an appearance of advanced antiquity despite its recent fashioning.

Priorities had clearly shifted for AfrI since 1991, when its chairman Don Mullan had declared in the *Irish Independent*: 'We don't want our Government erecting monuments of stone or of metal. The monument we want them to erect during this decade is the .7 percent of GNP which the United Nations has asked us to give in official development assistance.'[15] The urge to leave a permanent record in the landscape memorializing the Doolough tragedy, as well as creating a focal point for pilgrimage and AfrI's annual campaign, clearly proved too compelling to resist, and AfrI has since reaped the publicity benefits of this decision: since its construction the cross has become an important halt along the annual pilgrimage route and is a frequent stop-off point for organized tours of the area. In this one monument four historical experiences are collapsed, as indicated through its inscriptions on four sides: the Famine; Mahatma Gandhi and the struggle for Indian independence; Desmond Tutu and the 'road to freedom' in South Africa; and the Dunnes Stores labor dispute, which stemmed from the anti-apartheid movement. The date of unveiling allied the Famine with the ten-year anniversary of the Dunnes Stores strikes in 1984 and the ending of apartheid with Nelson Mandela's presidential election in 1994. The Doolough monument thus provides an example of how commemorations of Famine have functioned as a composite of the local, national, and global: here layering local memory of a specific nineteenth-century incident against AfrI's national agenda for overseas development aid, while referring to analogous contemporary political conflicts, and suggesting a modern Irish self-identity which is both multicultural and globally significant. The ideological flexibility of the Famine walk and monument has continued into the present, as a diverse array of causes continue to be grouped under the Famine banner: in 1994 the walk was led by Gandhi's grandson, Arun Gandhi; in 1995 by Guatemalan Mayan activist Juana Vasqeuz; in 1998 by war correspondent John Pilger; and in 1999 by Phan Thi (famously the subject of a 1972 Pulitzer-prize winning photograph in the aftermath of a US-led air attack on Vietnam).[16] In its most recent incarnation in 2007, the walk was aligned with the locally controversial Shell to Sea campaign and global climate change, under the theme 'Voice in the Wilderness: Erris, Gas and Global Warming.'[17]

The banners, speeches, erection of monuments, and symbolic leadership of the walks by renowned personages are all familiar components of Irish commemorative performance, regardless of the event being commemorated. Such ritualized walks owe something as well to long traditions of Irish religious pilgrimage to sacred sites, including the annual ascent of Croagh Patrick, located just a few miles from the Doolough Valley. As a deliberate and self-aware act, pilgrimage is a form of performance which establishes a relationship between the individual and a site, an act in the aggregate which may define a site's collective significance, a point AfrI has obviously understood thoroughly.

Yet AfrI's attempts to mold Famine memory to contemporary activism, no matter how laudable the cause, gloss that there is no unproblematic or neutral connection between the two. Visual juxtapositions of nineteenth-century engravings and contemporary photographs in AfrI's publication *Famine Is a Lie* (1995) present a troubling erasure of historical difference and deny the complicity of the viewer in such images. The manipulability of such images is exemplified by the insertion of a fictitious background in AfrI's reproduction of *Digging for Potatoes* (1849). Similarly, a newspaper advertisement for the 1991 Famine walk deploys an evolutionary metaphor featuring *Bridget O'Donnel and Children* (1849) in the queue.[18]

More seriously, in 1994 Cormac Ó Gráda challenged the veracity of the Doolough story as popularly recounted and instrumentalized by aid groups, claiming that 'The organizers' initial claim some years ago that "several hundred" perished in one night has no more foundations than the old tale about Queen Victoria's miserly relief donation of £5 ... By all means, use the Famine analogy to raise charity, but those concerned must get their facts right first.'[19] Certainly, Ó Gráda's concerns at historical distortion through the perpetuation of exaggerated – though compelling – stories seemed validated by public tendencies to

Figure 2   Famine Memorial, Action from Ireland, Swinford, Co. Mayo (1994). Photo by Emily Mark-Fitzgerald.

dramatize the Doolough incident: photographs of the Louisburgh Drama Group in period costume, wailing and staggering along the Doolough walk, appeared on the front page of the *Irish Independent* on 8 April 1991, with the accompanying article dramatically inflating the 1849 mortality figure to 5,000 people.[20] The line between leveraging and exploitation of the past to suit present needs is a fine one, and such spectacular and overtly theatrical re-enactments are particularly susceptible to distortion in the service of emotive affect, and subject to the same criticism frequently leveled at heritage reconstructions which offer viewers the opportunity to indulge in tragic fantasy under the guise of history.

The enfolding of Irish Famine memory within global humanitarian narratives was again enacted at the site of a second Famine monument dedicated by AfrI in Swinford, County Mayo the day after the Doolough unveiling. This monument, located behind the former Swinford work-house (now a geriatric hospital), was constructed on the former mass gravesite, itself marked locally by a slab monument of indeterminate age and origin. It is perhaps the most explicitly political monument to be found at a Famine mass grave in Ireland, featuring laser-etched portraits of Mahatma Gandhi and Michael Davitt separated by a St Brigid's Cross, as well as quotes from each. Through image and inscription the monument explicitly acknowledges Michael Davitt's visit to the Swinford mass grave before his creation of the Land League in 1879. The juxtaposition of Davitt and Gandhi makes for an unusual pairing in the Famine context, though each is instantly recognizable as an iconic crusader for social justice, and the Land League is a widely cited inspiration for Gandhi's land reform activities. However, the monument lacks any incorporation into a larger framework of local memory, despite its association with Davitt and real connection with his subsequent political activities, and its form reads as an uninspired variant on the bland modern graveyard marker. Tucked away behind the hospital and unseen by the public, its overt political allusions ring hollow, privileging two known historical figures (and the participation of Gandhi's grandson at the unveiling) over the many hundreds actually buried there.[21]

The connection of Davitt's Famine memory to his formation of one of Ireland's most significant political movements is, ironically, a subject of far greater historical consequence than Doolough's compelling yet historically fuzzy Famine story. However, Doolough's evocative setting, positioned along a well-traveled roadway, and its absorption into ritualized Famine walks, have combined to ensure a position of

Famine commemorative significance far surpassing Swinford's. The contrast reinforces the point that historical veracity need not be the primary factor in perpetuating memory or in the prompting of commemorative performance, and that the dramatic power of memorial performance and its political utility may well serve as a dividing line between history, heritage, and the sustenance of collective memories.

Skibbereen

Few place-names in Ireland are as intimately associated with the Famine as Skibbereen in County Cork. The town's immortalization in the popular turn-of-the-twentieth-century song 'Dear Old Skibbereen' has ensured its name's perpetual connection with the suffering endured during the Famine period. As a recurrent subject of outside media attention, Skibbereen's Famine past is unusually rich in surviving textual and visual representations. The central point of reference for several accounts is Skibbereen's mass grave in Abbeystrewery cemetery, where an estimated 8,000–10,000 are buried in nine mass burial pits. Though no evidence has been found to suggest that the Famine received any form of ongoing commemoration in Skibbereen in the post-Famine years, its memory was nonetheless an active one, prompting in 1947 a heated exchange between members of Skibbereen's Urban District Council (UDC), which made front-page news in the Cork-based *Southern Star* over a proposal by Mr Wolfe that congratulations be sent to Princess Elizabeth on the occasion of her impending marriage. In voicing their strident objection, several of the speakers invoked the centenary of the Famine that year and the local memory of its victims buried in the Abbeystrewery cemetery.[22] As in many other towns across Ireland, Skibbereen hosted annual commemorations of the Manchester Martyrs[23] of 1867 well into the twentieth century; such commemorations were famed for their staging of 'mock funerals' of the three executed men, complete with empty coffins and impassioned speeches extolling the heroism of Irish Nationalists.[24] In 1946 the *Southern Star* described the unusual incorporation of the Abbeystrewery site and its earlier 1887 Famine memorial into the local Manchester Martyrs' commemoration: after speeches in Irish, a decade of the rosary, and a parade to the cemetery, a wreath was ceremonially laid on the 1887 memorial.[25]

By the early 1990s dismay at the state of the cemetery and letters of complaint published in the *Southern Star* prompted the formal convening of Skibbereen's Famine Commemoration Committee in October

1992, of which several members had also been involved with the Manchester Martyrs commemorations since the 1950s.[26] By November 1992 the group sent notices to the local paper indicating their plans to erect a memorial and renovate the mass plots at Abbeystrewery.[27] The following year the committee's efforts gained momentum through the coordination of a Famine walk in Skibbereen by AfrI on 24 July 1993, which began at The Castle, Castletownshend and ended at Abbeystrewery. The announcement of the walk in local media outlined the committee's intentions and interests in relation to the 150th anniversary, describing Skibbereen as a 'focal point' and 'epicenter' for the anniversary, of 'special appeal to second and third generation Irish in England, Australia, the U.S.A. and Canada.'[28]

From the outset Skibbereen's commemorations were twinned with efforts to attract outside tourism to the area.[29] The committee's aspirations to establish Skibbereen as a center for the 150th commemorations translated into ambitious plans stretching beyond renovation of the graveyard into the creation of a 'Famine Heritage Trail' and a major interpretative center, supported by a feasibility study funded by the West Cork Leader Co-op (a major sponsor of the commemorative efforts). At a mass meeting held four months after the AfrI-led Famine walk, committee secretary Pat Cleary outlined the committee's objective to raise £125,000 for 'Phase One' of the project, the cemetery renovation and Heritage Trail, with the insistence that 'the cemetery will not be developed as a tourist attraction. It will instead be a place where visitors can pay tribute to the very many thousands of people who died during the famine.'[30] Despite Cleary's statement, chairman Noel O'Driscoll subsequently acknowledged tourism as a significant driver of the efforts:

> Skibbereen is widely recognised as having suffered more from the effects of the Famine than any other part of Ireland. Whilst unashamedly proud of our heritage, we decided to combine the major tourist and business potential of the project with the honouring of the memory of our sacred dead who are buried in unmarked graves in various graveyards in the district.[31]

Following the committee's expectation that the renovation and Trail would be ready by 1995, in time for the 150th anniversary, plans for Phase 2 of the commemorations were also outlined, in the form of a £2 million visitor center which would 'extend both ends of the tourist season, with widespread financial benefits for all section involved in

the business, plus creating extra employment.'[32] True to the committee's intentions, by 1996 the cemetery had been renovated and the
walking trail established, marked by a series of medallions at Famine
sites across the town, a viewing platform, and a map indicating their
location and history.[33]

At the cemetery the committee fulfilled its original plan and created
a new archway over the entrance, delineated the mass graves from surrounding plots and refurbished them, erected a large directional sign to
the cemetery, paved an entry plaza near the entrance, and placed
plaques along the inside wall of the entrance. The dedicatory panel at
the cemetery combines lines from 'Dear Old Skibbereen' with affirm-
ations of the exceptionalism of Skibbereen's suffering, again naming
the town as the 'epicentre of this horror,' which suffered more than
most other places. The original 1887 wrought iron memorial was
moved from its location at the foot of the mass grave nearest the
entrance and replaced by a Celtic cross, its base fronted with sponsored
commemorative bricks and a plaque exhorting visitors to 'pray for
the families whose names are recorded in this commemorative plot.'
Another monument was added in the form of eleven rectangular slabs
arranged in a semicircle, including five large slabs with inscriptions
fronted by six smaller plain slabs. The range of inscriptions on the five
slabs is perhaps indicative of a committee-based approach, lacking
cohesion and confusing in its mix of historical and contemporary
texts.[34] Unfortunately, despite the cemetery's significance to Skibbereen's Famine memorial activities, its contemporary monuments are
less than impressive: the profusion of plaques and monuments makes
for a cluttered memorial site with little visual distinction, or attention
focused on any particular aspect.

The second phase of the development, the establishment of the
Skibbereen Heritage Centre, was realized in 2000 at a final cost of approximately £600,000. The project's development was led by a combination
of the Office of Public Works, Cork County Council, Skibbereen UDC,
and the Skibbereen Famine Commemoration Committee. UDC member
Michael Dwyer echoed Noel O'Driscoll's 1993 comments on the layering
of Famine memory with the economic benefits of tourism to the area:
'It is important that we remember the past … but it's also important that
we look to the future with optimism and I believe this project will be a
tremendous boost to the town.'[35] Such comments on the conflation of
tourism opportunities with Famine remembrance across Ireland were certainly not isolated: correspondence relating to the erection of the Famine
monument in Ennistymon, County Clare in 1995 similarly noted that

'the strategic location of this Memorial was chosen largely because of its accessibility to approximately 500 tour buses each year and to numerous self-drive tourists.'[36]

Like the Heritage Trail, the center was created primarily as an engine of cultural tourism – a collision point of Famine memory and economic regeneration that would serve to push Skibbereen to the forefront as a national focal point for Famine commemoration. This intent was echoed in the Famine Commemoration Committee's failed efforts to locate the National Famine Memorial at their site, following an island-wide competition in 1995, managed by the National Famine Commemoration Committee under Minister Avril Doyle, which drew 65 applications from towns across Ireland. Yet the transformation of Famine spaces into tourist amenities or attractions inevitably effects some aestheticization and packaging of what is a complex, conflicted past. As John Lennon and Michael Foley have noted in their study of the multiplication of 'dark tourism' sites, the 'educative elements of sites are accompanied by elements of commodification and a commercial ethic which (whether explicit or implicit) accepts that visitation (whether purposive or incidental) is an opportunity to develop a tourism product.'[37] Skibbereen's Famine memory has long been held as a mark of exceptionalism for the area, referring (as its monument does) to the area as the 'epicentre of horror' – denying, of course, the impossibility that such a place could exist. Taking the historian's point of view, Cormac Ó Gráda has critiqued Skibbereen's uncomplicated embrace of its Famine legacy as another example of the Irish commemorations' blanket application of victimhood status to the population at large:

> Ignoring the shame and the guilt leaves the way open in due course for a version of famine history in which the descendants of those who survived all become vicarious victims ... a case in point is the crass proposal for a 'Wall of Remembrance' by Irish Famine Commemoration (Skibbereen) Limited, whereby 'we, the descendants of the Famine victims ... remember our kinfolk.'[38]

However, seen from another point of view, Skibbereen's Famine commemorations are but a contemporary link on the chain of ritualized memory which has centered on the Abbeystrewery cemetery since the nineteenth century. What was textually evoked and visually depicted in newspapers and books of the period remained alive through the proximate commemorations of the Manchester Martyrs, and has now been most recently transformed through the power and agency of the contemporary heritage industry. The attempts to move Skibbereen's association with the Famine from a local or regional framework to national significance may not have formally succeeded, but its intriguing layering of Famine commemorative performativity – from the evolution of burial procession to the Famine grave, to mock funeral of the Manchester commemoration, to AfrI's Famine Walk, and the performance of tourism through the Heritage Trail – suggests that Skibbereen has retained an intense, living identification with its Famine past which will continue to make it unusual amongst other Famine memorial sites in Ireland.

In the aggregate, what has unfolded from the command 'remember the Famine' is an eclectic mix of commemorative gestures, monumental and otherwise, confirming the suspicion that we cannot possibly locate a singular 'authentic' Famine experience. In an age of globalization and the reduction of complex historical realities into a consumable 'heritage,' the Famine remains a dislocation whose contradictions outnumber its certainties. We have moved no small distance from the solemn and sparse commemorations of the 1945 Fianna Fáil government to Michael Flatley's 2005 dance extravaganza *Celtic Tiger*, featuring an extensive Famine sequence complete with scantily rag-clad dancers, projections of burning cottages, and mock evictions. And yet, the productions of our time seem no less determined by the desire to inscribe them into our own (post-1990s) experience of modernity: 'The past is a foreign country whose features are shaped by today's predilections, its strangeness domesticated by our own preservation of its vestiges.'[39] In acknowledging and outlining the performative dimensions of 1990s Famine monumental commemoration, I have endeavored to demonstrate the indelible stamp present preoccupations have made on the construction of the Famine past, and the necessity of understanding the particular sociopolitical forces which have shaped these monuments. If collective self-presentation does not simply reflect but actually forms group identity, as suggested by so many different strands of performance theory, then a close examination of the various ways in which Famine memories matter, and to whom, will reveal no easy resolution of the Famine's meaning, but its ongoing disturbance of our present.

Notes

1   Paul Connerton, *How Societies Remember* (Cambridge: Cambridge University Press, 1989).

2 Joep Leerssen, 'Monument and Trauma: Varieties of Remembrance,' in *History and Memory in Modern Ireland*, ed. Ian McBride (Cambridge: Cambridge University Press, 2001), 204–22, 219.

3 Michel de Certeau, *The Practice of Everyday Life*, trans. Steven Rendall (Berkeley and London: University of California Press, 1984).

4 For an extended discussion, see Emily Mark, 'Memorials and Monuments to the Irish Famine: Commemorative Art and History' (PhD thesis, University College Dublin, 2007).

5 Cormac Ó Gráda, 'Making History in Ireland in the 1940s and 1950s: The Saga of *The Great Famine*,' *Irish Review* 12 (Spring/Summer 1992): 87–107.

6 Peter Gray and Kendrick Oliver, 'The Memory of Catastrophe,' *History Today* 51 (2) (2001): 9–15, 13.

7 Cormac Ó Gráda, 'After the Famine Fever,' *Irish Times*, 19 May 2001.

8 Mary Robinson, 'Cherishing the Irish Diaspora: Address to the Houses of Oireachtas on a Matter of Public Importance,' speech delivered in Dublin, 2 February 1995.

9 Don Mullan, ed., *A Glimmer of Light: An Overview of Great Hunger Commemorative Events in Ireland and throughout the World* (Dublin: Concern Worldwide, 1995), 32.

10 Action from Ireland (AfrI), *Famine Is a Lie* (Dublin: Action from Ireland, 1995).

11 Ron Eyerman, 'Performing Opposition, or, How Social Movements Move,' in *Social Performance: Symbolic Action, Cultural Pragmatics, and Ritual*, eds. Jeffrey C. Alexander, Bernhard Giesen, and Jason L. Mast (Cambridge: Cambridge University Press, 2006), 193–217, 207.

12 This role was subsequently assumed by Fine Gael TD Avril Doyle after a change of government in 1995.

13 AfrI, 3.

14 'Bishop Tutu's Fiery Failte,' *Irish Independent*, 6 April 1991; Tom Shiel, 'Famine Centre Opened,' *Irish Independent*, 8 April 1991.

15 Quoted in Shiel, *ibid.*

16 Margaret E. Ward, 'Child Symbol of War Joins AfrI Walk for Children of Conflict Horror,' *Irish Times*, 15 May 1999.

17 Michael Duffy, 'Famine Walk to Highlight Global Warming,' *Mayo News*, 17 May 2007.

18 *Southern Star*, 23 March 1991. *Digging for Potatoes* and *Bridget O'Donnel and Children* were two of the most widely reproduced Famine-era engravings during the 150th anniversary period. Both originally appeared in the *Illustrated London News* on 22 December 1849.

19 Cormac Ó Gráda, 'Satisfying a Great Hunger for Guilt and Self-Pity,' *Sunday Tribune*, 15 May 1994.

20 See Shiel, 1991.

21 AfrI's third monument is located at the Famine graveyard in Callan, County Kilkenny, also dating from 1994. The monument is engraved with a Christlike figure wearing peasant clothing and crucified on a pitchfork and spade; its inscription cites 'Ireland 1845/Bangladesh 1974/East Timor 1975/Brazil 1979/Ethiopia 1984/Somalia 1992/Angola 1994.'

22 'Royal Wedding: Proposal at Skibbereen Urban Council Meeting,' *Southern Star*, 8 November 1947.

23 In 1867 the Irish Nationalists William O'Mera Allen, Michael Larkin, and William O'Brien were captured during an attempted jailbreak in Manchester, which resulted in the death of a policeman and the freeing of two prominent members of the Irish Republican Brotherhood. The three men's impassioned speeches before the gallows and subsequent execution led to their canonization as Fenian martyrs and the construction of numerous monuments to their memory.

24 Gary Owens, 'Constructing the Martyrs: the Manchester Executions and the Nationalist Imagination,' in *Images, Icons, and the Irish Nationalist Imagination*, ed. Lawrence McBride (Dublin: Four Courts Press, 1999), 18–36.

25 'Manchester Martyrs: Annual Commemoration in Skibbereen,' *Southern Star*, 30 November 1946.

26 Interview with D. O'Sullivan, Treasurer, Irish Famine Commemoration, Skibbereen Ltd, 11 August 2007.

27 'Skibbereen Group Plans Memorial,' *Southern Star*, 7 November 1992; 'Famine Pit at the Abbey,' *Southern Star*, 12 November 1992.

28 'AfrI "Famine Walk" for Skibbereen,' *Southern Star*, 10 July 1993.

29 '"Skibbereen Story"–A Major Project,' *Southern Star*, 6 November 1993.

30 *Ibid.*

31 *Ibid.*

32 *Ibid.*

33 *The Skibbereen Trail: A Historical Walking Tour* (Skibbereen: Irish Famine Commemoration, Skibbereen Ltd, 1996).

34 The text is a melange, which includes extracts from Lady Jane Wilde's poem *The Exodus* (1871) and Rev. John O'Rourke book *The History of the Great Irish Famine* (1902), where he quotes Thomas Hood's famed *Song of the Shirt* (1843).

35 Eddie Cassidy, 'Visitor Centre to Recall Town's Tragic Past,' *Irish Examiner*, 11 April 1997.

36 J. J. Gallagher, letter from Office of the National Director of the Ancient Order of Hibernians in America to Dr Stephen Lalor, Secretary, Irish National Famine Commemoration Committee, 10 October 1995 (copy provided to the author by Noel Crowley, Clare County Librarian).

37 John Lennon and Michael Foley, *Dark Tourism* (London and New York: Continuum, 2000), 11.

38 Ó Gráda, 'Satisfying a Great Hunger for Guilt and Self-Pity.'

39 David Lowenthal, *The Past Is a Foreign County* (Cambridge: Cambridge University Press, 1985), xvii.

8
Performing 'the Troubles': Murals and the Spectacle of Commemoration at Free Derry Corner

Matthew Spangler

'But it's not a performance.' The tour guide turned to me and said it again, 'It's not a performance. It's the truth. We're telling our story. We're telling what really happened. Bloody Sunday, Battle of the Bogside: we're getting our story out there. That's what it's about.' We were standing atop Derry's seventeenth-century city walls, a group of nine foreign tourists, overlooking the Bogside, when I suggested to our guide that the area around Free Derry Corner resembles a stage set in performance. The guide was employed by the Museum of Free Derry's Bloody Sunday Centre to give hour-long walking tours of the Bogside and city walls, which offer panoramic views of Derry's historically Catholic and Nationalist neighborhood. Though he could not have been older than 30, and thus could not have lived through the events he referred to, the idea that their memorialization and public display might be termed a *performance* seemed to strike him as an offence.[1]

The specter of the Troubles haunts the Bogside. Bloody Sunday, in particular, has provided more inspiration for memorialization and performative response than perhaps any other event in Northern Ireland's long history of sectarian struggle. From U2's famous song, to Paul Greengrass's feature film, to the murals that now mark Free Derry Corner, the events of 30 January 1972 have been continually performed and re-performed over the last four decades. In the years prior to the event, tensions were high in this border city of 55,000 where 60 percent of the population lived in the mostly Catholic, working-class neighborhoods of the Bogside and adjacent Brandywell and Creggan, which in the early 1970s had an unemployment rate as high as 30 percent.[2] Derry hosted the first public demonstration of the Northern Ireland Civil Rights Association on 5 October 1968 and later was the site of the three-day Battle of the Bogside in August 1969,

100

when the Bogside and Creggan declared themselves free from British rule and erected makeshift barricades to keep out the police. Three years later, the British army broke through these barricades in an attempt to reassert control of these so-called no-go areas. With tanks and armored personnel carriers, 'Operation Motorman' (July 1972), which was also carried out in Belfast, was one of the largest British troop movements since the Second World War. But Bloody Sunday remains the Bogside's and perhaps Derry's most prominent historical event. The First Battalion Parachute Regiment's killing of 13 unarmed demonstrators[3] (another 13 were wounded, one of whom later died of his injuries) and its repeated memorialization has caused Bloody Sunday to go down in the narrative of global history as a profound symbol for the misuse of military power against a civilian-led demonstration – an event comparable, if not on the scale of its casualties then in its narrative authority, to the Paris Massacre of 1961 or Tiananmen Square, Beijing. For Nationalists, the term 'Bogside' brings to mind Northern Ireland's civil rights movement; for Republicans, it represents nothing less than the injustice of British rule.[4]

Today, the Bogside's Free Derry Corner is one of the city's most often visited tourist sites.[5] The short stretch of Rossville Street between Westland Street and William Street, where all of the shootings took place, is marked by eleven three-story wall murals depicting images associated with Bloody Sunday and the Troubles. Numerous statues, plaques, and other forms of public display commemorating civilian victims, politicians, and Republican heroes also mark the area. And there is the ubiquitously visible, white gable wall – perhaps *the* visual symbol of the Bogside – announcing that the visitor is now entering 'Free Derry.' Prominently placed at the entrance of the Glenfada car park, where several of the Bloody Sunday shootings took place, is the Museum of Free Derry and Bloody Sunday Centre, where the visitor is greeted by the sounds of gunshots and panicking crowds as a documentary video of Bloody Sunday plays on a continuous loop. Together, the murals, museum, and surrounding plaques, statues, graffiti, and other objects of memory-on-display constitute a panoply of oppositional narratives to the official ones so long maintained by the British government. This performative landscape does not so much *reflect* history as *constitute* it through specific acts of remembrance, storytelling, and display.

In labeling these material symbols of memory and commemoration 'performances,' however, I do not mean to suggest that they or the narratives they create are fabricated, disingenuous, or inconsequential; quite the opposite. As Victor Turner asserts, performance is 'making

Figure 3   Free Derry Corner with the Bogside Artists' murals 'The Petrol Bomber' (left) and 'Bloody Sunday' (right) in the background and commemoration to those who died in the H-Block hunger strike as well as previous hunger strikes in the foreground, June 2007. Photo by Matthew Spangler.

not faking.'[6] To call something a performance is thus not to malign it as artificial, for the lens of performance attends to the very real narratives of memory and history that such symbols constitute, sustain, subvert, critique, or naturalize. Performances are, in Michel de Certeau's words, 'tools manipulated by users,' and are the evidence of a creative agency that facilitates the construction of identity.[7] As the material expressions of culture, performances have the capacity to interject marginalized voices into global, national, and local public spheres, or redefine the interrelated parts of these public spheres all together in ways that might alter what is understood as social or cultural reality. Ultimately, performance provides an especially rich and charged space for encountering the complex narratives of history and identity in the making. Further, public spectacles, which themselves are fundamentally performative, provide a stage for what Diana Taylor calls 'the construction' (and I would add contestation) 'of communal identity.'[8] This chapter focuses on the performativity of public spectacles of commemoration at Free Derry Corner with a particular emphasis on the eleven wall murals that dominate the area and the narratives of identity and history that they create, sustain, or critique. Key to my argument here is that these murals are not *like* performances, they *are* performances.

Over the last two decades, performance and cultural studies scholars have increasingly come to view the act of displaying heritage as a performative one – that is, not only citational, but constitutive of particular narratives of being. Many of these analyses further situate public display within the context of tourism, in which both the selection and framing of the tourist object as well as the tourist's behavior are viewed as performances. Such an analysis extends from a former inclination of researchers to explain tourism through the medium of the 'gaze,' which itself is indebted to Michel Foucault's theories on the relationship between vision and power in medical and judicial settings.[9] More recently, theories of performativity have been used to analyze public display within heritage museums and other sites of cultural memory;[10] the display of souvenirs;[11] displays of tourism as social and political resistance;[12] the act of tourism as a collection of scripted and embodied acts;[13] tourist guides as performers;[14] the performance of display associated with 'post-tourism';[15] and second-person tourist performances, in which the audience is inserted into the historical drama and made to play a role in its recreation.[16] A uniting thread among these diverse studies is the idea that tourism itself provides an important cultural site for the display and subsequent narrative creation of identity, history, and memory. In the case of the Bogside, the process of narrative-making through the performativity of display is made especially rich, for the neighborhood is more than just a tourist site. It is the location of trauma, and as such, it occupies a highly exalted and even fetishized space within the narrative of Northern Ireland's sectarian and civil rights struggles. The site itself is sacred, made doubly so through the spectacle of public marking and commemoration, a process Dean MacCannell refers to as 'sight sacralization,' by which objects and places are ritualistically transformed into sacred sites through five phases: naming, framing, enshrinement, mechanical reproduction, and social reproduction.[17] The theatricality of commemoration, sacralization, and public display thereby creates a highly visible stage on which to showcase narratives of identity and memory.

Heritage displays, such as the collection of signs at Free Derry Corner, are never neutral. They are not 'the real thing' lifted from the past and inserted in the present; rather, those who construct them constitute the heritage object itself, as well as the narrative it tells through a creative process that is fundamentally theatrical. Because public memory is only knowable through signs and texts – literature, theatre, oral testimonies, murals, statues, plaques, maps, photographs, videos, or other forms of mechanical recording – once these objects are naturalized into the collective imagination, they possess a powerful authority to identify and shape past events into coherent narratives of history and truth. Barbara Kirshenblatt-Gimblett calls heritage museums 'agencies of display'[18] and argues that the act of publicly displaying heritage not only 'shows and speaks, it also *does*.'[19] It is this capacity to *do* – to bring into being specific narratives of history, memory, and identity – that reveals the performative power of such public displays. Insofar as the multitude of signs at Free Derry Corner resembles an elaborate, open-air stage set, this urban landscape of memory and commemoration draws on the capacity of performance to make and remake what is thought of as historical reality.

Even Derry's topographical landscape seems complicit in this performance, as the theatricality of conflict and power appears written on the city's hills, streets, and valleys. Sitting outside and below the high, canon-fortified walls and at the bottom of a large hill in an undesirable patch of bogland that was once under the waters of the River Foyle, the Bogside's very location connotes marginality. In the early 1600s, when Derry was largely a Protestant and Loyalist settlement, Catholics were forbidden from living within the city walls.[20] Loyalist narratives of the subsequent Siege of Derry (1688–89) have so effectively claimed the image of the walls as a defense of Protestant settlers from Catholic invaders that the walls themselves have become what Graham Dawson calls 'a symbol of Protestant domination and of [Catholics'] second-class status.'[21] In order to enter the Bogside from the city center, one must exit the walls, leaving behind the narrow, shop-lined streets that comprise the city's commercial heart and walk down a steep, often rain-sodden hill, past the Free Derry sign, and into a neighborhood of chipped paint and littered sidewalks, one very different from the tidiness of the hilltop only a few hundred yards away. Amplifying their symbolic value of authority and domination, in 1970, the British military established an observation post atop the portion of the walls that looms most directly over the Bogside (the observation post was dismantled in the fall of 2006). The most acute set designer could not create a more potent physical representation of sectarianism and the segregation of power than that which constitutes Derry's and the Bogside's topographical features.

While Derry's geographical landscape is comparatively immovable, the urban one is not. It is constantly being altered and remade, even as the specific acts of remaking posit a mimetic rhetoric of truth and unchangeability. The murals, plaques, graffiti, monuments, and other forms of public display that dominate the Bogside ostensibly reflect the past, but they, like all such performative archives, in fact, say more about the Bogside's present and future.

The most dramatic aspects of the Bogside's urban landscape are the eleven wall murals that line Rossville Street (at the time of writing, plans are underway for a twelfth). Images using a high degree of physicality, presentational poses, careful framing, and symbolism create striking theatricality. They borrow so much from the conventions of stage pictures that the murals might be grouped into two theatrical categories: those that depict scenes in *representational* mode and those that use *presentational* mode. The murals in representational mode show freeze-framed images of intense action, scenes in media res that are arresting in their visual power. The mural 'Bloody Sunday' (1997),[22] for instance, is a reworking of an iconic image of the Troubles: a photograph of Father Edward Daly, bent double to avoid flying bullets, waving a bloody handkerchief as he leads a group of men carrying the limp body of Jackie Duddy from the scene of the shootings, while an armed British soldier stands nearby on the words 'Civil Rights' scrawled across a blood-soaked banner. In 'The Petrol Bomber' (1994), the artists' first mural, painted for the 25-year commemoration of the Battle of the Bogside, a young boy, wearing a gas mask to protect against the CS gas canisters that have gone off behind him, prepares to throw a petrol bomb in the direction of the viewer. The mask makes the boy appear ant-like, menacing and otherworldly, a sort of human, animal, and machine hybrid, while in the background are soldiers in riot gear and the towering Rossville Flats, in flames and shrouded in smoke. According to the artists, this is the most often photographed of all their murals.[23] 'The Rioter' (2001) and 'Operation Motorman' (2001) depict individuals, one a civilian demonstrator the other a British soldier, in moments of intense action: the rioter is staring down an armored military truck, while the soldier is striking a closed door with a mallet. Finally, in 'The Runner' (2006), the most recent of the murals, three boys flee the scene of a British CS gas attack. The dynamic theatricality of these images conveys embodied movement circumscribed by and emerging through conflict, a conflict that is literally written on the bodies themselves. As acts of surrogation, these bodies not only stand for particular historical events, but also reinscribe on a continual basis the pain and trauma that this community maintains as a central aspect of its historical identity.

Other murals use a presentational form that is more subtle, though nonetheless theatrical. 'The Bloody Sunday Portraits' (started in 1997 and completed in 1999), for instance, shows the faces of the 14 civilian casualties ringed by a circle of 14 oak leaves (Derry derives its name from the Irish word *doire*, meaning oak grove surrounded by bogland). One of the most symbolic of the murals, 'The Death of Innocence' (1999–2000) depicts Annette McGavigan, a 14-year-old Bogside girl who was shot by a British soldier in 1971 while she was collecting rocks for a school project. There is a pile of rocks at her feet and, when the mural was initially unveiled, an unpainted butterfly in the upper left-hand corner and a rifle, pointed muzzled downwards, running along the left-hand frame of the mural. In the summer of 2006, the artists painted the butterfly bright purple and orange and broke the rifle, symbolic indications of the peace they believed was now close at hand. 'The Hunger Strike' (2000) depicts an image of Raymond McCartney, based on the famous photograph smuggled out of the Maze Prison in 1981 showing him suffering the effects of malnourishment. Although McCartney appears gaunt and drawn in the actual photograph, the mural downplays these features in the interest of making his image appear more imposing. With his long hair, beard, delicate face, and cloak-like blanket wrapped around his shoulders, he appears even Christ-like. In 'Bernadette' (1996), the artists' first mural painted in color, Bernadette McAliskey (Devlin, at the time) addresses a crowd during the Battle of the Bogside. And in a similar mural, 'Civil Rights' (2004), demonstrators face the viewer and carry banners that read 'One Man One Vote,' 'Jobs Not Creed,' and 'Anti Sectarian.' Finally, 'The Peace Mural' (2004), the only one of the eleven not to include human subjects, fuses the outline of a dove and an oak leaf on a vibrant, multicolored background. As performative gestures of memory, these murals use the techniques of stage imagery and dramatic point of view to endow specific individuals and events with narrative presence. They not only reiterate the past through citation of 'a thing done,' but insofar as they reconfigure, frame, and display these events, achieve something in the present ('a doing');[24] specifically, they constitute – rather than merely reflect – the identity of the Bogside through their acts of display and performed memory.

Painted by William Kelly, Kevin Hasson, and Tom Kelly, collectively known as the Bogside Artists, these murals join a tradition of mural painting in Northern Ireland – a performative 'genealogy'[25] – that began in earnest in the early 1900s when images of William III and other Orange symbols began to appear on gable walls in Protestant communities in working-class West Belfast.[26] Wall art in Derry's Catholic, working-class communities began with the 'blanket protest' in September 1976, in which H-Block prisoners in the Maze Prison, arguing that they were political prisoners and not criminals, refused to wear prison uniforms. Derry-born Mickey Devine, co-founder of the Irish National Liberation Army (INLA), was one of the most visible members of the protest. His death in June 1981, in the second hunger strike, sparked an explosion of mural painting in the Bogside as well as throughout Northern Ireland's Nationalist and Republican communities.[27] Today, Nationalist neighborhoods, such as the Falls Road and the Bogside, and Unionist ones, such as the Shankill Road and the Fountainside, are marked with a wide range of murals and other visual symbols of identity. As Neil Jarman puts it, 'Murals helped to transform "areas where Protestants lived" into "Protestant areas"' and likewise for Catholic areas.[28] It is this capacity to transform a neutral place into a Catholic, Protestant, Republican, or Loyalist space that indicates the performative power of murals in Northern Ireland.

But the Bogside Artists' murals differ from the broader tradition of mural painting in several respects. First, the muralists self-identify with their work. With a few exceptions, such as Bobby Jackson, whose murals in Derry's Fountainside were publicly maintained by his family for three generations, muralists in Northern Ireland – whether Protestant or Catholic – rarely identify themselves with their work. In contrast, the Bogside Artists sign their murals, maintain a website,[29] sell books, posters, and DVDs documenting their work, invite visitors to their Bogside studio, give frequent interviews, hold workshops for youth and various immigrant communities, and regularly travel to give public lectures for audiences around the world.[30] This public self-acknowledgement and indeed self-promotion makes the three Bogside Artists, who have been working together now for 14 years, substantially different from Northern Ireland's other generally anonymous mural painters.

Second, the Bogside Artists have distanced their murals from paramilitary culture in an attempt to perform an image of the Bogside that is outside sectarian politics. Through the cultivation of their public personas as antiwar as well as the selection and exclusion of certain forms of iconography in the murals, they have sought to perform the conflict within broader issues of global human rights, rather than local sectarian ones. 'The Rioter,' for instance, with the lone man staring down the armored personnel carrier, is an appropriation of the well-known image of the lone protestor in Tiananmen Square staring down the line of Chinese tanks. The murals do not contain images of harps, sham-rocks, or Irish language, an absence that is notable, even conspicuous, when compared to other murals in Nationalist neighborhoods depict-ing scenes from the Troubles. And in an indictment of Republican viol-ence, 'The Runner' contains a portrait of Charles Love, a 16-year-old Catholic boy, who was inadvertently killed by an IRA bomb at the Bloody Sunday commemoration ceremony in 1990. The artists describe their murals in contrast to what they call 'tribal-political' murals, pre-ferring to see their work as providing a voice for a marginalized com-munity, damaged by years of sectarian violence, to construct its own history through a creative space of emotional objectification and psychic healing.[31] The artists consult with community members during the 2–6 weeks it takes to paint a mural, and generally raise the funds – between £600 and £1,000 – directly from the community.[32] But despite the murals' imagery associated with global human rights and the absence of overt Republican iconography, they ultimately sustain conventional, Republican narratives, as the Catholic community remains the unwitting and repeated victim of the British army's combined acts of aggression. Moreover, when viewed in their topographical context alongside the Bogside's other forms of historical display – overtly sectarian murals, statues commemorating the H-block hunger-strikers and fallen Repub-lican icons, plaques detailing the events of Bloody Sunday, and graffiti lionizing the 'INLA' and 'Real IRA' – it becomes difficult not to read the Bogside Artists' work as enabling standard sectarian narratives of 'the Troubles,' despite their own statements to the contrary.

Finally, at a time when local governments throughout Northern Ireland are providing incentives for communities to paint over their murals,[33] the Bogside murals have become publicly sanctioned and cel-ebrated as official texts. A public commemoration ceremony, held on 31 July 2007 and attended by John Hume and Martin McGuinness, officially named the collection the 'People's Gallery,' a moniker that positions the murals as authentic, grassroots, and of the community. In a move that doubly marked the murals' theatricality, the city of Derry subsequently announced plans to train spotlights on them. As such, these murals lack the appearance of improvisation that marks so many others in Northern Ireland, and instead, perform an image of iconographic permanence.

Though like any performance, the murals are not static; rather, they are constantly evolving over time as they respond to present con-tingencies. The painting of the butterfly and the breaking of the gun in 'The Death of Innocence,' seven years after the mural was initially unveiled, exemplifies this fluidity. Similarly, in 'The Petrol Bomber,' the geographical outline of Ireland set within a circle on the front of the boy-subject's jacket was painted black by antiwar activists in May 2006 to symbolize opposition to the Irish government's policy of allowing US aircraft to stop over at Shannon Airport. The muralists initially condemned the antiwar activists for altering their mural on the grounds that neither they nor the community were consulted (though the muralists themselves are sympathetic to the antiwar campaign).[34] But in something of a gesture of solidarity, rather than repaint the outline of Ireland as it was, they blacked out the entire circle. Such mutations attest to the deeply performative capacity of these murals to appear permanent but to be in fact in active dialogue with present-day audiences about present-day concerns.

Above all, though, the murals and their attendant forms of display performatively mark the Bogside as an authentic and sacred site. A glass-cased map on Rossville Street, for instance, indicates the movement of the protesters and soldiers on Bloody Sunday. Numbers inside red circles indicate the location where each victim was shot and killed, while letters inside blue circles indicate the wounded. This textual reenactment – a 'printed repository of restored behavior'[35] – replays the events in a commemorative act of conservation, seemingly remembering it as it was. Visitors can then walk around the Bogside and imagine that they are standing in the exact locations: the exact spot where British soldiers lined up and aimed their guns; the exact spot where people crowded in a doorway for protection; the exact spot where Father Daly waved his blood-stained handkerchief. But there is, of course, an irony in staging the authenticity of such locations, for the rhetoric of mimetic fidelity becomes increasingly difficult to maintain as the city undergoes cosmetic changes with the passage of time. The ten-story Rossville Flats which, in photographs of Bloody Sunday, tower over the scene of the shootings, were demolished in 1989. Many of the streets have been changed so that they no longer correspond to the historical map. Glenfada Car Park today resembles nothing more than a mundane stretch of asphalt. Perhaps most representative of change are the tourists who now frequent the Bogside with cameras flashing, recording these spectacles of history on display.

But it is precisely through the selection, framing, and display of historical objects, on one hand, and the visitors' apprehension and recording of these objects, on the other, that make the Bogside an authentic site in ways that override material absence. Paradoxically, the more the Bogside is marked as an authentic site with plaques, murals, and statues

– the more it thus departs from the image of itself – the more authentic and indeed sacred it becomes. Even first-time visitors, who may know little about Northern Ireland's history and politics, on seeing this commemorative landscape with its copious murals, statues, and plaques, cannot help but feel they are crossing sacred ground. For many, this produces a sense of voyeurism and even 'tourist shame,' but ultimately one feels that one is encountering MacCannell's 'genuine society.'[36]

Increasingly, the spectacle of collective memory in and around Free Derry Corner is displayed in the context of global tourism. While the Derry Visitor and Convention Bureau features Free Derry Corner on nearly all of its tourist publications, the Northern Irish Tourist Board (NITB), desperate to mimic the success of its southern neighbor, focuses on sites that can more easily be read independent of sectarian conflict.[37] The NITB's website briefly mentions the Bogside murals, but says nothing about Free Derry Corner, placing much greater emphasis instead on other Derry attractions, such as the Guildhall, the Tower Museum, the ancient walls, and the Amelia Earhart Centre. In contrast, since at least the late 1990s, Gerry Adams and other Republican political leaders have recognized tourism as a way to develop Catholic, working-class areas. For four years now, Coiste Political Tours has been running daily trips through Republican areas of west Belfast led by former political prisoners.[38] The Bogside Artists recognize and embrace the fact that tourists travel to Derry to see their work, despite the fact that they did not create their murals to become tourist attractions.[39] But there is always the danger that the theatrical spectacle itself will displace the very real trauma of the events it represents. There is also the danger that, when combined with tourism, the spectacle of heritage will promote trivializing or exoticizing narratives of its object, despite the best attempts to the contrary. But this is why the lens of performance is so valuable. It allows us to perceive objects of commemoration, not as one-dimensional reflections of a fixed and already known past, but as complex performances of identity and memory in active dialogue with the exigencies of the present. Such an interpretive approach foregrounds their human-madeness, and above all, the fact that they constitute narratives of social reality for audiences in the here and now. As performances, these acts of spectacle and commemoration present images of how communities see themselves and want to be seen by others. They implicate the present and indicate possibilities for the future and, perhaps most importantly, for moving on without forgetting the past.

Notes

1 The described interaction took place in June 2006 during one of five research trips I took to Derry between 1994 and 2007. This project has been supported by grants from the College of Social Sciences Research Foundation at San José State University and the California State University.

2 Peter Pringle and Philip Jacobson, *Those Are Real Bullets: Bloody Sunday, Derry 1972* (New York: Grove Press, 2000), 28.

3 The 10,000 to 20,000 marchers were protesting Stormont's August 1971 decision to impose internment without trial, which, by early 1972, had resulted in the imprisonment of approximately 900 people, the vast majority of whom were Nationalists. See Don Mullan, *Eyewitness Bloody Sunday: The Truth* (Dublin: Merlin Publishing, 2002), xxvii.

4 The subsequent inquiry conducted by Chief Justice Lord Widgery found the soldiers innocent of wrongdoing in a report issued only eleven weeks after the event. Following 26 years of accusations that the Widgery Report was little more than a whitewash, on 29 January 1998, then Prime Minister Tony Blair announced the creation of the Saville Inquiry, which would revisit the events of Bloody Sunday and consider facts not reviewed by the initial one. Among other omissions, for instance, the Widgery Report did not include any statements made by those who were wounded on Bloody Sunday. The Saville Inquiry considered a massive amount of evidence, including 2,500 statements by witnesses, and thus far has cost the British state more than £182 million. At the time of writing (October 2008), the Inquiry has made public most of the transcripts from the interviews, but has yet to issue the eagerly awaited final report. More information on the Saville Inquiry can be obtained at http://www.bloody-sunday-inquiry.org.uk/index.htm.

5 The exact number of tourists who visit the Bogside every year is not known, but the Museum of Free Derry reported 14,500 visitors in 2007.

6 Victor Turner, *The Anthropology of Performance* (New York: PAJ Publications, 1986), 93.

7 Michel de Certeau, *The Practice of Everyday Life*, trans. Steven Rendall (Berkeley: University of California Press, 1984), 21.

8 Diana Taylor, *Disappearing Acts: Spectacles of Gender and Nationalism in Argentina's 'Dirty War'* (Durham, NC: Duke University Press, 1997), 29.

9 John Urry, *The Tourist Gaze: Leisure and Travel in Contemporary Societies* (London: Sage, 1990); Carol Crawshaw and John Urry, 'Tourism and the Photographic Eye,' in *Touring Cultures: Transformations of Travel and Theory*, eds. Chris Rojek and John Urry (London: Routledge, 1997), 176–95; David Crouch and Nina Lübbren, eds. *Visual Culture and Tourism* (Oxford: Berg, 2003).

10 Bernard J. Armada, 'Memorial Agon: An Interpretive Tour of the National Civil Rights Museum,' *Southern Communication Journal* 63 (1998): 235–43; Carole Blair, 'Contemporary U.S. Memorial Sites as Exemplars of Rhetoric's Materiality,' in *Rhetorical Bodies*, eds. Jack Selzer and Sharon Crowley (Madison: University of Wisconsin, Press, 1999), 16–57; Tim Edensor, *Tourists at the Taj: Performance and Meaning at a Symbolic Site* (London: Routledge, 1998); Victoria Gallagher, 'Memory and Reconciliation in the Birmingham Civil Rights Institute,' *Rhetoric and Public Affairs* 2 (1999), 303–20; Barbara

Kirshenblatt-Gimblett, *Destination Culture: Tourism, Museums, and Heritage* (Berkeley: University of California Press, 1998); Jennifer Iles, 'Recalling the Ghosts of War: Performing Tourism on the Battlefields of the Western Front,' *Text and Performance Quarterly* 26 (2) (2006), 162–80; David W. Lloyd, *Battlefield Tourism: Pilgrimage and the Commemoration of the Great War in Britain, Australia and Canada, 1919–1939* (Oxford: Berg, 1998).

11 Lisa L. Love and Nathaniel Kohn, 'This, That, and the Other: Fraught Possibilities of the Souvenir,' *Text and Performance Quarterly* 21 (1) (2001): 47–63.

12 Phaedra Pezzullo, 'Touring "Cancer Alley," Louisiana: Performances of Community and Memory for Environmental Justice,' *Text and Performance Quarterly* 23 (3) (2003): 226–52.

13 Michael S. Bowman, 'Looking for Stonewall's Arm: Tourist Performance as Research Method,' in *Opening Acts: Performance in/as Communication and Cultural Studies*, ed. Judith Hamera (Thousand Oaks, CA: Sage, 2005), 102–33; Jane Desmond, *Staging Tourism: Bodies on Display from Waikiki to Sea World* (Chicago, IL: University of Chicago Press, 1999); Tim Edensor, 'Performing Tourism, Staging Tourism,' *Tourist Studies* 1 (1) (2001): 59–81; Tim Edensor, 'Staging Tourism: Tourists as Performers,' *Annals of Tourism Research* 27 (1) (2000): 322–44.

14 Michael S. Bowman, 'Performing Southern History for the Tourist Gaze: Antebellum Home Tour Guide Performances,' in *Exceptional Spaces: Essays in Performance and History*, ed. Della Pollock (Chapel Hill, NC: University of North Carolina Press, 1998), 142–58; Elizabeth C. Fine and Jean Haskell Speer, 'Tour Guide Performances as Sight Sacralization,' *Annals of Tourism Research* 12 (10) (1985): 73–95.

15 Scott Magelssen, 'Making History in the Second Person: Post-touristic Considerations for Living Historical Interpretation,' *Theatre Journal* 58 (2) (2006), 291–312; Andrew Wood, '"What Happens [in Vegas]": Performing the Post-Tourist *Flâneur* in "New York" and "Paris,"' *Text and Performance Quarterly* 25 (4) (2005): 315–33.

16 Susan C. Haedicke, 'The Politics of Participation: Un Voyage pas comme les Autres sur les Chemins de l'Exil,' *Theatre Topics* 12 (2) (2002): 99–118; Megan Sanborn Jones, 'Reliving the Pioneer Past: Mormon Youth Handcart Treck Re-enactments,' *Theatre Topics* 16 (2) (2006): 113–30; Scott Magelssen, '"This is a Drama. You Are Characters": The Tourist as Fugitive Slave in Conner Prairie's "Follow the North Star,"' *Theatre Topics* 16 (1) (2006): 19–34.

17 Dean MacCannell, *The Tourist: A New Theory of the Leisure Class* (New York: Schockehn Books, 1976), 44–5.

18 Kirshenblatt-Gimblett, 1998, 1.

19 *Ibid.*, 6.

20 Brian Lacey, *Siege City: The Story of Derry and Londonderry* (Belfast: Blackstaff Press, 1990).

21 Graham Dawson, 'Trauma, Place and the Politics of Memory: Bloody Sunday, Derry, 1972–2004,' *History Workshop Journal* 59 (1) (2005): 151–78, 158.

22 Dates refer to the year in which each mural was initially completed.

23 On 20 June 2006, I interviewed William Kelly and Kevin Hasson, two of the three painters, who collectively call themselves the Bogside Artists (William's brother Tom Kelly is the third).

24 See Elin Diamond, 'Introduction,' in *Performance and Cultural Politics*, ed. Elin Diamond (London: Routledge, 1996), 1–14, 1.

25 Joseph Roach, *Cities of the Dead: Circum-Atlantic Performance* (New York: Columbia University Press, 1996), 25–30.

26 Bill Rolston identifies 1908 as the specific date when Loyalist murals began to appear. See *Drawing Support 2: Murals of War and Peace* (Belfast: Beyond the Pale, 1998), i.

27 Neil Jarman's 'Preface' to *Murals: The Bogside Artists* (Derry: Guildhall Press, 2001), 6–8.

28 Neil Jarman, 'Painting Landscapes: The Place of Murals in the Symbolic Construction of Urban Space,' in *Symbols in Northern Ireland*, ed. Anthony D. Buckley (Belfast: The Institute of Irish Studies, 1998), 81–98, 84.

29 See www.bogsideartists.com; for additional photographs of their work, see http://cain.ulst.ac.uk/bogsideartists/menu.htm.

30 The Bogside Artists have given lectures in Australia, the U.S., and Europe. (Interview, 20 June 2006).

31 Interview, 20 June 2006; see also William Kelly, Kevin Hasson, and Tom Kelly, 'Manifesto' and 'Frequently Asked Questions,' in *Murals: The Bogside Artists* (Derry: The Guildhall Press, 2001), 34–6 and 104–5.

32 Interview, 20 June 2006.

33 Benoît Lety, 'Tourism: A Continuation of Conflict by Other Means,' *Le Monde Diplomatique*, January 2008, 15.

34 Interview, 20 June 2006.

35 Roach, 1996, 140.

36 MacCannell, 1976, 10 and 155.

37 According to the NITB, 1.9 million foreign tourists visited Northern Ireland in 2006 compared to 7.4 million in the Republic, which also reported ten times the revenue of the North with 4.7 billion. See 'Visitor Tourism Performance 2006,' http://www.nitb.com/article.aspx?ArticleID=1536 and Fáilte Ireland, 'Tourism Facts 2006,' http://www.failteireland.ie/getdoc/36f2d08a-c59b-482f-91b4-9f25f25ac3bd/Tourism-Facts-2006 (both accessed 8 July 2008).

38 Lety, 2008, 15.

39 Interview, 20 June 2006.

9

St Patrick's Purgatory and the Performance of Pilgrimage

David Cregan

Victor and Edith Turner's book *Image and Pilgrimage in Christian Culture* (1978) is considered to be the most influential text in the anthropological work that connects pilgrimage with meaning in culture.[1] Interestingly, the Turners chose the Irish pilgrimage of St Patrick's Purgatory at Lough Derg in County Donegal as a particular field of study, additionally making numerous references to the pilgrimage to Croagh Patrick in County Mayo. Lough Derg is classified as an archaic site because evidence exists to prove that it has survived as a sacred destination through a variety of religious practices and traditions. As a result of the adaptability of its spiritual significance *Image and Pilgrimage in Christian Culture* asserts that Lough Derg, and other places like it, allows the pilgrim to make connections between contemporary experience and a perceived connection with persistent ideas and ideals of the more ancient and perceivably numinous past.

The Turners' work on pilgrimage creates an inroad for an examination of important religious or cultural traditions from the perspective of performance studies by creating a paradigm for the interpretation of collective ritual action and what that action indicates in relation to social, historical, and cultural transformation. While the number of Roman Catholics in Ireland attending Sunday mass dropped to below 50 percent[2] in the past decade, the number of Irish taking on the journey of pilgrimage has increased. Despite the extreme physical conditions that the pilgrim must endure at Lough Derg, or the environmental challenges that must be conquered at Croagh Patrick, thousands of Irish people enter into these ancient practices closely associated in more modern times with Roman Catholicism. In fact, the website for St Patrick's Purgatory addresses 'frequently asked questions': 'I do not attend church regularly; can I do the pilgrimage?'[3]

In his book *The Ritual Process: Structure and Anti-Structure*, Victor Turner introduces the notion of liminality to differentiate between the ordinary of everyday and the extraordinary of specific rites of passage such as ritual or pilgrimage. Turner relies on the previous work of anthropologist Arnold van Gennep, who defined these important transitional moments for humanity as marked by three distinct phases: separation, margin or liminal, and aggregation. Turner outlines van Gennep's stages thus:

> The first phase (of separation) comprises symbolic behavior signifying the detachment of the individual or group either from an earlier fixed point in the social structure, from a set of cultural conditions (a 'state'), or both. During the intervening 'liminal' period, the characteristics of the ritual subject (the 'passenger') are ambiguous; he passes through a realm that has few or none of the attributes of the past or coming state. In the third phase (reaggregation or reincorporation), the passage is consummated ... he is expected to behave in accordance with certain customary norms and ethical standards binding on incumbents of social position in a system of such positions.[4]

These three phases will form the analytic paradigm through which I shall analyze the increase in participation in pilgrimage in Ireland and its relationship to the normative religious practice of participation in institutional church obligations, out of which pilgrimage has traditionally grown.

Ritual theories often support a primitivism which presupposes an instinctual tendency for deism in humans. Consequently, much of the language used is uncritical of the possibility of the social construction of what is sometimes framed as spiritual intuition. This spiritualism, or belief that the spiritual and material worlds are distinct from each other, is often expressed in social science discourse through rather theological language – language that supports the idea that the spiritual is more instinctual than the material, and thus truer.

St Patrick's Purgatory, more commonly referred to by its geographical location, Lough Derg, is situated approximately four hours from the metropolitan center of the Republic of Ireland, Dublin, and two hours from the metropolitan center of Northern Ireland, Belfast. The island itself is small, consisting of a church and a few shelters for pilgrims, including a dormitory. The prayers said as part of the pilgrimage remain virtually the same today as they did hundreds of years ago: the Apostles' Creed, the Our Father, and the Hail Mary. However, the required periods of time spent on the island and some of the ritual practices have been altered. Sometime around the fifteenth century the length of time on the island was reduced from fifteen to nine days. Today, the most common pilgrimage lasts three days. Records detail that pilgrims ate bread and drank water once a day, but in the time when the purgatorial ritual of the cave still existed pilgrims did not eat for 24 hours before entering, and not at all while inside. Upon exiting the cave the renewed soul would submerge into the cold waters of the lake three times as a symbol of their purgation. The Irish seemed to be drawn to the radical ascetic nature of the demanding ritual and practice of this pilgrimage, and while the modern pilgrimage has been significantly modified, and in cases reduced to one day, its expectations appropriately test the comfort level of the more privileged citizens of post-Celtic Tiger Ireland.

In *Lough Derg: St Patrick's Purgatory* (1944) Alice Curtayne provides some interesting insight into the first phase of van Gennep's model of pilgrimage, detailing why the pilgrim is drawn out of his or her own ordinary social context and into the extraordinary experience of the pilgrimage. Curtayne's language reveals the archaic and primordial attraction, and offers an understanding of what continues to be alluring about this challenging experience to Irish people who today are far less attracted to the normative religious practices of Catholicism, which traditionally motivated the Irish to make this sacrificial journey. Curtayne explains the transition:

> The most attractive aspect of the island routine is that it is a complete suspension of normal living. There is no meal served here in the formal sense, and the usual daily routine of bed, dress and toilet is rudely dislocated. Then of course there are no telephones to distract, or wireless programmes to assail the nerves. There is a complete absence of the fuss, clatter and compulsory absorption in petty trifles that make up the confusion of everyday life. All of that bustle, so frequently mistaken for achievement, all that hugger-mugger, is left behind on the mainland and the pilgrim steps into new air.[5]

The idea of stepping into 'new air' rhetorically illustrates the first phase of the pilgrimage in which the very atmospheric experience of the individual is altered and society and culture are radically reconfigured. The necessary steps destabilize the subject and reawaken reactionary impulses dulled by routine or, as eluded to by Curtayne, the steady hum of technology; a notion all too familiar to the contemporary Irish citizen as mobile phones and computers dominate their time and focus.

The journey from civilization to nature is a movement away from the social or cultural into the primal. What drives people to want to detach from their routines and submit themselves to the rigor and discomfort of the pilgrimage, for a pilgrimage is not a holiday? In particular, what aspects of contemporary Irish culture and society are supporting the steady practice of Irish pilgrimage during a historical period in which formal or institutional religious identification is markedly on the decline? In 'The Territory of the Anthropology of Pilgrimage' Alan Morinis illuminates the yearning for an experience of the sacred which he claims motivates these types of esthetic journeys:

> Pilgrimage is born out of desire and belief. The desire is for solution to problems of all kinds that arise within the human situation. The belief is that somewhere beyond the known world there exists a power that can make right the difficulties that appear so insoluble and intractable here and now. All one must do is journey.[6]

What is interesting here is Morinis's use of the word desire. Desire implies want or need, but Morinis separates this notion from the concept of belief. Belief has the cognitive associations concomitant with an intellectual assent to something such as faith, but desire is more primordially associated with instinct or impulse. 'To want' varies vastly from 'to desire.' Desire implies an almost irresistible or uncontrollable movement toward something. If it can be accepted that desire, not necessarily faith, is at the heart of what draws the individual into the action of pilgrimage, then the Irish historical and contemporary attraction to sacred journey can be seen to transcend the ideology of doctrine or the structure of institution in order to tap into a more ancient yearning associated with the human quest for meaning. In an age where science and education promise enlightenment, pilgrimage reflects an alternative ethereal impulse.

Morinis defines pilgrimage as 'a journey undertaken by a person in a quest of a place or a state that he or she believes to embody a valued idea.'[7] Once again, there is a valuable point of distinction here in the search for significance in the performance of Irish pilgrimage. The history of foreign interest in Lough Derg is clearly associated with the supernatural quality of place or geographical location. Its natural surroundings have seen little change since the fifth century when St Patrick, the patron saint of Ireland, was said to have passed a challenging spiritual threshold alone on the island. The pilgrimage is traced back to the fourth century, and the Annals of Ireland contain a record which describes the existence of this sacred site and its challenging rituals dated as far back as 784. The virtues of this primordial pilgrimage were extolled in poetry and mythology throughout Europe in the Middle Ages and is, in fact, the only spot in Ireland mentioned specifically on a fifteenth-century map of the world. The belief that the cave on the island is a doorway to another world drew nobility from the continent who wished to gain a glimpse of a supernatural place. And yet, distinctly, the Irish were historically noted to be drawn to the extreme nature of the ascetic practices of this location rather than the immediate temporality of the mystical cave. Beginning in 1704, when Catholicism was officially repressed by the British Protestant Parliament, access to the island was prohibited, yet thousands flocked to the shores of Lough Derg. In this sense it would seem that the pilgrimage was incomplete without the arrival on the island. What is, in fact, unique about the Irish interest in St Patrick's Purgatory is the distinction Morinis makes between place and state. Clearly Irish pilgrimage valued place but privileged state. While the signifier of place – arrival at a particular location – was unavailable, the supernatural quality of state was undesignated or uncontrolled by conventional human politics. And so we are left with an insight into the Irish attraction to sacred journey and pilgrim practice despite a distrust or even distain for organized religions. Irish pilgrimage privileges the primordial draw of existential desire and the subjective aspiration of individual transformation and it is, perhaps, these forces which are beckoning temporary detachment from the luxury of wealthy and prosperous contemporary Ireland to the physical, psychological, and spiritual struggles of sacred journey.

Following Victor Tuner's analysis of van Gennep's stages of pilgrimage it is interesting to begin to examine the actual ritual practices involved. Today St Patrick's Purgatory is open to pilgrims from June 1 to August 15. The current practice involves three days, beginning at 11 am on the first day and ending before noon on the third day. The pilgrim is expected to have abstained from the consumption of any food from the midnight before arrival. Having crossed to the island by a special ferry, pilgrims remove their shoes and remain barefoot for the rest of the pilgrimage. Once on the island a sequence of prayers called Stations are performed. Lough Derg is considered a penitential pilgrimage, focusing on the absolution of sins. The central penitential practice of the retreat is the all-night vigil. The pilgrim is required to remain awake from the time of arrival until the evening of the second day. Pilgrims are given one Lough

Derg meal each day, which consists of dry toast or oatcakes and black tea or black coffee.

The actions performed by the pilgrims are ancient and highly ritualized. The entire body is engaged in this sacred performance in which discomfort is clearly a primary aim. The pilgrim must begin the practice of the Stations immediately. The Stations are prayers which consist of the repetition of the Roman Catholic Profession of Faith or Creed, the Our Father, and the Hail Mary. The Stations begin with a visit to the Blessed Sacrament contained within the Basilica built on the island. This is a piece of the Eucharistic bread believed by Catholics to be the real presence of Jesus. From here, the pilgrim proceeds to St Patrick's Cross, just a few yards from the entrance to the church. Upon arrival the pilgrim kneels and recites the Our Father, the Hail Mary, and the Creed once. The pilgrim then proceeds to St Brigid's Cross, an inset on the wall of the Basilica. Here they kneel and repeat three Our Fathers, three Hail Marys, and the Creed. The pilgrim then walks to the edge of the water with his or her back to the Basilica and the crosses. With arms outstretched an ancient prayer of renunciation of the world and Satan is repeated to invoke the pilgrim's earlier baptismal commitment. Alice Curtayne describes this dramatic spiritual moment thus:

> This repetition of the baptismal vow is a reaching back again towards baptismal innocence and is the usual ritual of retreats. But here in the special circumstances it takes on an entirely new meaning. Recited in the open, while facing the airy spaciousness of mountain, sky and water, the pilgrim has the impression of having reached some complete solitude, despite the fact that there is probably a queue of people awaiting their turn beside him.[8]

Again, the primordial call away from the constructed nature of culture and society is emphasized and acted in order to access new or renewed meaning in the life and experience of pilgrimage.

Having renounced the world, the pilgrim turns back to the Basilica, circling it four times while completing seven decades of the Rosary and the Creed. From here the pilgrim proceeds to the ruins of six ancient, beehive-shaped monastic cells. What remains of these holy structures is a rough circle of boulders which once served as the foundation to the structure which has long since disappeared. Each cell is dedicated to a Celtic saint: Brendan, Brigid, Columba, Molaise, Catherine, and Dabheoc, respectively. The cells are commonly referred to as Beds and are surrounded by jagged sloped rocks. At each Bed the pilgrim recites three Our Fathers, three Hail Marys, and one Creed. These prayers are recited in order first while walking three times around the outside of the Bed, again while kneeling at the entrance, and a third time while walking around the inside, and one final time while kneeling at a rugged cross erected at the center of each cell. The conditions on the island are, more often than not, rainy. The pilgrim performs these rituals in their bare feet resulting in fatigue, sore feet, and knee pain. After having done the circuit of all six Beds the pilgrim returns to the water's edge and repeats five Our Fathers, five Hail Marys, and the Creed standing, and then again kneeling. Returning to St Patrick's Cross and kneeling, one Our Father, one Hail Mary, and the Creed are said. To complete the Station the pilgrim goes back into the Basilica, kneels before the tabernacle containing the real presence of Jesus, and says five Our Fathers, five Hail Marys, and the Creed, which is offered for the intentions of the Holy Father in Rome. At this stage the pilgrim's fast may be broken. This entire process is repeated four more times in the outdoors. This is an intensely physical penitential ritual through which the performing body suffers both fatigue and pain.

The central penitential practice of the retreat is the all-night vigil. In order to help pilgrims to stay awake there is the constant recitation of prayers. As pilgrims process *en masse* around the periphery of the Basilica the final four Stations are repeated. There are 15-minute breaks between each Station during which time pilgrims can step outside the Basilica and, perhaps most significantly, converse with one another. The rigorous practices of the pilgrimage create solidarity among its participants, and pilgrims are encouraged to support one another and help each other to stay awake as the morning approaches.

The vigil on St Patrick's Purgatory may, in fact, be the location of the power and impact of the performative qualities of pilgrimage. In his article 'Performances: Belief in the Part One is Playing' Erving Goffman defines the term 'performance' thus: 'all the activity of an individual which occurs during a period marked by his continuous presence before a particular set of observers and which has some influences on the observers.'[9] Goffman's notion of presence and impact on actor and observer provides interesting insight into the particularly social aspects of Irish ritual and pilgrimage. Performance on St Patrick's Purgatory is physically challenging for the individual, but also requires a communal adherence to the tightly choreographed routines of the ritual requirements. In order to achieve the rigorous demands of the Stations pilgrims must be orderly and patient rather than merely self-motivated or individually goal-oriented. In fact, through the action of pilgrimage, one is both actor and observer in a well-blocked performance of bodies.

With the arrival on the island, the removal of shoes, and the execution of the symbolic action required at Lough Derg, the pilgrim is most certainly detached from their previous routines and reoriented into a new set of social structures. With the repetition of the ritual prayers and actions the pilgrim is resituated in the culture of the pilgrimage. The actions deliver the pilgrim into Victor Turner's description of van Gennep's second stage, liminality.

It is through compliance with expected performance that the ritual subjects place themselves in the social state of neither here nor there. What does it mean to be neither here nor there? When entering into the pilgrimage the pilgrim accepts the instructions and the concurrent challenges with a certain degree of passivity. Following in the footsteps of millions who have come before them and falling into line with fellow pilgrims, the individual accepts the ambiguity and uncertainty of this new social experience in the hope of reaching an encounter with something akin to divinity. Turner writes: 'It is as though they are being reduced or ground down to a uniform condition to be fashioned anew and endowed with additional powers to enable them to cope with their new station in life.'[10] The performance of pilgrim ritual, therefore, is an aspirational rehearsal for transformation in the life left behind before the journey.

During the liminal stage of pilgrimage social signifiers that divide and classify one person from another are temporarily dissolved into social solidarity. The removal of shoes upon entry in St Patrick's Purgatory is just such a social leveler. While the removal of shoes most certainly represents an entry onto sacred ground and holy humility this collective requirement also stimulates a level of camaraderie. Pilgrimage offers alternative structures indicative of social life and during the liminal period new cultural alternatives are permitted to take shape. Turner describes the new social structures that emerge during the liminal period of pilgrimage as 'unstructured or rudimentarily structured and relatively undifferentiated *comitatus*, community, or even communion of equal individuals who submit together to the general authority of elders.'[11] What Turner refers to as 'the general authority of elders' illuminates a modern deferential to a version of primordial wisdom discernible in the archaic type of pilgrimage St Patrick's Purgatory is classified as by Turner. In this sense, the pilgrimage to Lough Derg could be interpreted as a performance of the past, and in the Irish context, a glimpse of the pilgrim over his or her shoulder as the waves of modernity pull the Irish subject into the world of the global market.

Posture, movement, even timing and rhythm are essential for the completion of the pilgrim's journey. Dance theory provides an illuminating correlation between the highly choreographed rhythms of the body during St Patrick's Purgatory and the archaic impulse inherent in this journey, which continues to draw thousands of Irish people. In her article 'The Dancer of the Future' Isadora Duncan describes how movement is primary in revealing the unencultured nature of the human being:

> The movement of the waves, of winds, is ever in the same lasting harmony. We do not stand on the beach and inquire of the ocean what was its movement in the past and what will its movement be in the future. We realize that the movement peculiar to its nature is eternal to its nature. The movement of free animals and birds is always in correspondence to their nature ... It is only when you put free animals under false restrictions that they lose the power of moving in harmony with nature, and adopt a movement expressive of the restrictions placed about them.[12]

Duncan weaves movement and nature together, allowing for an interpretation of the pilgrim performance that struggles to free the pilgrim from the 'restrictions placed around them' through choreography of ritual. This is perhaps best illustrated in the practices of St Patrick's Purgatory when the pilgrim turns away from the constructed elements of the sacred island such as the Basilica and, with arms outstretched, renouncing the material world while facing the virtually unchanged landscape of the surrounding area at Lough Derg.

The various movements which constitute the performance of pilgrimage are movements of hope – not simply a desire for the retrieval of a more primitive and thus more 'natural' self. The type of harmony sought by the pilgrim as the individual's body submits to the alternative movements of ancient sacred choreographies is a unity of body and soul, a desire to belong to the community of humanity over the commodities of commercialism. Like a dancer the pilgrim's body expresses hope through movement. The Turners describe it thus:

> It has become clear to us that liminality is not only *transition* but also *potentiality*, not only 'going to be' but also 'what may be,' a formulable domain in which all that is not manifest in the normal

day-to-day operations of social structures … can be studied objectively, despite the often bizarre and metaphorical character of its contents.[13]

This theory asserts that the action, and perhaps even the rise in popularity of the pilgrimage in contemporary Irish cultural practice, is a sociologically quantifiable performance that actively demonstrates a movement away from individualism towards community.

The idea that pilgrimage is not simply transition but also potentiality provides insight into the contemporary fascination with pilgrimage in Ireland and the apparently contradictory disinterest in institutional religious practice. In Curtayne's book on St Patrick's Purgatory from the 1940s the pilgrim practices are clearly a deepening of the ritual routines of practicing Catholics in Ireland at that time. She describes the unity in diversity which characterized the pilgrim experience in mid-twentieth-century Ireland: 'There is a unifying factor, moreover, which makes the crowds to be observed on Station Island more interesting than crowds that gather anywhere else in the world: a common spiritual purpose binds them all; they are all penitents.'[14] For most of the previous century Irish people were united by a sense of morality and religious vision. In the light of disappointment in the Roman Catholic Church the mythic power of Catholicism has been fragmented and no longer necessarily serves as the existential impetus that drives the pilgrim toward journey.

It might be argued that the Irish pilgrim no longer merely seeks sacred journey for repentance or even to grow in a traditional spiritual sense. Is the Irish pilgrim then simply an existential tourist? Is the pilgrimage a type of supernatural voyeurism in which the pilgrim seeks just one more exotic experience to add to their postmodern to-do list? Clearly, St Patrick's Purgatory will not satisfy the tourist's need for pleasure or pampering. We have already established that pilgrim travel has a unique character, but how does it function in the concrete experience of esthetic challenge?

Performance and meaning collide most obviously through the ritual associated with making or completing the pilgrimage. Performance and ritual share a dependence on symbol as metaphor. In his book *Rite Out of Place: Ritual, Media, and the Arts* Ronald Grimes describes what he calls a ritual metaphor: 'A ritual metaphor is a drastically embodied symbol, one in which symbol and symbolized are simultaneously identified and differentiated.'[15] Ritual metaphor provides access to meaning in its association with the sacred rather than the secular.

Consequently, the ritual actions of St Patrick's Purgatory, with its differentiation in location and custom from the outside world, embody an existential expression of meaning that reflects a deeper search for identity because they are framed within religious meaning. Lough Derg literally stages a world of action and language to differentiate itself from the outside world in order to shed new light on the significance of life. In this sense, contemporary interest in pilgrimage in Ireland could be interpreted as part of the postmodern package of New Age Spirituality and its focus on individual enlightenment.

If it can be accepted that the modern pilgrim is subject to postmodern worldviews and is shaped by the move toward individualism advocated by commercialism and globalization, then it is clear that Turner's third paradigm in the pilgrim's progress, aggregation, is where a slippage occurs in more contemporary analyses of why pilgrimages are still performed in the changing spiritual light of the modern world. In the final stage the pilgrim is reintroduced to society with the expectation of effecting change. But what if the pilgrim is not associated with the ongoing relationship with the institutional church that historically characterized pilgrimage? The action and evolution of the pilgrimage is a symbolic metaphor for the action and evolution of society and culture. The ascent to institutional structures of spirituality and faith has been disassembled in contemporary Ireland, but the desire for something beyond the material has not been erased in this rejection. Belief in the Church has traditionally been correlated with belief in God, an idea that has, on the surface, made it appear that the Irish have lost their historically characteristic belief in the Divine. And yet desire for the something divine has propelled the institutionally rebellious intellect of the Irish spirit into the bodily performance of innate sacred desire in the form of pilgrimage in Ireland. Pilgrimage has, perhaps, become the most widely acceptable site of the performance of faith in modern Ireland as the market mentality collides with the instinct of centuries of profound spiritual inheritance. The cultural walls of the Church in Ireland have crumbled and the Irish, as they have so often done in the past, return to the natural, the archaic, and the performative to connect with something spiritual.

Notes

1 Victor Turner and Edith Turner, *Image and Pilgrimage in Christian Culture: Anthropological Perspectives* (New York: Columbia University Press, 1978).
2 'Irish Mass Attendance Below 50%,' *Catholic World News* online, www.cwnews. com/news/viewstory.cfm?recnum=44521 (accessed 11 July 2008).

3 'FAQs: Three Day Pilgrimages,' *Lough Derg: Bringing You the Gift of Hope* website, http://www.loughderg.org/module.cfm/opt/0/page/faqs/area/FAQs (accessed 16 June 2008).

4 Victor Turner, *The Ritual Process: Structure and Anti-Structure* (Chicago, IL: Aldine, 1969), 94.

5 Alice Curtayne, *Lough Derg: St Patrick's Purgatory* (Dublin: Burns Oats & Washbournes, 1944), 179–80.

6 Alan Morinis, 'Introduction: The Territory of the Anthropology of Pilgrimage,' in *Sacred Journey: The Anthropology of Pilgrimage*, ed. Alan Morinis (Westport, CT: Greenwood Press, 1992), 1–27, 1.

7 *Ibid.*, 5.

8 Curtayne, 1944, 168.

9 Erving Goffman, 'Performances: Belief in the Part One Is Playing,' in *The Performance Studies Reader*, ed. Henry Bial (London: Routledge, 2004), 59–63, 61.

10 Turner, *The Ritual Process*, 95.

11 *Ibid.*, 96.

12 Isadora Duncan, 'The Dancer of the Future,' in *The Twentieth-Century Performance Reader*, eds. Michael Huxley and Noel Witts (London: Routledge, 2002), 171.

13 Turner and Turner, 1978, 3 (emphasis in original).

14 Curtayne, 1944, 178.

15 Ronald L. Grimes, *Rite Out of Place: Ritual, Media, and the Arts* (Oxford: Oxford University Press, 2006), 97.

Part III
Political Performances

10
De Valera Performs the Oath: Word, Voice, Book, and Act
Anne Pulju

On 11 August 1927, over 40 Fianna Fáil politicians entered Leinster House in small groups. Eamon de Valera was the last to enter the office of the Clerk of the House, accompanied by Frank Aiken and Dr James Ryan. The Fianna Fáil leader then spoke to the Clerk in Irish, reading from a prepared note. Translating his own words, de Valera recounted his statement for Dáil Éireann in 1932: 'I said: "I am not prepared to take an oath. I am not going to take an oath. I am prepared to put my name down in this book in order to get permission to go into the Dáil, but it has no other significance."'[1] The book into which de Valera put his name contained the signatures to the Oath of Allegiance which was a prerequisite to taking a seat in Dáil Éireann. This signature book was, de Valera discovered, covered by another book, prompting further maneuvering, as observed by Aiken and Ryan:

> Mr. de Valera picked up the Bible which was lying on the book containing the oath, carried it to the other end of the room, and placed it on the couch there. He then went back, signed his name on the line pointed out by the Clerk, at the same time covering the writing above the line with some papers he held in his hand.[2]

De Valera added his name to those of the other members of his political party who had previously been elected to Dáil Éireann yet refused to take their seats. With the signatures, one of the most contentious situations in modern Irish history came to a sudden, abrupt end.

The convoluted manner in which de Valera finally signed his name to the Oath reflects the complexity of the discursive role of the Oath and its varied interpretations in Irish culture. In this chapter, I will argue that de Valera's words and actions on this occasion can be understood within the context of performance studies as an attempt to ensure that his encounter with the Oath was not seen as a binding performative statement or gesture. His skillful use of symbols and language, which drew on alternative systems of authority, meant that the attempt was largely successful, with major implications for Irish society. As a pivotal point for the modern nation-state, the taking of the Oath constitutes one of the most significant performative moments in Irish history. De Valera's Oath proves particularly rewarding as an object of investigation due to the fact that it was a uniquely contained performance in both physical and temporal terms, yet was surrounded by remarkable rhetoric which explicitly engaged with questions of performance that are sometimes obscured in historiographic narratives.

The Oath: war over words?

Commentators have sometimes been surprised at the weight the Oath of Allegiance carried in the Treaty negotiations which ended the Anglo-Irish War. At times the Oath seemed more crucial than even the apparently more down-to-earth question of partition of the northern counties. To consider the Oath as a mere empty gesture, however, would ignore not only its genuine discursive power, but also its involvement with the practical issue of how closely the new Irish state would be tied to Britain. The Oath ultimately included in the Treaty (and the one to which de Valera would sign his name) was not precisely an Oath of Allegiance to the British Crown; it required Dáil members to swear allegiance 'to the Constitution of the Irish Free State' and *fidelity* 'to H.M. King George V ... in virtue of the common citizenship of Ireland with Great Britain and her adherence to and membership of the group of nations forming the British Commonwealth of Nations.'[3] The Oath and the Treaty were still too much for Republicans, however, and political and military schism resulted. R. F. Foster argues: 'the break with the irreconcilables came on a form of words.'[4] The immediate consequence of that break, the Irish Civil War, resulted in many hundreds of deaths.[5]

The words of the Oath remained potent even after Cumann na nGaedheal, the pro-Treaty party, won the war. As the Free State's stability and prospects for survival increased, de Valera began to hold discussions with fellow Republicans about the pragmatic benefits of taking the Oath, paving the way for his 1926 break from Sinn Féin and founding of Fianna Fáil. After the June 1927 election, however, in which Fianna Fáil made a strong showing, those elected to the Dáil refused to take the Oath and their seats. In what Tim Pat Coogan calls a 'dramatic scene' and a 'mock attempt' designed for publicity purposes, the Fianna Fáil members visited Leinster House *en masse* on 23 June, only to be denied entry to the Oireachtas.[6] The party then began proceedings to have the Oath requirement removed from the Free State constitution by popular referendum. Extraordinary circumstances, however, intervened when Kevin O'Higgins was assassinated on 10 July. Emergency legislation passed in response included a requirement for Dáil candidates to swear they would take the Oath and their seats if elected, and the abolition of the referendum process for amending the Constitution. Seeing no future for Fianna Fáil outside the parliamentary system, de Valera secured unanimous consent of the elected deputies to enter the Dáil.

Although both contemporary and historiographic reactions to Fianna Fáil's *volte face* were mixed, the import of the event is undeniable. As The Earl of Longford and Thomas P. O'Neill argue in their authorized biography, 'De Valera's performance, however one interprets and assesses it, made it certain that parliamentary democracy would in fact prevail.'[7] The signing of the Oath opened the door to the political stability that would, finally, ensure a lasting independent Irish state, aided by the particular circumstances of de Valera's performance.

Politics as performance

Performative qualities in definitive events of modern Irish social history have often been acknowledged. Contemporary political performances like Bertie Ahern's interviews and public addresses are merely the latest of Fianna Fáil's dramatic appeals to the public. Even before the founding of the party, de Valera himself was described as a play-actor in a derogatory sense by General Sir Nevil Macready, British politician and son of the great actor William Charles Macready. Referring to a 1921 meeting, Macready calls de Valera 'one who would always play to the gallery and lose himself in a maze of insignificant detail.'[8] While de Valera's acting is, for Macready, cause for criticism, this description does highlight a significant issue in considering de Valera and his impact. Specifically, Macready captures the extent to which de Valera, as a historical agent, consciously and carefully attempted to manipulate the terms of his performances. De Valera's Oath was performed not only in the moment that his pen crossed the paper, but also in the planning, in the descriptions he subsequently issued, and in the rehashing of the event in the media and the books of history.

Performance theory can be useful in the analysis of politics in a variety of ways, including approaches like Clifford Geertz's 'symbolic action,' which focus on the interpretation of 'acted saying – a corona-tion, a sermon, a riot, an execution.'[9] Also applicable are the 'social drama' theories of Victor Turner, which describe a pattern through which crises of 'morality, law, custom, or etiquette, in some public arena' precipitate societal breaches.[10] Rituals may then be employed as 'adjustive mechanisms'[11] in order to reintegrate the community. History suggests that, in Turner's terms, the taking of the Oath served as a 'ritual process of redress'[12] which helped to heal a deep division in Irish politics and society, despite de Valera's attempts to minimize the power of the ritual at the time.

I swear; I perform

The theories of philosopher J. L. Austin also inform analysis of these events, because they offer ways to understand how symbols and rituals function together through the power of words. Austin's *How to Do Things with Words* (the published version of his 1955 lecture series) defines a 'performative' as an utterance that in itself *does* something, in contrast to the merely descriptive 'constative' utterance. Austin's exam-ples of common performatives include phrases such as 'I do' (as in a wedding), 'I name' (as in a christening), 'I bet,' and, crucially to the present discussion, 'I promise' and 'I swear.'[13]

Austin's theory goes to the heart of de Valera's concerns about taking the Oath: simply put, the politician feared that signing the paper would have the effects of a performative statement. Having previously regarded the taking of the Oath as a performative promise of allegiance to Britain, he now – when forced into the Oath by pragmatic circum-stance – did everything he could to render the performative powerless. His words and actions before, during, and after the performance of the Oath-taking ritual represented an attempt to alter the circumstances of his performance sufficiently to cause the public audience to read the performative as, at best, nonexistent, or failing that, as what Austin would term 'void' and thus nonbinding.

In Austin's terms, speaking or signing one's name to the statement 'I do solemnly swear true faith and allegiance to the Constitution of the Irish Free State as by law established and that I will be faithful to H.M. King George V' would in itself be an action that established a relation between the speaker, the Constitution, and the king. By con-trast, the Fianna Fáil statement published in the newspapers on the morning of the Oath-taking, written by de Valera with only minor changes from the party, argued:

> It has … been repeatedly stated, and it is not uncommonly believed, that the required declaration is not an oath; … that, in short, it is merely an empty political formula which deputies could conscientiously sign without becoming involved, or without involving their nation, in obligations of loyalty to the English Crown … The Fianna Fáil deputies hereby give public notice in advance to the Irish people, to all whom it may concern, that they purpose to regard the declaration as an empty formality.[14]

Austin addresses arguments like this when he imagines a skeptic who suggests that the performative power of an 'I promise' statement is reliant on the performer's intentions: 'Surely the words must be spoken "seriously" so as to be taken "seriously"?'[15] Austin replies that this distinction between word and subjective intention is invalid, as 'accuracy and morality alike are on the side of the plain saying that *our word is our bond*.'[16]

Austin notes, however, that the speaking of words is usually not the only component of a performative utterance:

> Speaking generally, it is always necessary that the *circumstances* in which the words are uttered should be in some way, or ways, *appropriate*, and it is very commonly necessary that either the speaker himself or other persons should *also* perform certain *other* actions, whether 'physical' or 'mental' actions or even acts of uttering further words.[17]

The circumstances of the Oath-signing were arranged by the Saorstát Éireann government to be 'appropriate' to a certain set of meanings, that is, to pro-Treatyites' understanding of the Oath as an important signifier of allegiance to the Constitution. The Oath was a serious matter, undertaken in a manner both efficiently businesslike and solemn, with the presence of the New Testament reminding the overwhelmingly Catholic legislators of the weight of their words and actions. The circumstances were not necessarily, however, what one might expect from an imperial vow, not spoken aloud or signed in public, not invested with any particular pomp and circumstance. Owen Dudley Edwards suggests that the circumstances were thus a crucial factor in de Valera's entry into the Dáil, and by extension in the shaping of the future course of Irish politics: 'had he been forced to take the oath with full panoply ... he had apparently determined to refuse and devote himself to the revival of the Irish language.'[18] For the first Free State Dáil in 1922, the Oath had been administered in the chamber by the Speaker, but in 1923 the process was changed to a simple signature in the Clerk's chambers in order to avert Republican protest. Thus, while de Valera and his party must be credited with making a decision that greatly contributed to the stability of the modern Irish nation-state, credit is also due to the Free State officials who did not force public display upon the Fianna Fáil Oath-takers, but accepted them into governmental proceedings in the course of an otherwise normal day. This very mundane nature of circumstance, however, offered room for interpreting the oath as something less than a binding performative.

Austin contends that a performative that is not carried through to its fulfillment is not a lie; rather, it is 'unhappy' or 'infelicitous.'[19] Without solely crediting individual agency, he notes that inappropriate circumstances can cause a performative to be questionable from the moment it is first spoken. He writes:

> It is obviously necessary that to have promised I must normally:
> (A) have been heard by someone, perhaps the promisee;
> (B) have been understood by him as promising.
> If one or another of these conditions is not satisfied, doubts arise as to whether I have really promised, and it might be held that my act was only attempted or was void.[20]

Eager to have his act perceived as 'void' from the beginning, yet deeply aware that it would be heard worldwide, de Valera did his best to ensure that his audience would not understand his action as promising. Later in his lectures, Austin terms the phrase 'I swear' an 'illocutionary' act, defined as a speech-act that requires performance for some other person and carries with it certain conventional commitments or obligations.[21] Certainly, de Valera never had any intention of carrying out the commitments that would customarily be expected of a citizen taking an oath of allegiance. And once taken, de Valera's Oath was not greatly tested by obligations to Constitution, King, or Commonwealth, even while he violated the terms to which he had signed his name by attempting to legally destabilize the status of all three of those bodies *vis-à-vis* Ireland.

Additional circumstances of the Oath ceremony could have been called 'inappropriate'; among these were the ways the books and papers at the scene were used. The use of a signature rather than a spoken promise did not in itself constitute inappropriateness. Austin explicitly acknowledges the signature as an alternative to the use of the spoken 'I' in the performative utterance, and de Valera's anxiety over the Oath ritual revealed a similar sense of reading a signature as metonym for individual subject. Using papers to render his name momentarily floating in a blank space constituted de Valera's attempt to deny a relationship between the words of the Oath and the inked signature left as tangible trace of the event. In effect, he attempted to eliminate the Oath statement from the scene entirely, substituting his own script with both the Irish words he spoke and the words he and his companions published before and after the event. As W. B. Worthen points out, however, performance is not limited to textually based events.[22] Even when text does underlie performance, an excess of meaning can destabilize the meanings that agents and rituals work to convey. The fact that de Valera left the ceremony vowing to burn the Oath book one day suggests that his self-belief could not entirely overcome the weight of countering symbol and discourse.

Iteration, agency, and authority

I argue that de Valera's Oath-signing ritual is best read as the attempt of an individual subject to manipulate the discursive power of performative statements and symbolic, ritualized actions. One response to this argument must be to question how much power an individual subject has in circumstances that are always imbued with the weight of prior performances. Jacques Derrida and Judith Butler have both commented on this issue, Butler emphasizing the performative's 'citation of a prior and authoritative set of practices'[23] – with the result that, as Derrida writes, that the subject's intention 'will no longer be able to govern the entire scene and system of utterances.'[24] In the case of the Free State Oath, the swearing drew on a long history of authoritative practices, including the succession of Oaths of Allegiance that had been political issues in Ireland over hundreds of years. The presence of Catholic symbols evoked the additional authority of religious ritual. De Valera, conscious of the power of history and symbol, had to destabilize the power not only of the Free State government he had previously declared illegitimate, but also of long Irish history and cultural practice.

Thus, rather than simply stating his personal intentions, de Valera used what agency he had to engage with prior authoritative practices that could stand as alternatives to those cited by the Oath-swearing ritual. Using the Irish language to speak the words with which he sought to redefine the meaning of the signature, de Valera cited history and authority different from those conveyed by English. Other authoritative practices were suggested by symbolic books. Homi Bhabha highlights the power of 'the emblem of the English book ... as an insignia of colonial authority' with particular regard to the forced adoption of the English language and authoritarian systems.[25] While Bhabha's books and de Valera's are not equivalent, it is reasonable to suggest that the paper-covered book of the Oath represented the embodiment of English imperialism to the nativist de Valera. The Bible, by contrast, represented an authority system de Valera generally chose to acknowledge. The removal of the Testament to the other side of the room suggests that, despite all his maneuverings, de Valera feared that his action was still in some violation of a higher authority whose symbol might be tainted by close proximity to – or witnessing of – the scene.

In negotiating the Oath, de Valera claimed for himself the authority of Irish identity, explicitly disidentifying with Britain, while attempting to divorce the situation from any relevance to religion. He also employed his own established public persona, what R. F. Foster calls his 'aura of austere and incorruptible authority.'[26] His past as a teacher, his reputation for stern logic, his dramatic Republican history, his role as husband and father, and his function as a visible symbol of whiteness, maleness, and Catholicity all made reference to normative systems of belief that were acceptable to the nation.

Uptake and reaction

The aftermath of Fianna Fáil's decision to take the Oath suggests that de Valera's manipulation of circumstance was quite successful with its audiences. Nonetheless, Fianna Fáil did face some mockery. The pro-Treaty *Irish Times* wrote on 12 August 1927 that the party's reasoning was 'palpably absurd,' and sure to win 'contempt.'[27] The skeptics of London's *The Times* opined that 'few will be deceived by such a palpable piece of face-saving'[28] and, in an editorial, questioned 'the borders of perjury.'[29] In a similar vein, the *New York Times* wondered why, if the Republicans saw the Oath as an 'empty formality,' they expressed 'long and fervid horror about swallowing it?'[30] Certain historians have likewise raised eyebrows at Fianna Fáil's sudden turn from the moral high road to political pragmatism. J. J. Lee describes 'the Soldiers of Destiny shuffl[ing] into Dáil Éireann,'[31] while R. F. Foster dryly notes that the solution of the 'empty formula' had been 'forecast five years before, appositely enough by the Professor of Metaphysics of University College, Dublin.'[32]

Such criticism did not cause substantial damage to Fianna Fáil's fortunes. John Regan suggests that 'what appeared to be a ridiculously contrived and worthless symbolic gesture' rightly 'should have divided the party and alienated much of its grass roots.'[33] And yet, the party was not divided; its voters were not alienated. *The Times* described the Irish public as 'bewildered' by this 'confusing and unexpected' series of events, but bewilderment did not lead to substantial rejection.[34] True, Fianna Fáil met with unexpected failure in its immediate attempt to take power through a coalition with Labour, and Cumann na nGaedheal maintained its plurality in the next general election, held in September. But Fianna Fáil's showing was stronger than ever, winning 57 seats.

The public was not deceived into accepting Fianna Fáil's 'empty formula' rationalization out of whole cloth, as subsequent sarcastic comments, and indeed support for the eventual removal of the Oath attested (for if it were a mere empty formula, why was removal necessary?). But neither was the public deceived as to de Valera's motives, for most observers, even many republicans, could accept the argument that the opposition's participation in the political system was a necessity. Pragmatism had by this point a decided appeal to a populace that had had its fill of real-life tragedy.

The performance of the Oath continued to reverberate in de Valera's political career. He insisted to the Dáil in 1932, during a debate over removing the Oath from the constitution, 'I have never taken an oath – never. No man who knows what an oath is will say I have.'[35] Having escaped the explicit performative 'I swear,' de Valera continued to engage with performative discourse in avowing 'I have never taken an oath' an example of the kind of statements Eve Kosofsky Sedgwick calls 'periperformatives,' utterances that 'are *about* performatives and ... cluster *around* performatives.'[36] Performative and periperformative issues came to the fore again when de Valera visited Dublin's German Embassy in order to sign a book of condolence upon the death of Adolf Hitler in 1945. Negative reaction soon found the Taoiseach insisting that his signature must not be interpreted as metonymically representing any commitment from the Irish state to the German state. At the same time, the possibility that he was in fact pursuing a symbolic reaffirmation of the independence of the Irish nation suggests that he had once again carefully manipulated the circumstances of a performative event in order to achieve specific political ends.

De Valera's performances echo in the contemporary acts of his political descendants in Fianna Fáil. For example, Taoiseach Bertie Ahern, pressed by the Mahon Tribunal on 20 September 2007 to clarify comments he had previously made under oath about his financial dealings, was admonished for making 'statements ... offered for some alternative purpose' beyond answering the questions asked.[37] The same day, when asked what was in his mind on an occasion when he shifted money between accounts, Ahern replied: 'listen, Mr O'Neill, with the greatest of respect, we are here the two of us to a large gallery [*sic*], talking about contemplation ... It didn't matter what I contemplated.'[38] Ahern's protestations that his thoughts and motives should *not* be relevant to an audience's interpretations of his actions stand in contrast to de Valera's argument. At the same time, however, Ahern's 'statements' and his reinterpretations of his comments under oath point to a deep and ongoing implication with performativity, as do the media appeals to the public that the *Irish Independent* called 'dum-downed [*sic*] showbiz politics.'[39] Our understanding of Ahern's performances, like those of de Valera, might benefit from a consideration of their complex negotiations with explicit performative gestures and less obvious periperformative utterances, as parts of the strategies with which political agents attempt to manage the impact of their words and actions.

Notes

1   Eamon de Valera, Statement, *Dáil Éireann Debates*, Vol. 41, 29 April 1932, http://historical-debates.oireachtas.ie/D/0041/D.0041.193204290005.html (accessed 2 May 2008), sect. 1102.

2   Statement by Frank Aiken and James Ryan, 23 September 1927, quoted in the Earl of Longford (Frank Pakenham) and Thomas P. O'Neill, *Eamon de Valera* (London: Hutchinson, 1970), 256. This authorized biography quotes de Valera's statement to the Clerk as follows: 'I want you to understand that I am not taking any oath nor giving any promise of faithfulness to the King of England or to any power outside the people of Ireland. I am putting my name here merely as a formality ... no other meaning is to be attached to what I am doing' (256). Patrick Murray, in his article 'Obsessive Historian: Eamon de Valera and the Policing of His Reputation,' calls the Longford and O'Neill book 'authoritative,' but also notes that 'the authors are essentially vehicles for de Valera's transmission of his view of his history' (*Proceedings of the Royal Irish Academy* 101C [2001]: 37–65, 63). I am conscious not only of the biases of these biographers, but even more so, of de Valera's own purposes in controlling his record. Thus, while I rely, as have many historians, on de Valera's own translations and descriptions of the Oath-taking ritual (the most widely disseminated accounts of the events), I am less concerned with their historiographic accuracy than with their function as types of performance in themselves.

3 Anglo-Irish Treaty, 6 December 1921, Documents on Irish Foreign Policy Series, http://www.nationalarchives.ie/topics/anglo_irish/dfaexhib2.html (accessed 10 June 2008).

4 R. F. Foster, *Modern Ireland 1600–1972* (New York: Penguin, 1988), 506.

5 Approximately 800 Free State soldiers were killed; anti-Treaty losses, although undocumented, were probably considerably greater. See Michael Hopkinson, *Green Against Green: The Irish Civil War* (Dublin: Gill & Macmillan, 1988), 272–3.

6 Tim Pat Coogan, *Eamon de Valera: The Man Who Was Ireland* (New York: HarperCollins, 1995), 399.

7 Longford and O'Neill, 1970, 258.

8 Nevil Macready, *Annals of an Active Life*, Vol. II (London: Hutchinson, 1924), 574.

9 Clifford Geertz, 'Blurred Genres: The Refiguration of Social Thought,' *American Scholar* 49 (1980): 165–79, 173.

10 Victor Turner, 'Social Dramas and Stories about Them,' *Critical Inquiry* 7 (1) (1980): 141–68, 149.

11 *Ibid.*, 158.

12 *Ibid.*, 158.

13 J. L. Austin, *How to Do Things with Words*, 2nd ed. (Oxford: Oxford University Press, 1975), 1–11.

14 Eamon de Valera and Maurice Moynihan, *Speeches and Statements by Eamon de Valera, 1917–73* (Dublin: Gill & Macmillan, 1980), 150.

15 Austin, 1975, 8.

16 *Ibid.*, 10 (emphasis in original).

17 *Ibid.*, 9 (emphasis in original).

18 Owen Dudley Edwards, *Eamon de Valera* (Cardiff: GPC Books, 1987), 114.

19 Austin, 1975, 22.

20 *Ibid.* (emphasis in original).

21 More particularly, 'I swear' functions in illocutionary fashion as a 'commissive,' a statement that 'commit[s] the speaker to a certain course of action' (157).

22 W. B. Worthen, 'Drama, Performativity, and Performance,' *PMLA* 113 (1998): 1093–107.

23 Judith Butler, 'Burning Acts: Injurious Speech,' in *Performativity and Performance*, eds. Andrew Parker and Eve K. Sedgwick (New York: Routledge, 1995), 196–227, 205.

24 Jacques Derrida, 'Signature Event Context,' in *Margins of Philosophy*, trans. Alan Bass (Chicago: University of Chicago Press, 1982), 307–30, 326.

25 Homi Bhabha, 'Signs Taken for Wonders: Questions of Ambivalence and Authority Under a Tree Outside Delhi, May 1817,' in *The Location of Culture* (London: Routledge, 1994), 102–22, 102.

26 Foster, 1988, 526.

27 *Irish Times,* 12 August 1927, 6.

28 *The Times,* 12 August 1927, 10.

29 *Ibid.*, 11.

30 *New York Times*, 12 August 1927, 16.

31 J. J. Lee, *Ireland 1912–1985: Politics and Society* (Cambridge: Cambridge University Press, 1989), 155.

32 Foster, 1988, 526.
33 John Regan, *The Irish Counter-Revolution 1921–1936* (New York: St Martin's Press, 1999), 274.
34 *The Times,* 12 August 1927, 10.
35 Eamon de Valera, Statement, sect. 1100.
36 Eve Kosofsky Sedgwick, *Touching Feeling: Affect, Performativity, Performance* (Durham, NC: Duke University Press, 2003), 68 (emphasis in original).
37 Transcript, 20 September 2007. Tribunal of Inquiry into Certain Planning Matters and Payments, http://www.planningtribunal.ie/images/SITECONTENT_738.pdf, (accessed 2 May 2008), 120.
38 *Ibid.,* 143.
39 'Politics Is All Showbiz, So Bertie Takes to Airwaves Before Dail,' *Irish Independent*, 27 September 2006, http://www.independent.ie/national-news/politics-is-all-showbiz-so-bertie-takes-to-airwaves-before-dail-80358.html (accessed 2 May 2008).

11
Between the Living and the Dead: Performative 'in-betweens' in the Works of Alastair MacLennan

Carmen Szabó

In his article 'Between Memory and History: *Les Lieux de Mémoire*,' French historian Pierre Nora discusses the fundamental change in the relationship between history and memory, the living and the dead, that took place during the Enlightenment. Nora observes that the basis for this profound alteration in the social and material relations with the dead and the increasingly pronounced distinction between intimate memories and public histories is the substitution of what he calls 'places of memory' (*lieux de mémoire*), 'the artificial sites of the modern production of national and ethnic memories,' for 'environments of memory' (*milieux de mémoire*), 'the behavioural retentions of unscripted tradition, in which the dead, taking the form of ghosts and ancestral spirits, once participated more actively.'[1] There is a stringent need to recapture the spaces of memory through (re)performing them, in an attempt to channel the 'ghosts and ancestral spirits' through effigies, in a séance that could make sense of our fragmented, troubled present.

Nora's use of the word 'effigy' follows Joseph Roach's discussion of the term, not as a noun that focuses on 'a crudely fabricated image' of a person, but as a verb, an action that means 'to evoke an absence, to body something forth, especially something from a distant past.'[2] The recapturing of memory moves away from the stiffness of the image and becomes an action, an actuation – it becomes performance. These spectacles of memory and death have been described by Nora as 'moments of history torn away from the movement of history, then returned; no longer quite life, not yet death, like shells on the shore when the sea of living memory has receded.'[3] These sets of actions open up an almost physical connection between past and present, helping to re-imagine communities and giving them the potential comfort of belonging to a global community.

This chapter considers two actuations by Northern Irish performance artist Alastair MacLennan as effigies against the theoretical background created in the space between places and environments of memory. The terms in which I understand the relationship between space, art, and memory underscore my reading of MacLennan's actuations. Site-specificity, performance, spatiality, found objects, and the retrieval of Northern Irish or European memory all come into play when discussing MacLennan's *Body of Earth* (1996) and *Coming to Meet* (1996). MacLennan's artistic achievement must also be contextualized within the framework of Northern Irish site-specific performance and the identity discourse that marked the arrival of new theoretical mindsets determined by postcolonialism.

As MacLennan's actuations are closely related to the fragmented spaces of the Northern Irish urban landscape, it is important to identify a theoretical scaffolding that encourages the awareness of our perpetual performance of place. In his book *The Practice of Everyday Life*, Michel de Certeau identifies the spatial complexity of the sign within the framework of the modern urban landscape. The walker is able to produce meaning through a continuous interpretation of transitory spaces which impact on the predetermined horizon of expectations. The city becomes part of a simulation structure because it is always in the absence of the original that representation can take place.[4] Or, as Rosalind Krauss has demonstrated, the meaning of originality is dependent on the copy, the forgery, the counterfeit.[5] However, within the boundaries of the modern city, Jean Baudrillard's[6] simulation pattern becomes a determining feature: mapping exists before the spatial construct and the matrix of simulation defines the interpretation of signs, thus vitally influencing the resulting meaning. In such circumstances, to represent the place is to construct a removal from it, to bracket it off from the intricate maze of the cityscape.

Art is traditionally associated with the gallery, an institutional and thus political space that defines the value of the aesthetic object and validates its position within the matrix of the artistic exhibition. The object becomes art when placed within the boundaries of the gallery, a space marked by the paradox of conferring aesthetic meaning within a theoretically nonpolitical space constructed on political foundations. Opposed to the artistic haven of the gallery and the museum, the city encapsulates the complexity of anticipation and memory, the city as palimpsest, as Walter Benjamin would characterize it,[7] as paper that has been written upon twice, the original having been erased. In comparison with the apparently 'pure' space of the gallery, the city appears as a real, cultural-semiotic space, overdetermined by multiple readings but at the same time as a space that is so overtly political that it almost denies artistic readings. Site-specific art attempts to use this theoretical differentiation by analyzing the process of 'writing over' the city and the way in which the space resists being written upon. The process of inscribing and decoding the multilayered structures of the modern city transforms the cityscape into an artscape of meaning.

When discussing site-specific art, Nick Kaye reminds the reader that site-specificity is linked to the incursion of 'surrounding' space or 'real' space into the viewer's experience of the artwork. The spectator is displaced from the comfortable environment of the gallery into the familiar but nevertheless disturbing space of the city, which is rendered 'strange' by the artwork. This strangeness of art outside the boundaries of the gallery changes the view of the city from a physical space of everyday life into a mental space of aesthetic perception.[8]

The aesthetic object moves out of the gallery and into the political space in an attempt to destabilize the latter, creating a closer link between the space, the object, and the beholder. Thus, within the framework of the political space, a non-place emerges. The idea of non-place is derived from a negative connotation of the place, some sort of negative quality of the place, which could be translated as an absence from itself caused by naming and by the political and historical determinations of the place. According to anthropologist Marc Augé, 'non-place and place are like palimpsests on which the scrambled game of identity and relations is ceaselessly rewritten.'[9] The gallery reiterates the notion of non-place in the non-sites exposed within its walls. The gallery as an initial ideal space of art becomes political by incorporating images and objects of external sites, bracketing them off from their real space and repositioning them within the gallery. Through this reversed process of defamiliarization, the everyday object or its photographic representation becomes part of the aesthetic performance.

Fredric Jameson argues that postmodern art and architecture are symptomatic of the dilemma in which the resolution of the individual's practice into a 'known' spatial, social, or ideological totality has come under question.[10] This postmodern condition of the artistic space is also reflected in notions of identity that move from the binary opposition self-other, through hyphenated identities, towards a hybrid identity which refuses homogeneity and thus encourages multiplicity and fragmentation. The performance itself becomes a hybrid of the place and the public. Within this context, the non-site becomes an abstract mapping of absent spaces within the space of the gallery and there is a continuous confrontation between the two, given the attempt of the gallery to limit the site – to engulf and assimilate it, thus erasing it. The importance of the non-site becomes vital within the discourse of contemporary art by trying to point to the site, tracing boundaries within the space of the gallery and enhancing the aesthetic reception of the site.

In an article on the work of the American photographer David Wojnarowicz, Robert Sember discusses a collection of photographs taken in the Chaco Canyon in the New Mexico desert. A national park, the Chaco Canyon contains hundreds of partially excavated ruins attributed to the Anasazi people, the ancestors of Puebloan Native Americans living in the south-west of the US today. Determined by a past for which we have no clear historical narrative, the space of the desert is reinterpreted and reappropriated by the photographer. Using the photographic paradox of presence and absence, past and future, Wojnarowicz engages in excavating the moment, reading himself into the texture of the ruins, which are both 'disturbingly present and uncomfortably silent.'[11] MacLennan's *Body of Earth* (1996) and *Coming to Meet* (1996) both attempt, like Wojnarowicz's work, to capture the tensions between myth and fact; between different versions of histories; between present, past, and future – tensions that constantly trouble our epistemologies.

The hybridities that determined the theoretical landscape of the 1980s and 1990s inform MacLennan's own biography: born in Scotland, Alastair MacLennan has been living and working in Belfast since 1975. In a 1987 interview with Declan McGonagle for *Performance Magazine*, he observed his existence in Belfast as a continuation of his position as an outsider during his childhood in Scotland:

> My parents are from North West Scotland (with Irish connections). I was brought up in the South. Cultural differences were like chalk and cheese. Growing up, I felt an 'outsider' looking in, and an 'insider' looking out.' There were double-take overlays. These I now use.[12]

Both his geographical existence 'on the edge of Europe' and his position as an outsider within Northern Ireland determined the artistic credo of his work, initiating an interesting negotiation between the pronounced locality and isolation of Northern Ireland during the years of the Troubles and a global, multicultural artistic space he previously experienced both as a student at the School of the Art Institute of Chicago and as an artist exhibited throughout Europe.

The cultural atmosphere of Northern Ireland in the 1980s was characterized by a flurry of postcolonial readings, which attempted to renegotiate the binary oppositions of self/other and center/margin, by pushing identity discourse toward a trendier and at least theoretically viable hybridity and multiplicity. The renegotiation of the colonial binary opposition of center/margin re-imagined and re-inscribed the previously marginalized Northern Irish urban landscape as 'center' in a space where previous definitions of centrality were crumbling, diluted in a sea of centers that announced the coming of postmodernist fragmentation. As MacLennan explained to McGonagle:

> Concepts which formulated centres are now obsolete. New wave communications and information media now contribute to the disintegrating stranglehold of centres built by, and for, redundant technologies and attitudes. 'Centres' are becoming peripheries, peripheries... 'centres.'[13]

Within a political structure that, in reality, was still firmly based on binary oppositions, MacLennan's art attempted to reach out not only to the local communities, but also to the larger structures of European art. As it happened with other artistic ventures in that period in Northern Ireland (including the Field Day Theatre Company, Charabanc Theatre Company, as well as artists such as Willie Doherty, Victor Sloan, or Paul Seawright), there was a need to expand the spatial and political limitations of Northern Ireland and to integrate the artistic voices of the province within an emerging, modern European artistic identity. If, from a theatrical point of view, the underlying agenda was that of translation and adaptation of European classics to a Northern Irish voice, witnessing an intended inclusion of Northern Ireland in the 'cradle' of Western civilization, artists like Doherty (or MacLennan for that matter) tried to find parallels with the Northern Irish situation within the communal history and memory of Europe. For Alastair MacLennan art does not only open up the space of memory, it also closes the gaps between nations and identities. His growing concern about the existing gulf between aesthetics and ethics created a view of art as 'skill in action, where skill is the resolution of conflict.'[14]

In his book *The Government of the Tongue*,[15] Northern Ireland's Nobel prize-winning poet Seamus Heaney stated that poems cannot stop tanks in their tracks or bombs from exploding; however, what artistic works can and should do is to get involved in the political process, to question and challenge the political realities, to make people aware.[16] The idea of awareness becomes very important in MacLennan's works. His actuations and installations transform the familiar spaces of the city into places of memory made strange through 'naming.' This process induces the creation of what Marc Augé describes as 'non-sites.'

The social and political involvement that MacLennan's works encourage follows the ideas put in artistic practice by artist Joseph Beuys, who explored the issue of artistic 'action' from the point of view of artistic responsibility. Through his 'social sculptures,'[17] Beuys refused to give in to the attempts of the masses to perpetuate themselves with images of beauty, images that can only remind one of the familiar and fail to initiate any thought but that of pleasure in the comfortable and accepted. This becomes the creed of the postmodern artist as underlined by Jean-François Lyotard:

> Those who refuse to reexamine the rules of art pursue successful careers in mass conformism by communicating, by means of the 'correct rules,' the endemic desire for reality with objects and situations capable of gratifying it.[18]

Both the creation of non-sites and that of Beuysian social sculptures involve, within the creation of artistic meaning, the idea of alienation. In his response to MacLennan's actuation *Still Tills*, featured in the National Review of Live Art in 1990 at Glasgow's Third Eye Centre, Tim Etchells (founder of theatre/performance company Forced Entertainment and member of the NRLA panel) commented: 'Some things are hard to quantify. Of course it is not the smell of that performance by Alastair MacLennan that I have in my head. The thing I carry with me still is its marvelous disquiet. Its disturbance of my ordinary. Its made-me-think-again-ness. Its pit of questions. Its everyday made strange.'[19]

MacLennan also destabilizes the institution of the gallery and makes spectators aware of their environment by the challenges directed against their horizon of expectations. Following in Marcel Duchamp's footsteps, MacLennan uses found objects with an overtly political purpose. He questions and challenges the presumptions about art's public and private function. He carefully arranges found objects as triggers of memory, as spaces of remembrance. The simplicity of a name on a piece of paper or announced from a loudspeaker within a historically charged environment opens up endless possibilities of representation. The names of the dead, uttered or written, create force-fields that invoke the spirits of history and trigger the mechanisms of memory.

Body of Earth was an actuation/installation specifically made for the Project Arts Centre in Dublin in 1996. It commemorated the lives of those lost through political violence during the Northern Irish

Figure 4 *Body of Earth*, Project Arts Centre, Dublin, 1996. Courtesy Alastair MacLennan.

Troubles of 1969–96. Issues of loss, conflict, and absence were raised through means of visual and audio triggers based on 'naming the dead.'

The title *Body of Earth* evokes the memory of the Jewish myth of the Golem, the body of earth brought to life through naming. It becomes an environment of memory where the painful absence of the named dead is balanced by the ghostly images of the viewers reflected in the mirror plating fixed along the four walls of the gallery, brought to life through the naming of the long list of the victims of the Troubles. The presence of absence is displayed in the specially constructed chest-high table heaped with earth and following the full length of one diagonal in the gallery space. The telluric force of the earth brought into the gallery is set against the continuous audio reminder of the names of the dead. The viewers walking through the space become implicated in the work and complete the artistic representation by constituting the link between image and sound. The space of memory is created through the viewers not as an escape, not as transportation to a beyond, but as a heightened awareness of the here and now. The gauze that delimitates the space of the performance acts both as wall, as barrier and also, through its transparency, encourages the spectators to engage in a quest for memory.

Luke Clancy comments in his review of the installation in the *Irish Times*:

> Visitors enter this room, with its low gauze false ceiling, through a small parting in the cloth, and they are immediately faced with a long white cloth-covered bench, as evocative of an operating table as an altar. Instead of an etherised patient, or the fixings of transubstantiation, the bench supports a mound of rubbled earth, formed into a kind of elongated pyramid. On either side of this main structure two smaller, similar tables bear further pyramids of sifted earth and ashy soil. Each of these smaller structures is penetrated by a bowed wooden ladder and is decked in slender black and white ribbons.[20]

In even tones, a male and a female recite, in alphabetical order, a list of names. This list initiates the process of remembering which represents the only possibility of getting to terms, if not escaping the gruesome reality of the Troubles.

The living process of creating artistic meaning becomes central to MacLennan's actuations. The found objects that he introduces in the space of the gallery ('some institutional-looking glass, a triangle of gleaming chrome dishes ready to collect specimen tissue or shrapnel, a zimmer frame for those who can stumble away, as well as various other scraps and a fan of black in-soles'[21]) become fundamental not as props but as 'activated paintings,' as environments of memory that follow the artist's credo of 'making art as a living process without the necessity of physical residue for sale.'[22] The long list of names that rolls from the speakers is an audio reminder of the close relationship between past, present, and future. Resembling the elusive ruins of David Wojnarowicz's photomontages, the names bring forth the remains of memory only to return to their earthly tombs after each naming. However, this is the essence of MacLennan's art: the objects and the sounds are channeled through the conscience of the viewers in order to create the process of memory which initiates action and involvement from the spectators. An important and unusual characteristic of *Body of Earth* is the absence of the artist. MacLennan's choice of removing the body of the artist from the environment creates an open possibility for the viewers to experience the 'memory machine' without the comfortable mediation of the artistic presence. The viewers have to negotiate their own movements within the environment, and their own unmediated choices determine their artistic experience.

The publication of *Coming to Meet (an artist's book)*[23] coincided with the exhibition *Body of Earth* at the Project Arts Centre. *Coming to Meet* enhances and complements *Body of Earth* by extending the list of the victims of history to Europe. The atrocities of the Holocaust are reflected, simply, in a photographic meditation upon the names of Jewish women found on labels in a deconsecrated synagogue in Prague. The names of the dead are now written, not spoken, creating a visual image that reminds the viewer of the shared histories of Europe and the ethics of the use of power between individuals, regardless of geographical space.

The space from where the labels were retrieved is thus described by MacLennan in the book:

> During the Nazi occupation, the synagogue Na Palmovce, Prague 8, Liben, was closed and transformed into a storage room for the confiscated property of the Jewish community. After World War Two, the synagogue began to fall into ruin. In the depopulated Jewish ghetto it became used as a warehouse. In the 1950s, the nearby Jewish cemetery was radically reduced, and in 1960 it was completely filled over with earth, totally destroyed.[24]

From the ruins of this space of memory, the labels baring the names of Jewish women have been retrieved from an upstairs balcony.

The process of retrieval becomes an archaeological excavation of memory, closely connected to the artistic process in *Body of Earth*. In the latter, the voices uttering the names of the dead were conjuring up ghostly images from the past, re-created from the bodily presence of the viewers. The untouched mound of earth filling the space of the gallery appeared as a space of remembrance from which immaterial names would spring up through utterance. On the contrary, the photographic collection included in *Coming to Meet* is characterized by silence. The names have been taken from the ground and revealed in the open palm of the artist. The 24 images represent, against a blurred background of grey earth, the artist's palm, open and empty at first; then holding a large number of labels, some with names written in black ink. Among the beautiful calligraphies appear names like Ester, Rachel, Sarah, Ruth, and Jahvel, creating a strong link between an ancient, biblical spirituality and the painful reality of loss and history. While on some of the labels the writing is very clear, others are empty or washed and blurry, enhancing the idea of memory as incomplete retrieval from the darkness of history.

What we see are, as in Wojnarowicz's photographs mimicking the ruins of the Anasazi people in the Chaco Canyon, traces, remains, ruins that cannot be comprehended as a totality but only as fragments of pre-existing lives, theirs and ours, many of them impossible to retrieve. The idea of trace that can be related to MacLennan's photographs in *Coming to Meet*, as semiotic and political trigger of memory, is closely related to the idea of trace as appears in cultural semiotics. The meaning of the spoken, written, or visual sign can be read in the very texture of the representational gesture, and yet every expression always appears as a *trace*. Meaning is slippery and is based on the absence of something that has to be evoked. The notion of trace becomes a decisive tool in establishing the play of meanings within the process of artistic communication. The trace provides the freedom of interpretation, of decoding the message of the artistic phenomenon because it includes in the ideology of the sign a liminal space, a 'free' zone where the audience and the participants in the production are allowed to apply their own points of view to the aesthetic object.

However, there is a double determination of this space. On the one hand, it can be considered as a zone of free interpretation, where the meaning is created and re-created constantly, thus allowing the basic elements of culture to be renewed and re-interpreted. On the other hand, this freedom can become dangerous and it can be infested by manipulated meanings, hidden in the free zone, and thought by the receivers to be genuine. These booby-trap-like meanings represent the main tool for a successful ideological propaganda. Nevertheless, the importance of the trace is overwhelming in any cultural semiotic analysis given the freedom it provides to the communication process. Umberto Eco relates the idea of the trace to the politicization of the representational, artistic space. In his book *A Theory of Semiotics*,[25] Eco relates the production of signs and the subjects producing them to the cultural codes of a given society, codes already existing or in the process of creation. Thus, his semiotic theory links the concepts of society and culture by using the terms footprint and cart-trails, resembling the term trace discussed above. For Eco, the study of semiotics resembles exploring a forest where cart-trails or footsteps modify the explored landscape, so that the description of the explorer must also take into consideration 'the ecological variations that he has produced.'[26]

In the photographs collected in *Coming to Meet*, the explored landscape is modified by the presence of the artist's body, even though fragmented as only the artist's hand appears in close-up. The combination between the remains, the found objects, and the body of the artist through holding the labels in his hand increase the interpretative value of the trace. The body, even though photographed, still conveys a present-ness, a reality that is transmitted to the viewers. The photographs become environments of memory, activated installations.

Works like *Body of Earth* (1996) and *Coming to Meet* (1996) remind us of Tadeusz Kantor's 'Theatre of Death,' based on the reconstruction of memory composed of discrete, mutually unconnected 'photographic plates.'[27] By staging the space of memory, Kantor's 'Theatre of Death' staged regions of memory inhabited by the dead and the mechanisms of memory replaced the games of fiction, very much like Pierre Nora's 'environments of memory.' MacLennan translates the principle of Kantor's theatre into his actuations, bracketing off snapshots of memory and creating through them an environment that challenges both our individual and collective responsibilities. According to his own confession, MacLennan creates performances or installations for particular locations, 'allowing the nature of the locality itself to "inform" the work.'

Alastair MacLennan's actuation works encourage and trigger a new level of involvement from the spectators through a continuous 'attack' on the senses. He rewrites the institutional spaces of the gallery but also those of Belfast (in *Naming the Dead*, for example, in 1998) a city that, like Walter Benjamin's Berlin, begins to learn how to interpret its painful history within the framework of the European community. MacLennan's art initiated and continues to sustain a movement in Northern Irish culture towards hybridity, multiplicity, and a post-humanism.

Notes

1 Pierre Nora, 'Between Memory and History: *Les Lieux de Mémoire*,' *Representations* 26 (Spring 1989): 7–25.
2 Joseph Roach, *Cities of the Dead: Circum-Atlantic Performance* (New York: Columbia University Press, 1996), 36.
3 Nora, 1989, 12.
4 Michel de Certeau, *The Practice of Everyday Life* (Berkeley: University of California Press, 2002 [1984]), 120.
5 Rosalind Krauss, *The Originality of the Avant Garde and Other Modernist Myths* (Cambridge, MA: MIT Press, 1985).
6 Jean Baudrillard, *Simulations* (New York: Semiotext[e], 1984).
7 Walter Benjamin, *The Arcades Project* (Cambridge, MA: Harvard University Press, 2002).
8 Nick Kaye, *Site-Specific Art: Performance, Place and Documentation* (London: Routledge, 2000), 65–6.
9 Marc Augé, *Non-Places: Introduction to an Anthropology of Supermodernity* (London: Verso, 1995), 72.

10 Fredric Jameson, *Postmodernism or the Cultural Logic of Late Capitalism* (London: Verso, 1991).

11 Robert Sember, 'Seeing Death: The Photography of David Wojnarowicz,' in *The Ends of Performance*, eds. Peggy Phelan and Jill Lane (New York: New York University Press, 1998), 31–51, 40.

12 Alastair MacLennan, quoted in 'I See Danger,' interview by Declan McGonagle, *Performance Magazine* 47 (1987), http://vads.ahds.ac.uk/collections/maclennan/interviewperformance.htm (accessed 24 April 2008).

13 *Ibid.*

14 *Ibid.*

15 Seamus Heaney, *The Government of the Tongue: The 1986 T. S. Eliot Memorial Lectures and Other Critical Writings* (London: Faber and Faber, 1989).

16 *Ibid.*, 64.

17 For a theoretical analysis of 'social sculpture,' see Volker Harlan, ed., *What is Art? Conversation with Joseph Beuys* (London: Clairview, 2004). Beuys's 'social sculptures' include *The End of the Twentieth Century* (1983–5, Tate Modern, London); *7000 Oaks* (1982, Kassel, Germany); and *Palazzo Regale* (1985, Museo e Gallerie Nazionali di Campodimonte, Naples, Italy).

18 Jean-François Lyotard, 'Answering the Question: What Is Postmodernism?' in *The Postmodern Condition: A Report on Knowledge* (Minneapolis: University of Minnesota Press, 1984), 71–84, 75.

19 Tim Etchells, 'Comments on the National Review of Live Art,' *Performance Magazine* 63 (March 1991), 16–17, 16.

20 Luke Clancy, 'Alastair MacLennan at Project Arts Centre,' *Irish Times*, 4 January 1997, http://www.ireland.com/newspaper/ireland/1997/0104/97010400112. html (accessed 24 April 2008).

21 *Ibid.*

22 *Ibid.*

23 Hilary Robinson, ed., *Coming to Meet (An Artist's Book)* (Dublin: Project Press, 1996).

24 Alastair MacLennan quoted in Hilary Robinson, 'Introduction,' in *Coming to Meet (An Artist's Book)* (Dublin: Project Press, 1996), 2–4, 3.

25 Umberto Eco, *A Theory of Semiotics* (Bloomington: Indiana University Press, 1976).

26 *Ibid.*, 34.

27 Tadeusz Kantor, *A Journey through Other Spaces, Essays and Manifestos, 1944–1990* (Berkeley: University of California Press, 1993), 108.

12

Jus Soli/Jus Sanguinis: The Biopolitics of Performing Irishness

Matthew Causey

Introduction

Several recent and unsettling performances of Irishness demonstrate the violence, aesthetic re-interpretations, and laws being promoted to define, restrict, and control Irish identity. In this chapter I consider three disparate events: 1) the Unionist organization Love Ulster march and subsequent 'Republican' protests and riots that took place in Dublin in 2006; 2) the centenary in 2006 of Samuel Beckett's birth and the manner in which scholars and the Irish government, through its Department of Arts, Sports and Tourism, attempted to reaffirm or reclaim the author for Ireland as Irish; and 3) the 2004 amending of the Irish constitution by voter referendum to restrict citizenship to children of non-nationals born in the Republic unless they have a least one parent who has been lawfully resident in the state for three of the last four years. Each of these events suggests an uneasy relationship of elements of contemporary Ireland to new models of Irish identity and represents unique strategies for control. The struggle exists at the level of personal and cultural identity, but spreads out to economic concerns of cultural tourism, which markets an authentic branding of Irishness. The most illustrative and perhaps disquieting of my examples is the 27th constitutional amendment and its criteria for Irish citizenship, which was approved by 79.2 percent of the voters in a turnout of 59.9 percent of the electorate. The amended constitutional require-ment for Irish citizenship represents a switch from a territorial politics of geography (of place) to a biopolitics (of life). In legal terminology it is a transition from *jus soli* (right of the soil) to *jus sanguinis* (right of blood). In effect, what these events and legislation enact is a situation in which citizenship and identity cannot be performed but can only be transferred, bestowed, inherited, i.e., controlled.

I will apply two cultural/philosophical models to analyze the problem. First, I will draw on Giorgio Agamben's notion of biopolitics to suggest how these events can be read as a conversion from a politics of performance that privilege an autonomous subject and citizenry toward the establishment of power whose regime is that of the life of the subject. Following on the later work of Michel Foucault, Agamben suggests that biopolitics constructs power not on the territorial but rather on the body, on the 'bare life,' as Agamben would put it, of the individual.[1] Agamben's biopolitics helps us understand the tendencies of cultural and legal systems to disenfranchise the performative, the autonomy of the subject, the sovereignty of the citizen, and instead insist on a prior biological imperative. Second, I will engage Alain Badiou's model of a performable subjectivity loosened from the restrictions of identity and his critiques of the fraught logic of identitarianism and minoritarianism. Badiou's clearest example of this type of subjectivity is outlined in his book on St Paul in which he discusses how the model of subjectivity within the early Church suggested that identity has no relevance to being a Christian, but rather to the event of Christ, which supersedes law and biological determinants.[2] No matter an individual's gender, race, politics, nationality, or any element of identity, with faith in the event, and a commitment to live a life in fidelity to that event, one's subjectivity is constructed. Subjectivity is a performance – not a biological predetermined reality. My argument here is that elements of contemporary Irish culture and law call on a biopolitics of identity, which are verified in the occurrence of biological certainty and are thereby more easily contained and controlled. Thus, I am suggesting that issues surrounding these performances of Irishness are biopolitical problems in which life is the locus of power, while promoting a model of subjectivity made possible by emphasizing and legalizing the performative.

Love Ulster

On 25 February 2006 riots occurred in central Dublin during a controversial Love Ulster march scheduled to run from Parnell Square at the Garden of Remembrance to Leinster House, the seat of Dáil Éireann (National Parliament of Ireland). The parade was due to march down O'Connell Street and in front of the General Post Office (GPO), a building well known for its importance in the events of the 1916 Easter Rising. Love Ulster is a Unionist organization based in Northern Ireland whose mission, as stated on the group's website, includes 'a campaign for Unionist unity' and an 'end to government concessions to Irish nationalism/republicanism.'[3] The march was organized in cooperation with Families Acting for Innocent Relatives (FAIR). FAIR was 'formed as a non-sectarian, non-political organization to work in the interests of the innocent victims of terrorism in South Armagh.'[4] The event was the first Loyalist march in the Irish republic since Partition in 1921 and such a combination of Unionist agendas marching in the capital of the Republic of Ireland was surely to meet with resentment and protest. The Love Ulster marchers were numbered at 350 and the protestors, organized by the Republican party Sinn Féin, were counted at 300.[5] The marchers carried banners and placards noting the violent deaths allegedly caused by Republican paramilitary groups. Multiple video clips of the march and the riots, news reports, and even musical tributes are currently available on YouTube.com.[6]

The march barely began before it was met at the Parnell monument at the top of O'Connell Street by protestors who set upon the marchers, gardai (police), and reporters, hurling bricks, lumps of concrete, bottles, several petrol bombs, and firecrackers. There were 41 arrests and 14 injured taken to hospital, including six gardai. The march was halted, but the disturbances continued. The violence erupted in several other locations in the city center, including O'Connell Bridge, Aston Quay, Fleet Street, and Temple Bar before the rioters dispersed. The worst of the damage occurred in the Nassau Street area where three cars were burnt out, windscreens were smashed, and businesses had their windows broken. Ironically, it was a day on which Dublin was hosting high-profile and tourist-friendly events: the Six Nations rugby tournament and the Jameson Dublin International Film Festival. The city was crowded with tourists and sightseers.

On the day of the march, Mongolian immigrant to Dublin, Khosbayar Ganbold, who called himself Michael so as not to confuse the locals, was working as a clerk at a city center convenience store on Westland Row, which runs along the east end of Trinity College and intersects with Nassau Street. During the riots a group of men entered the store, stole alcohol, and fled, pursued by Khosbayar. On the street a gang of at least ten men turned on Khosbayar, beat him to the ground, broke a bottle over his head, and used a metal chair to beat him. His workmates Robert Hu and Ze Wang came to his rescue. According to *Irish Independent* reporter Anne-Marie Walsh, 'A Mongolian man has told how two Chinese workmates saved his life when he was set upon by a gang of men during last Saturday's riots in Dublin city centre.' The report claimed that Khosbayar Ganbold thought he would die in the suspected racist attack. He stated: 'Maybe it was a racist attack, who knows. I haven't told my family at home – I'm not sure what to do about that.'[7] I knew Khosbayar and I spoke with him about the event. There was no indication that the attack was racially motivated and, in fairness, it may be that the gang who attacked him were local thugs and opportunists, more intent on stealing alcohol than attacking immigrants. Nonetheless, a gang of young Irish men attacking a Mongolian immigrant does carry all the hallmarks of a racist attack. The 2006 *Rough Guide to Ireland* suggested that Ireland is 'one of Europe's most backward places when it comes to racism.' The *Guide* stated that Irish society is homogeneous, 'remarkably conservative,' and 'seemingly untouched by developments in more tolerant societies. In Belfast, too, there has been a major attempt by loyalist gangs to "cleanse" the city's ethnic population, targeting mainly the local Chinese community.'[8] The racism and resentment that accompanies an increase in immigration is a common pattern globally. Ireland is no exception.

The Dublin Love Ulster parade, like so many marches in the North, was a spectacle of Loyalist identity, territorial ownership, and power, which when placed within the *mise-en-scène* of the GPO, O'Connell Street, and the capital of the Republic was a volatile mix. The organizers stated they were only attempting to give voice to their family members, friends, and neighbors who were victims of Republican paramilitary groups. However, the ideological signs of Unionism were fairly obvious. Ireland's internal divisions were clearly exhibited in the Love Ulster march and subsequent protests and riots, which emphasized confrontation to difference and otherness (Loyalist/Unionist, Protestant/Catholic, North/South). These spectacles of parades, protests, and riots can tend to exacerbate and fuel anger toward those who embody difference and otherness.

Even though the protests were marked by violence, personal injury, and property damage, Paul Cullen in the *Irish Times* seemed to underplay the significance of the events:

> It was a very Irish riot. No one killed, thankfully. No one seriously injured. Shoppers ambling peacefully down Grafton Street while a mob rampages up Nassau Street. Missiles thoughtfully left out for the rioters on a building site on O'Connell Street. More cleaning staff to sweep up after the trouble than riot police to prevent it happening.[9]

Perhaps framing the disturbances as a rather benign occurrence in this way is a matter of inadequate reporting or knowledge as there was no mention in the *Irish Times* of Ganbold's attack. Cullen sought to explain the rioter's sense of social alienation which leads to such violence.

> What is evident is the alienation of a specific sector of youth from the rest of society. Lack of education, drugs, male violence, the growth of gangs, a lack of role models and the influence of television may all be factors.[10]

Cullen argues that a factor in the riots was the rioters' lack of sense of a coherent Irish identity. Socioeconomic deprivation in some quarters of a waning Celtic Tiger Dublin is obvious, with multi-generational families living on social welfare and housed in crowded council estates. According to the Social Inclusion Unit of Dublin City Council, nearly one in every five people in Ireland (19 percent) is deemed to be living in poverty; in Dublin some 91,700 people are in income poverty.[11] It would be foolish to deny that the socioeconomic conditions that see so many excluded from the prosperity contribute to the antisocial behavior. However, could it be argued that the actions of the rioters were not a result of a cultural alienation and an absence of a community identity, but rather of an all too clear sense of identity based on a minoritarian logic, which performs a celebration of an exception, a unique status of a minority for whom special rules apply? Is the spectacle of the parades of visibility and identity, an *ourselves alone* ethos, a manner of intensifying resentment to otherness and difference?

Richard Kearney in his 1997 *Postnationalist Ireland*, written in the era of the Good Friday Agreement (1998), makes a proposal suggesting a new Europeanism and joint sovereignty solution of multiple identities within Northern Ireland.[12] He notes that the monarchical nationalism of the British and republican nationalism of the Irish would be indefinitely incompatible. John Harrington, in a gloss of Kearney, states that 'Ireland's salvation would, thus, depend on its completing a developmental trajectory from colonial dependence, to nationalist independence, then onwards and upwards to European interdependence.'[13] Harrington argues that Kearney's proposal for a postnationalist Ireland has been realized through the developments of Northern Ireland in the post-Good Friday Agreement era. However, because of economic growth, increasing immigration, and neoliberal policies, a new model afforded by Agamben's biopolitics is required to critique the current functions of state power.

As introduced above, contemporary French philosopher Alain Badiou goes a step further in thinking through the problem of identity and minority. He disputes aggressively the minoritarian and identitarian logic of so much of contemporary cultural theory. He considers what we might model as a subject devoid of identity and asks us to imagine a radical subject outside the late capital logic of minoritarianism. According to Badiou, Western culture is ruled by the order of victimized subsets which ironically find support in the democratic strategies of capital. Positioning an identity is to map a market share.

> Whence catastrophic pronouncements of the sort: only a homosexual can 'understand' what a homosexual is, only an Arab can understand what an Arab is, and so forth. If, as we believe, only truths (thought) allow man to be distinguished from the human animal that underlies him, it is no exaggeration to say that such minoritarian pronouncements are genuinely barbaric.[14]

Badiou is seeking to 're-found a theory of the subject that subordinates its existence to the aleatory dimension of the event as well as to the pure contingency of the multiple being without sacrificing the theme of freedom.'[15] He seeks to know the 'law capable of structuring a subject devoid of all identity and suspended to an "event" whose only proof lies precisely in its having been declared by a subject.'[16] This type of subjectivity is performative, creating identity not from minority status of biological markings but from attachments to events. There is in the model a call to historicity and action that builds an autonomous and free subject.

Both Kearney and Badiou are making suggestions on how to move through the impasse of the conflicts precipitated by logic and demands of identity. Samuel Beckett long ago critiqued the reliance and realities of identity in a radical aesthetic still ahead (or outside) of its time. 'I, say I. Unbelieving,' is how Beckett considers the cul-de-sac of identity in his novel *The Unnamable*.[17] However, in Beckett's art the struggle exists between the impossibility of ever knowing the 'I' and its being while nonetheless playing through the necessity and undeniability of its presence. How does Beckett's philosophy square with a Love Ulster march? When a radical denial of being and identity is subtracted from a political struggle for visibility what is the remainder?

The Beckett centenary

Several weeks after the Love Ulster march black banners hung from the lampposts of city center Dublin. The sculpted face of Beckett looked down from each banner on a city not surprisingly unsure of its rapid rise in all things cultural and financial. The flags fluttered in celebration of Beckett's birth centenary in a century that might well be known as the museum of centennial celebrations falling as it will after such momentous happenings of the twentieth century with the firsts of modernism, technology, and atrocities. All the black banners – both a tribute and a marketing target for Irish cultural tourism – for an artist whose profound darkness transcends any attempt at the 'feel good' factor of most tourist/cultural campaigns. One can imagine, alongside the slogan that Ireland is the 'land of one thousand welcomes,' the admonition that 'infinite emptiness will be all around you, all the resurrected dead of all the ages wouldn't fill it, and there you'll be like a little bit of grit in the middle of the steppe.'[18] However, what Beckett has to say, what his words express about the horrors and misdirections of existence, was perhaps for the organizers of the centennial celebrations less a concern than the geography of his early years. The tourist gaze was directed to the marking of the place, a locating of the trace: here is Foxrock where he was born, there is the college room where he slept, a plaque placed, and a tour group alerted. What was to be sold, in the form of film festivals, exhibitions, CD releases of readings of the prose, theater productions, new editions of the collected works, and academic conferences was not only the profundity of Beckett but also the identity demonstrated through the traces of the land and the blood of the family – *jus sanguinis*.

Academic interest in Beckett's Irishness is nothing new, and books such as Eoin O'Brien's 1986 *The Beckett Country* indicate the research pursued on the influence and echoes of the geography, culture, and people of Ireland in Beckett's writing.[19] However, Beckett's theater, prose, and poetry works are commonly known to radically question perception, existence, and identity. Such theatrical images as characters reduced to only a mouth (*Not I* [1972]), or buried in the ground up to their neck (*Happy Days* [1961]), or confined in a technological memory (*Krapp's Last Tape* [1958]), signify, in part, a tenuous relation to self and identity. Anna McMullan writes that

> Beckett's theater may serve as a potent crucible for rethinking the borders of Irishness, as it incorporates Irish memories and histories, but refuses to posit a unitary cultural sphere or world that would exclude other histories or non-normative

subject positions, or naturalize the categories of identity and otherness.[20]

McMullan reads in Beckett not only a profundity and intensity of Irish identity, but a simultaneous questioning of that position. She notes that an

> aesthetics of dehiscence in Beckett's postwar writing testifies to the cultural and geographical dislocation of his move to France and of writing in the French language, to the shattering effects of the personal and historical trauma of the war, and to the impossibility of articulating such experiences within existing normative structures of identity, representation, and perception.[21]

McMullan's thoughts on Beckett's critique of identity are not isolated. Hamm in *Endgame* asks:

HAMM: Clov.
CLOV *(absorbed)*: Mmm.
HAMM: Do you know what it is?
CLOV *(as before)*: Mmm.
HAMM: I was never there.
(Pause.)
Clov!
CLOV *(turning towards Hamm, exasperated)*: What is it?
HAMM: I was never there.
CLOV: Lucky for you.
(He looks out of window.)
HAMM: Absent, always. It all happened without me. I don't know what's happened.
(Pause.)
Do you know what's happened?
(Pause.)
Clov!
CLOV *(turning towards Hamm, exasperated)*: Do you want me to look at this muckheap, yes or no?
HAMM: Answer me first.

CLOV: What?
HAMM: Do you know what's happened?
CLOV: When? Where?

HAMM *(violently)*: When! What's happened? Use your head, can't
you! What has happened?
CLOV: What for Christ's sake does it matter?
(He looks out of window.)
HAMM: I don't know.[22]

Hamm asks Clov if he knows what has happened. He fears he was
absent while whatever took its course went on about it. He was never
there. His identity and being are to be as easily forgotten and mis-
placed as the gray world outside. But the marchers on the streets of
Dublin 2006, like the revolutionaries in Jean Genet's *The Balcony*, are
not interested in the illusions, games, and philosophies of an academic
and artistic minority. They are instead demanding to be seen, heard,
and recognized. And, of course, riots ensued.

During the Love Ulster march I happened to be in the Samuel
Beckett Theatre at Trinity College filming a section of a postgraduate
workshop production of Beckett's *Endgame* which was continuing its
limited run that night as part of the centenary events. The location
of the Beckett Theatre within the walls of the college grounds was
encircled by the march and the onslaught of sirens from the disturbances prevented any filming taking place that day. While we
were playing amongst a theatrical questioning of identity, essence,
and being, outside on the streets another performance was being
staged, whose mission in part was to foreground identity, essence, and
being.

The Trinity performance of *Endgame* that night went ahead as
planned, even though the College had been in a security lockdown
during the day. The performance was received in a remarkably different manner from the earlier run. On previous nights the audience
was widely amused at Clov's window and ladder slapstick and seemingly focused on the philosophical problematics of Hamm's incess-
ant theorizing; however, that night the feel of the performance and
its reception was subdued, depressed. Perhaps the players and the
spectators had experienced a bit of the shock that accompanies
watching a city momentarily slide toward violence and anarchy,
perhaps it was in recognition that Beckett had been right that
these tribal identities, which races, minorities, nation states, and
individuals often celebrate, are fabrications and cultural constructions that can be easily forced toward an unspeakable or
unnameable position which seems alarmingly close to the face of
fascism.

Amending the constitution

On 11 June 2004 and nearing the approach of the centenary of Bloomsday (more centennial fever) the Irish electorate voted on a referendum to restrict access and tighten the qualifications for Irish citizenship. The vote was to amend Article 9 of the 1937 constitution and would become the 27th amendment. Article 9.2.1 now states:

> Notwithstanding any other provision of this Constitution, a person born in the island of Ireland, which includes its islands and seas, who does not have, at the time of the birth of that person, at least one parent who is an Irish citizen or entitled to be an Irish citizen is not entitled to Irish citizenship unless provided for by law.[23]

The referendum was proposed by then Minister of Justice Michael McDowell, who made reference to 'baby and citizenship tourism' and the claims by the three main Dublin maternity hospitals that immigrant women were arriving in the Republic to give birth to their babies and themselves into Irish and EU citizenship.[24] The referendum and the legislation have been critiqued as racist. A Radio Telefís Éireann (RTÉ) poll of 'yes' voters confirmed that suspicion:

> A third of 'yes' voters interviewed stated that they 'were motivated by anti-immigrant feelings,' 36 per cent felt the country was being exploited by immigrants, and 27 per cent felt there were too many immigrants in the country.[25]

The biopolitics of the constitution of the 1937 Irish state has been routinely criticized. John Harrington, in 'Citizenship and Biopolitics of Post-National Ireland,' writes:

> The constitution certainly imposed a set of distinctive biopolitical tasks upon the independent Irish state, aimed at cultivating and developing the nation through the bodies of its population. Women were to be confined to the home; the Roman Catholic church dominated education and culture; the inhabitants of Northern Ireland were arrogated to the nation in spite of partition; Irish was to be revived as the official language of the state. As such the constitution expressed the high point of nationalist hegemony in independent Ireland.[26]

Philosophers such as Richard Kearney and legal scholars like Harrington historicize a transition in Ireland from a nationalist hegemonic and irredentist agenda under the leadership of Eamon de Valera (Taoiseach 1932–48), to the postnationalist, neoliberal, pro-European, consumerist attitude of Bertie Ahern (Taoiseach 1997–2008) with new state systems of controls and exclusions. For Harrington, though, both periods exhibit questionable strategies of biopolitics. What was necessary in the struggle for an Irish free state required biopolitical strategies in the control of the life of the citizen in order to draw from the individual their time and labor in service of the economic and social goals of the state. The 1937 constitution was a document of biopolitical controls aimed at establishing authority on the *bare life* of the citizens of the Republic. The document focused much of that control on women, who were relegated to duties of procreation and the household. However, postnationalist Ireland is increasingly liberal, with improved women's rights and vastly enhanced economic conditions. Yet, with that affluence and prosperity has come a growing immigration population. The development from nationalist to postnationalist Ireland is such that 'where earlier battles for self-assertion and self-preservation were fought at the frontier, the new struggle is within: a "race war" against internal threats to national progress.'[27]

Anxiety over asylum seekers' 'citizenship tourism' and 'baby tourism' led to the legal and constitutional developments over the means by which immigrants gain Irish citizenship. Harrington cites the 2003 decision of the Supreme Court in *Lobe v. Minister for Justice, Equality and Law Reform* as a critical development in the manner in which the state controls immigration and citizenship. The decision found in favor of the Minister against two families of Nigerian and Roma descent whose children were born in Ireland during their failed bids for asylum. Family rights, so central to the 1937 constitution, were diminished in favor of the protection and authority of the state against a perceived immigration threat. The conclusion drawn by Harrington and seconded by this author is that the contemporary postnationalist Ireland is 'a different beast to de Valera's state, which was ontologically subordinated to the will of the people and the law of God. What marks the Irish state out as such is no longer its exceptional virtue or piety, but the powers of exclusion and expulsion which it shares with all states receiving immigrants and asylum seekers.'[28] What is being legislated is a new but similar repressive system of the *bare life* of the immigrant who is now unable to perform their citizenship *jus soli* but instead suffers a racial exclusion *jus sanguinis*.

Conclusion

What do these events of march/riot, aesthetic appropriation, and law and citizenship suggest? What comes from the triangulating of their effects? It is not unusual for people to march in redress of perceived injustices or for protests to turn violent. It is common for a population to exhibit varying levels of xenophobia and seek to scapegoat new arrivals. It is standard practice to market a country as an attractive tourist destination through a forced celebration of its artists. I have argued that these legal, aesthetic, and political performances indicate a shift toward biopolitcal systems of control, away from a placing and a performance of the autonomous citizen toward state control of *bare life*. Perhaps listening to Beckett's negative philosophy of identity and the self while appreciating his deep responsiveness to locale, dwellings, and geography might help our understanding. Perhaps looking to the exclusions brought forth from the discussed legislation or appreciating the effects of our manic spectacles of identity might open a thinking through of subjectivity, citizenship through a performed right of the soil, *jus soli*, and not the right of the blood, *jus sanguinis*.

Notes

1   Giorgio Agamben, *Homo Sacer: Sovereign Power and Bare Life*, trans. Daniel Heller-Roazen (Stanford, CA: Stanford University Press, 1998).
2   Alain Badiou, *Saint Paul: The Foundation of Universalism*, trans. Ray Brassier (Stanford, CA: Stanford University Press, 2003).
3   'Home page,' LoveUlster.com, in association with *Shankill Mirror*, http://www.loveulster.com (accessed 6 June 2008).
4   'Welcome to FAIR.' FAIR: Families Acting for Innocent Relatives, http://victims.org.uk/s08zhk/index.php?option=com_content&task=view&id=1&Itemid=2 (accessed 6 June 2008).
5   Patsy McGarry, 'Dublin's Descent into Violent Chaos,' *Irish Times*, 27 February 2006, http://www.ireland.com/newspaper/ireland/2006/0227/ 1140626821020.html (accessed 6 June 2008).
6   Search terms of 'love, ulster, riots' on YouTube.com listed eight videos of the event: *YouTube – Broadcast Yourself*, http://youtube.com/results?search_query= love+ulster+riots&search_type= (accessed 6 June 2008).
7   A. M. Walsh, 'Brave Workmates Saved My Life after Frightening Attack by Racist Gang of Thugs,' *Irish Independent*, 1 March 2006, http://www.independent.ie/national-news/brave-workmates-saved-my-life-after-frightening-attack-by-racist-gang-of-thugs-105349.html (accessed 6 June 2008).
8   R. Mac Cormaic, 'Guidebook Criticises Ireland as "Backward" on Racism,' *Irish Times*, 23 March 2006, http://www.ireland.com/newspaper/ireland/2006/ 0523/1146660079474.html (accessed 6 June 2008).

9   P. Cullen, 'Anatomy of a Very Irish Riot,' *Irish Times*, 4 March 2006, http://www. ireland.com/newspaper/newsfeatures/2006/0304/1141298075218.html (accessed 6 June 2008).

10 *Ibid.*

11 Social Inclusion Unit, *Not Just Something from the Rare Oul Times ...: Social Inclusion Handbook, A Guide for Staff* (Dublin: Dublin City Council, 2007), http://www.dublin.ie/dcdb/social-inclusion/publications.htm (accessed 6 June 2008).

12 Richard Kearney, *Postnationalist Ireland: Politics, Culture, Philosophy* (London: Routledge, 1996).

13 John A. Harrington, 'Citizenship and the Biopolitics of Post-nationalist Ireland,' *Journal of Law and Society* 32 (3) (2005): 424–49, 426.

14 Badiou, 2003, 12.

15 *Ibid.*, 4.

16 *Ibid.*, 5.

17 Samuel Beckett, *The Unnamable*, in *The Beckett Trilogy: Molloy, Malone Dies, The Unnamable* (London: Calder, 1997), 291–418, 293.

18 Samuel Beckett, *Endgame*, in *Samuel Beckett: The Complete Dramatic Works* (London: Faber and Faber, 1986), 89–134, 109–10.

19 Eoin O'Brien, *The Beckett Country: Samuel Beckett's Ireland* (London: Faber and Faber, 1986).

20 Anna McMullan, 'Samuel Beckett's Theatre: Liminal Subjects and the Politics of Perception,' *Princeton University Library Chronicle*, eds. Michael Cadden, Paul Muldoon, and Gretchen Oberfranc, 68 (1 & 2) (2006), 450–64, 434.

21 *Ibid.*, 435.

22 Beckett, *Endgame*, 128–9.

23 Department of the Taoiseach, *Constitution of Ireland/Bunreacht na hÉireann*, http://www.taoiseach.gov.ie/index.asp?docID=243 (accessed 6 June 2008).

24 Mark Brennock, 'Masters Urged Tighter Controls on Immigration,' *Irish Times*, 22 April 2004, http://www.ireland.com/newspaper/ireland/2004/0422/1079399194316.html (accessed 6 June 2008).

25 Harrington, 2005, 448.

26 *Ibid.*, 424–5.

27 *Ibid.*, 429.

28 *Ibid.*, 441.

Part IV

Gender, Feminism, and Queer Performance

13

Ghosting *Bridgie Cleary*: Tom Mac Intyre and Staging This Woman's Death

Charlotte McIvor

This is for all consarned, cos what's strayed from the accounts is Bridgie's story is a love story, which fact needs te be roundly stated. These is not trivyel matters, thank you.

Bridgie, *What Happened Bridgie Cleary* by Tom Mac Intyre[1]

'For the love of God,' James Kennedy said to Michael Cleary, according to his own testimony, 'don't burn your wife!'

'She's not my wife,' Cleary replied, 'She's an old deceiver sent in the place of my wife. She's after deceiving me for the last seven or eight days, and deceived the priest today too, but she won't deceive anyone anymore. As I beginned it with her, I will finish it with her!'

The Burning of Bridget Cleary: A True Story by Angela Bourke[2]

Bridget Cleary's burning to death in 1895 indexes a moment of transition in Irish modern history that has consistently been subject to morbid fascination, but only recently critically engaged. Whilst suffering from a mysterious illness, Bridget was accused of being possessed by a fairy spirit by her husband and members of her extended family.[3] Despite her protestations, her husband and the others subjected her to a fairy trial of an invasive series of cures, including dousing her with urine and force-feeding her bitter herbs. After several days' 'treatment,' in an alleged final attempt to rid Bridget of the spirit, her husband, Michael, doused her in paraffin and held her over their household fire. This final, brutal act resulted in Bridget's death and led to a public trial in Her Majesty's Court in County Tipperary. Bridget was 26 years old.

A contemporary re-examination of Bridget's case was initiated by Angela Bourke's *The Burning of Bridget Cleary: A True Story* in 1999 with Joan Hoff and Marian Yeates's *The Cooper's Wife Is Missing: The Trials of*

169

Bridget Cleary following in 2000. These studies are distinguished by their extensive engagement with archival materials and efforts to discover what *really* happened, drawing on other shorter pieces of scholarship that had appeared over the years.[4] Public interest has increased since 1999 as a result of these studies, and in November 2005, Radio Telefís Éireann (RTÉ) produced a new documentary entitled *Fairy Wife: The Burning of Bridget Cleary*, directed by Adrian McCarthy, in their 'Hidden History' series.[5]

During a *Morning Ireland* interview with Adrian McCarthy on 21 October 2005, RTÉ played an audio clip from *Fairy Wife*. It featured the voice of a young Irish girl telling the story as if it were a fairy tale, and not a historical event. When she gets to the moment of Bridget's burning, she says, 'that got rid of the fairy. The beautiful girl disappeared too.'[6] By filtering the events through the perspective of a soft-voiced child telling a story, McCarthy highlights the convergence of myth and history in the remembering of Bridget's story and its repeated retelling. Since the case hit the press more than a century ago, the macabre focus on Bridget's death has positioned her life somewhere between a fairy story of a 'beautiful girl' who disappeared and became the subject of a lurid penny dreadful and a once living woman who exposes the contradictory nature of almost 'modern' Ireland.

Bridget's death at the hands of her family, the public response to this act at the time, and its subsequent memorialization through writing, performance, and verbal discourse constitute a rich series of sites in which to consider Ireland's relationship to its colonial past and notions of modernity, as well to interrogate the politics of gender and nascent Irish Nationalism in 1895, and the after-effects of these formations in the early twenty-first century. The retellings of the story of Bridget Cleary should not be understood merely as attempts to set the record straight about her life and death, but also occasions to perform constantly revised versions of Ireland's own history at the *fin-de-siècle* through her shadowy figure.

Echoing the continued fascination with Bridget's life, well-known Irish playwright, novelist, and poet Tom Mac Intyre's *What Happened Bridgie Cleary* premiered at the Peacock Theatre in April 2005.[7] This run was followed by a tour of Ireland in June and July 2005. In his theatrical version of events, the 'true' story is revealed as a love quadrangle between Bridget Cleary, her husband, Michael, and two men rumored to have been her lovers, including the local eggman.[8] Does resurrecting Bridget as a ghostly but embodied presence in performance and focusing on her sexuality grant her new power to speak, or simplify the dynamics at work surrounding her death?

Joseph Roach designates the process by which a culture 'reproduces and re-creates itself ... *surrogation.*'[9] He argues that surrogation will never completely succeed because collective memory 'works selectively, imaginatively and also perversely.'[10] Bridget is remembered and performed as a fairy story by the little girl who introduces McCarthy's documentary, but the content of her history bespeaks a far greater complexity which, through studies such as Bourke's, reveals the sociological content of Irish myth in the late nineteenth century. Roach's 'genealogies of performance,' which refer to the 'the historical transmission and dissemination of cultural practices through collective representations,'[11] offer a way to locate the multiple revisions of the story of Bridget Cleary as a cultural practice that goes beyond scholarly innovations to expose shifting concerns in Irish studies and the Irish theater. He charges genealogies of performance with having the power to attend to 'counter-memories,' or 'the disparities between history as it is discursively transmitted and memory as it is publicly enacted by the bodies that bear its consequences.'[12] But does Cleary's ghostly theatricalized presence ensure that the story is told in her favor?

Bridget Cleary and Ireland at the edge

Bridget Cleary's death occurred at a moment of radical change. The Home Rule movement was reorganizing after the downfall of Charles Stewart Parnell, and Irish cultural nationalism was appearing on the horizon, in the persons of W. B. Yeats and Lady Augusta Gregory, among others. Additionally, changes in the population following the Great Famine of the 1840s, which had 'swept away the rural poor who were most attached to traditional lifestyles, from speaking Irish to believing in the fairies,'[13] led to a shift in worldview that was purported to be leading Ireland in the direction of the modern disenchanted world. While Ireland was certainly not trying to distance itself from the Catholic faith in 1895, the perception was that non-Christian fairy stories were dying out and needed to be preserved by members of the burgeoning Irish Literary Revival and folklorists. These stories belonged to a vanishing present, rather than to the horizon of the future.

The clash of the Irish fairy world with the public courts and 'modern' world of Her Majesty's laws in Ireland through the trial over Bridget's death was framed as reflecting Ireland's very relationship to modernity and potential for development, especially as it related to Ireland's capacity for self-governance. The role of the anti-Irish press was considerable. Bourke writes:

> Representing a young woman as innocent victim and her tormentors – the men of her own community – as benighted and dull-witted peasants – these newspapers constructed a narrative which juxtaposed the incomprehensible, primitive superstitions of a colonized people with the rationality and enlightenment of Victorian British justice.[14]

In this account, Bridget is appropriated for the righteousness of the British cause, and the case is deeply gendered as a tragedy of the primitive that can only be solved by the death of myth and the control of the Irish people by the 'more rational' British. The isolated incident in Ballyvadlea, County Tipperary performed the imagined violent potentialities of the backwardness of the so-called Irish peasantry for the benefit of the anti-Home Rule and pro-British constituencies.

Angela Bourke argues that the body of folklore and fairy stories employed as evidence and explanation for the death of Bridget Cleary can best be understood as a vernacular strategy employed by Irish people in Bridget's community. She writes: 'Viewed as a system of interlocking units of narrative, practice, and belief, fairy legend can be compared to a database: a premodern culture's way of storing and retrieving information and knowledge of every kind, from hygiene and child care to history and geography.'[15] According to Bourke, the veracity of fairy beliefs is thus not at stake. Rather, it is a question of the manner in which the vocabulary of this belief system functions to shape and enable actions. This reading of the rhetorical strategies of rural folklore recuperates the reductive narrative of those in the British press who pointed to the brutality of these pagan beliefs as signaling the savagery of the Irish people at large. Bourke's emphasis on tracing 'interlocking units of narrative, practice, and belief' draws attention not only to the performative strategies of communication required to express oneself in the language of fairy belief, but to the very performance involved in interpreting this deliberately inscrutable information through projecting intentions onto the actors in the Bridget Cleary case.

When Hubert Butler suggested in 1960 that: 'Eyes that are dim with tears are not particularly perceptive; focused on the fairies, they never give the eggman his due,'[16] he hinted that the potential erotic mysteries of Bridget's life were obscured by an obsession with explaining fairy belief. Despite a focus on the grisly nature of Bridget's death and her decidedly female body (as wife, as daughter, as Catholic Irish woman), Butler rightly identifies that a consideration of Bridget as sexually transgressive or supernatural would not only destroy her status as victim of a crime, but condemn the Irish themselves, and particularly Irish women, as aberrant at a moment when depictions of Irish primitivism, degeneracy, and effeminacy were already flush in the British and American presses.[17] Butler thus diagnoses repression in the accounts surrounding Bridget's case, particularly around matters of sexuality.

The omission of speculations about Bridget's own potential complexities in previous treatments is precisely what Bourke, Hoff and Yeates, and McCarthy pick up on. Yet, following Butler, Tom Mac Intyre goes as far as to make Bridget's complex *sexuality* the focus of his piece, conflating her sexuality with her complexity as a (gendered) subject in late nineteenth-century Ireland. Writing in the *Irish Times,* Belinda McKeon noted: 'Bridgie Cleary, in Mac Intyre's eyes, chose the wrong path, to be with her husband, rather than with the man she truly loved – and for that she paid the price ... what happened afterwards left scars on his psyche as well as on her ruined body.'[18] Mac Intyre certainly gives 'the eggman [more than] his due,' yet this revelation does not lead to a happy ending. Instead, the play ends with Michael Cleary, Bridgie Cleary, and William Simpson, local Anglo-Irish groundskeeper and other suspected lover, in a seemingly interminable silence.

Bourke observes that, 'The story of Bridget is firstly one of "domestic" violence,'[19] but the 'domestic' was complicated in the Cleary case by the invocations of fairy forces at work. As Butler suggests, the language of fairy belief may have been used to deflect focus from both the erotic and the domestic angles of the case in favor of puzzlement about the beliefs of 'the Irish people.' The performance of puzzlement in the British and Irish press over language of fairy belief and its repercussions in the realm of criminality and Ireland's modern image displaces Bridget's body and its citations of gendered (and sexual) anxieties even as it obsesses over them. Mac Intyre foregrounds the erotic within the domestic, but does this retrieval accomplish only a further objectification of Bridget's body through a focus on the sexual?

Haunting performances: a theater of 'seething presences'

Mac Intyre has attested that questions of Irish women's psyches are foremost on his mind when he is writing plays. In a 2001 interview with Fiach Mac Conghail, Mac Intyre characterizes theater in Ireland as 'daddy-theater':

> Writing that isn't dripping from the unconscious bores me very quickly – that's what I call 'daddy-writing.' As we all recognize by this hour, the desperate need in the contemporary psyche is for the grip of the patriarchal goosestep if you like, to be marvelously mitigated and for the males who run the show to bring up, way, way up, the female energy. Now when that happens, the possibility of beautiful play is there.[20]

Mac Intyre's goal is to carve an authoritative space for the Irish female on the stage by accessing what he terms the 'unconscious' for 'female energy.' He characterizes this energy as sensual and erotic earlier in the interview, citing German choreographer Pina Bausch as a reference point. The notion of the unconscious conjures images of the dark, eternal feminine as a site where erotic and universal truth can be accessed, a theme familiar in other canonical Irish writing, such as in the work of W. B. Yeats.[21] Yet, this dark 'female' unconscious cannot simply be understood as a site of desired power, it is also a place of danger for those who fear female 'energy.' Rather than empowering, this conception of 'female energy' has often been used to demonize women like Bridget and sanction violence against them for the very reasons Mac Intyre is celebrating. Yet, he also states:

> For me, what I'd say consistently that I am seeking to have swirling, dancing inside the container is the desperate contemporary male need to make contact with the female magic, which I mentioned before and that's where it's at, it seems to me.[22]

The rhetoric of fairy folklore explored here through the case of Bridget Cleary has been argued by Bourke and others as a desperate need by the male (and possibly even female) to control 'female magic.' Nevertheless, by resurrecting Bridget as a dramatic persona, Mac Intyre asserts her place as witness in the theoretical record surrounding her case. He highlights the need to control female magic as what he believes to be the very unconscious of not only the case surrounding her death, but Irish theater and society at large.

Hence, Bridget as social figure reveals the way in which the female body in late nineteenth-century Ireland became the repository for a number of anxieties about Irish modernity on a wider scale.

Her body was lamented as the victim of backward savagery, but her 'seething presence'[23] has prompted inquiries that have returned her body and psyche to the center of the very debates that previously excluded her. This repositioning draws attention to the containment of aberrant or unruly female sexuality which was constitutive of early modern Irish national formations, as attested to by the purified figure of Mother Ireland or Eamon de Valera's later constitution enshrining the role of women in the home as mothers and caretakers. Mac Intyre's lament for Bridget's misunderstood desires places her center-stage at a moment of enormous change in Ireland's modern history and makes Michael Cleary and William Simpson suffer her forgiveness, perhaps as stand-ins for an archetypal Irish masculinity that has consistently ignored or deified figures like Bridget out of a fear of contact with 'female magic.'

Yet, Bridgie's actual historical death in the context of fear of 'female magic' troubles Mac Intyre's simplistic invocation of 'female magic' as the panacea for the androcentric Irish theater in 2005. The stasis presented at the conclusion of this work reveals the limits of his argument by his own hand, and reveals that rather than simply resurrecting Bridgie as witness, he asks her 'love story' to bear the weight again of the repressed desires expressed through the case. 'Female magic' is portrayed as trapped in the limbo of the afterlife, and expressible only in the service of recounting a stilted romance. Perhaps, however, this stasis is finally intended to stir the audience rather than its prisoners onstage.

What Happened [to] Bridgie Cleary ['s voice?]

In *What Happened Bridgie Cleary*, we encounter Bridgie after death, blissfully alone and at work in the afterlife. Her space is soon invaded, however, by the appearance of her former lovers. Yet, in defiance of all previous accounts, Bridgie is permitted the space to speak in the first person. Freddie Rokem writes:

> Theatre about historical events generally focuses on a character with knowledge (sometimes even too much knowledge), where the victimized survivor is given the position of witness. This witness is able to tell the spectators something about the experiences previously hidden behind the 'veils' of his or her past and now through the performance, revealed to the spectators. The cathartic processes activated by the theatre performing history are more like a 'ritual' of

resurrection, a revival of past suffering, where the victim is given the power to speak about the past again.[24]

Bridget is certainly resurrected through Mac Intyre's play; she is removed from the position of 'victim' and granted the dubious role of 'witness' as the pressure is put on Michael Cleary and William Simpson to explain themselves to her, rather than the other way around as in the final days of her life and in the ensuing controversy.

Marvin Carlson categorizes theatrical practice as having a 'ghostly quality.' His writing about the 'ghostly quality' of theater emphasizes its ability to synthesize historical and cultural events in its story-telling.[25] The audience gathers together in the theatrical space to hear familiar stories, experience familiar emotions, and engage with a well-known event in order to find comfort in these stories or emotions, or perhaps to move past them, purged of their effects. Although catharsis cannot be trusted as a transformative act with unequivocally radical consequences, Carlson argues that the mode of reception particular to the form has unique possibilities:

> The conditions of the theatrical event, enacted not only in a brief period of time, but before a mass audience, provide none of the opportunity for reflection or rereading offered by novels or lyric poetry and thus encourage the use of materials somewhat familiar to an audience for ease in reception.[26]

Beyond this utilitarian view of the use of 'familiar' stories in theater, it can perhaps be argued that when familiar stories are retold in new ways, they potentially push at the borders of an audience's accepted lexicon of knowledge.

Thus, in Mac Intyre's play, when Bridgie revises the still circulating rhyme 'Are you a witch or are you a fairy / Or are you the wife of Mikey Cleary?' to say instead 'I was never a witch, never a fairy / I was once wife to a man called Cleary,'[27] she subverts a phrase perhaps familiar to the audience. In the theatrical space, which does not permit much room for 'reflection or rereading,' a new history is created in the moment and circulated among the audience. By staging the effects of Bridget Cleary's conjectured love affairs onstage, Tom Mac Intyre restores contemporary corporeality to Bridgie by staging the ghost as a body in conversation with the evolved contemporary critical discourse over her death. The metatheatrical nature of the piece positions Bridgie as very aware of her audience and demands their participation. She challenges them: 'BRIDGIE (*to audience, coldly alert*): Only what was Bridgie Cleary *doin'* there that night – waitin' for te be made a herring of?'[28] This question is really never answered by the play – perhaps she was overwhelmed by sickness as has been suggested by Bourke, Hoff, and Yeates, or by a broken heart for not having the strength to follow Phildy Reddan[29] down the road. Her address to the audience suggests, however, that this is a question *they* should continue to contemplate rather than she alone.

Just as Belinda McKeon refers to 'the scars on his [Michael Cleary's] psyche as well as on her ruined body,' Mac Intyre emphasizes the scars and insecurities of the men, such as a painful rash on Michael's hands that references the demands of his profession as well as the lingering effects of the violence he has committed with them. Bridgie's violated body is *de*-spectacularized by the exclusion of its visibility in the flesh or discussions of the ordeal but *re*-spectacularized through Mac Intyre's emphasis on her story as a sensual 'love story.' Bridgie controls access to all information in this version, physical and emotional, yet she is seemingly damned to share space with the men whose psychological scars cannot really finally displace the damage done to her body. This move by Mac Intyre is representative of the bind that Bridgie was placed in during her life and urges the audience to engage with the hopelessness of this position, and perhaps address it in the present.

As Bridgie unconsciously (or so it seems in the performance) recites and revises a popular rhyme circulated about her death up to this day, history is being rewritten in the moment. The conflicted access to memory shared by all the characters in *What Happened Bridgie Cleary* embodies the amount of access we have to these events as spectators, even when face to face with the historical figures. Performance allows Mac Intyre to move beyond a mere 'retelling' of the history to activate the gaps in this story by staging its hauntings. By presenting the possibilities of all these absences and incompletes in conversation with the contemporary critical discourse concerning her death, Bridget is granted a new authority, and the record of her death is staged as dialogic.

Mac Intyre's play launches a critique which demands an acknowledgment of 'genealogies of performance' that inform and create cultural memory in relation to contemporary needs. Acknowledging the power and inconsistencies of Mac Intyre's Bridgie points us toward a history that is embodied and incomplete, enchanted and starkly realistic. Through the performing body, contact is forced not only with the ghosts of the past in the present, but with those of the future, as we consider how 'Bridgie' is continually created anew and in whose interests.

Notes

1 Tom Mac Intyre, *What Happened Bridgie Cleary* (Dublin: New Island/ New Drama, 2005), 93.

2 Angela Bourke, *The Burning of Bridget Cleary: A True Story* (New York: Penguin, 1999), 124.

3 She exhibited flu-like symptoms: chills, fever, joint pain, and an unwillingness to eat or drink. See Bourke, *ibid.*; and Joan Hoff and Marian Yeates, *The Cooper's Wife is Missing: The Trials of Bridget Cleary* (New York: Basic Books, 2000). At the end of the ensuing public trial, Michael Cleary was convicted of manslaughter, while the other involved parties – her father, Patrick Boland, his sister, Mary Kennedy, her sons, James, William, Patrick, and Michael Kennedy, and her father's cousin, Jack Dunne–were convicted of 'wounding' Bridget.

4 Before this resurgence of interest, various articles had been published, including Hubert Butler's 1960 essay 'The Eggman and the Fairies,' in *Independent Spirit: Essays* (New York: Farrar, Straus & Giroux, 1996), 169–79; and Thomas McGrath's 'Fairy Faith and Changelings: The Burning of Bridget Cleary in 1895,' *Studies*, 71 (Summer 1982): 178–84. More recently, RTÉ produced a documentary directed by Pat Feeley called *The Burning of Bridget Cleary* (aired 10 April 1995). Carlo Gébler published a novel based on the story entitled *The Cure* (London: Hamish Hamilton, 1994), and in 1995 Tony Butler's 'The Burning of Bridget Cleary: The 100th Anniversary' appeared in *The Nationalist* (25 March 1995).

5 McCarthy is also currently producing a feature-length film about the case.

6 *Fairy Wife: The Burning of Bridget Cleary*. dir. Adrian McCarthy (Ireland: Wildfire Films, 2006).

7 I was not able to attend the original run, but accessed a tape of it at the Peacock through the Abbey Theatre's archive in June 2006. All comments that follow on the performance are based on my viewing of the tape.

8 Butler implies that Bridget's death may have been brought on by an affair she had with a traveling eggman which angered her husband, with fairy possession only serving as the pretext for her punishment. Bourke also refers to persisting rumors that Bridget Cleary had a lover at the time of her death (40–3, 97–9, 106, 120, 150). William Simpson was the Anglo-Irish groundskeeper residing near her home who is named as one of her potential lovers by Bourke (97, 107, 150), as well as by Hoff and Yeates (94–7).

9 Joseph Roach, *Cities of the Dead: Circum-Atlantic Performance* (New York: Columbia University Press, 1996), 2 (emphasis in original).

10 *Ibid.*, 3.

11 *Ibid.*, 25.

12 *Ibid.*, 25–6.

13 Diarmuid Ó Giolláin, 'The Fairy Belief and Official Religion in Ireland,' in *The Good People: New Fairylore Essays*, ed. Peter Narváez (Lexington: The University Press of Kentucky, 1991), 199–214, 205.

14 Angela Bourke, 'Reading a Woman's Death: Colonial Text and Oral Tradition in Nineteenth-Century Ireland,' in *Postcolonial Discourses: An Anthology*, ed. Gregory Castle (New Malden, MA: Blackwell, 2001), 433–57, 434.

15 *Ibid.*, 433.
16 Butler, 1995, 178.
17 See Steve Garner, *Racism in the Irish Experience* (London: Pluto Press, 2004); and Noel Ignatiev, *How the Irish Became White* (New York: Routledge, 1995), among others.
18 Belinda McKeon, 'Between Two Worlds,' *Irish Times,* 21 April 2005, 16.
19 Bourke, 1999, 235.
20 Quoted in Fiach Mac Conghail, 'Tom Mac Intyre in Conversation with Fiach Mac Conghail,' in *Theatre Talk: Voices of Irish Theatre Practitioners*, ed. Lilian Chambers, Ger FitzGibbon, and Eamon Jordan (Dublin: Carysfort Press, 2001), 307–14, 309.
21 For an in-depth discussion of these themes in Yeats's writings, see Elizabeth Butler Cullingford, *Gender and History in Yeats's Love Poetry* (Cambridge: Cambridge University Press, 1993).
22 Quoted in Mac Conghail, 2001, 311.
23 Avery Gordon writes: 'If haunting describes how that which appears to be not there is often a seething presence, acting on and often meddling with taken-granted-realities, the ghost is just the sign, or the empirical if you like, that tells you that a haunting is taking place. The ghost is not simply a dead or a missing person, but a social figure, and investigating it can lead to that dense site where history and subjectivity make social life,' in *Ghostly Matters: Haunting and the Sociological Imagination* (Minneapolis: University of Minnesota Press, 1997), 8.
24 Freddie Rokem, *Performing History: Theatrical Representations of the Past in Contemporary Theatre* (Iowa City: University of Iowa Press, 2000), 205.
25 Marvin Carlson, *The Haunted Stage* (Ann Arbor: University of Michigan Press, 2004), 4.
26 *Ibid.*, 23.
27 Mac Intyre, 2005, 6.
28 *Ibid.*, 81.
29 This is the name given to the elusive eggman in Mac Intyre's play.

14
Challenging Patriarchal Imagery: Amanda Coogan's Performance Art

Gabriella Calchi Novati

It is worth remembering that the first figure to be invested by the deployment of sexuality, one of the first to be 'sexualised,' was the 'idle' woman. She inhabited the outer edge of the 'world,' in which she always had to appear as a value, and of the family, where she was assigned a new destiny charged with conjugal and parental obligations.

Michel Foucault[1]

Womanhood in Ireland: a sociocultural issue

Amanda Coogan exhibits a specifically Irish dilemma about the female body turned into a public display of the feminine abject through her contemporary performance art. Although Coogan's visual and symbolic focus on the female body is influenced by her training with the artist Marina Abramović, the contextualization of Coogan's work within a specifically Irish pattern of female construction and representation reveals its deepest significance. Coogan carefully foregrounds her own subjectivity, stating that 'before being a performance artist, I am a white, blond, blue-eyed, Irish woman.'[2] Her disclaimer highlights the semiotic peculiarity of the body, an undeniably central aspect of her work. Coogan's statement echoes Elizabeth Grosz's claim that 'bodies are always irreducibly sexually specific, necessarily interlocked with racial, cultural, and class particularities' and that 'being a body is something that we must come to accommodate psychically, something that we must live.'[3] The essence of Coogan's work, with its postmodern indifference to any kind of distinction between high and low culture, is neither an object nor an act, but the relationship between her shamelessly exposed body and the Irish patriarchal logic of gender.

This chapter examines key issues in the Irish sociocultural context as they relate to several examples of Amanda Coogan's performance art, including the *Madonna* series: *Madonna in Blue* (2001), *Madonna III* (2001), *The Sacred Heart* (2002), and the companion piece *The Fountain* (2001). Coogan offers a feminist critique of the 'lived body,' a body 'interwoven with and constitutive of systems of meaning, signification and representation.'[4] What we immediately witness through Coogan's body in performance is the physical disclosure of an outdated neurosis concerning the explicit female body[5] and its intertwining with sexuality, which is arguably still present in the Irish context.[6] That said, it is important to acknowledge the sociocultural transformation of and legal advances for women in Ireland over the past 40 years. The Anti-discrimination (Pay) Act in 1974 and the Employment Equality Act in 1977 attempted to erase the discrepancy produced by a gendered discrimination in salaries and employment.[7] In 1973 the 'marriage bar,' which in the past forced Irish women, once married, to retire from several fields related particularly to the civil service, nursing, and teaching, was abolished, while in 1986 the ban on night work and Sunday work was cancelled.[8] It was only in 1995 that the passing of the divorce referendum lifted the ban on divorce in Ireland. As Mark Cassidy, Eric Strobl, and Robert Thorton note, 'the origins of anti-discrimination legislation within the European Economic Community (EEC) were primarily economic rather than social,' explaining that 'prior to Ireland's entry into the EEC, explicit wage discrimination against females had been justified on the grounds that the male was the primary source of income for a family.'[9]

The Irish state, however, still exercises its patriarchal 'right' to legislate over the female body by subordinating women's reproductive rights. Pat O'Connor argues that 'contraception and abortion illustrate the many attempts made by the Irish state to maintain control over women's bodies,'[10] explaining that it was only in 1993 that 'condoms were made available in vending machines.'[11] The ban on abortion in the Republic of Ireland[12] was reinforced through three abortion referenda in 1983, 1992, and 2002.[13] The 1992 and 2002 referenda, however, widened the debate about the legalization of abortion in the Republic. While O'Connor claims that the Irish anti-abortion legislation mirrors 'the role of the state in reflecting and reinforcing the status of women as child bearers,'[14] Ruth Fletcher sees 'the constitutional prohibition of abortion, and the discourses which justify it, drawn on nationalism's representation of the self-sacrificing mother as an emblem of Ireland.'[15] Through a postcolonial reading of the issue,

Fletcher attempts to unravel the complexity of the abortion debate in Ireland by highlighting the tremendous importance of Catholicism as 'a particular maker of Irish nationality' and pointing out that 'anti-abortion efforts to make a "pro-life" stance a symbol of Irishness have drawn on and reconstructed this historical association between Catholicism and Irish nationalism.'[16] The Catholic Church promoted the Virgin Mary as the unique archetype of the new national Irish woman: 'the chaste, modest and humble virtues of Irish women and mothers grew apace with their penitential devotion to the Our Lady ... an ideal-type figure that was fecund and female and yet remained virgin and pure.'[17] This analysis illustrates the oxymoronic coupling of virginity and motherhood. The political and cultural struggle over the signification of the sexually resonant female body underpins Amanda Coogan's works, where a tension to find a new way to signify woman-hood is divorced from a patriarchal frame.

Woman as mother and Madonna

Barry Collins and Patrick Hanafin explain how Irish law constructed the image of woman as living embodiment of the newborn nation and the dichotomized depiction of woman as either mother or virgin. They note that the 1937 Constitution of Ireland, 'despite its predominant universalist ethos, also makes formal distinctions between men and women, recognizing the "special" role of woman.'[18] Article 41.2.1 states that: 'in particular, the State recognises that by her life within the home, woman gives to the State a support without which the common good cannot be achieved,' adding in 41.2.2 that 'the State shall, there-fore, endeavour to ensure that mothers shall not be obliged by econ-omic necessity to engage in labour to the neglect of their duties in the home.'[19] While much legislation has been revised (equality in wages, contraception, etc.), Article 41.2 remained unchanged in 2008, exem-plifying the 'phallocentric' nature of the Irish Constitution.[20]

Collins and Hanafin state that the 1937 Constitution had 'the enor-mous task' to establish 'not just a widely accepted set of constitutional principles, but the production of a document that could define a new national identity.'[21] Inherent in that identity is the constituted role of woman as mother. Furthermore, they highlight that 'the most notable (if not over-determined) of the range of national images embedded in the 1937 Constitution is that of the mother,' adding that 'given ... the patriarchal tone of the 1937 Constitution, it would appear that the new state was conceived ... with the role of woman largely confined to the private sphere, as home-maker, wife and mother.'[22] The Constitution offers no effective public acknowledgment of women as independent individuals: thus far woman has been regarded 'not as an autonomous person but as a site of contest,'[23] with not even a legally recognized agency on her own body, as the strict anti-abortion legislation in the Republic of Ireland demonstrates.

These complex dynamics have continued to severely restrict the position of women in Irish society. Tom Inglis argues that although contemporary Ireland experiences sexuality in a different and more liberal way, 'there are relatively few women who have become famous representatives of the new, sexually liberated Irish woman.'[24] In contrast, Inglis draws attention to those women who, instead of becoming famous, 'have become infamous for having transgressed traditional conventions.'[25] Such women have broken the sacred and symbolic Irish equation 'woman equals mother' by violently stepping outside the nationally accepted image of womanhood.

It is worth noting that the equation 'woman equals mother' has consigned 'woman' to a passive position within the symbolic order. Woman is signified but does not have any power of signification; she is relegated, via the libidinal realm of heterosexist desire, into a very strict biological or ethereal role. The application of Freud's theory as expressed in 'On the Universal Tendency to Debasement in the Sphere of Love' to the Irish patriarchal legacy reveals the unconscious mechanisms that lie beneath the symbolic mother (virgin)/whore dichotomy. According to Freud, the dichotomy virgin/whore occurs when men are trapped in the psychological impossibility to love and desire at the same time: 'where they love they do not desire and where they desire they cannot love.'[26] As a consequence, their 'love consists in a psychical *debasement* of the sexual object, the overvaluation that normally attaches to the sexual object being reserved for the incestuous object and its representatives.'[27] In Ireland this psychological split occurred as a direct consequence of the idealization and idolization of womanhood that originates in the notion of woman as spiritual creature, mother-Éire. This was the post-Independence model adapted from republican propaganda that the Irish government, working hand in glove with the church hierarchy, used to define the image of Mother Nation.

The powerful influence wielded by the Catholic Church in the Republic, both in directing the ethical and social values of Irish society, and in generating a Manichean-like imagery in which woman could be identified only among the realm of sinner or saint, penitent or nun, whore or Madonna, has been exhaustively analyzed.[28] The operation, until 1996, of the Magdalene Laundries – 'voluntary' institutions open for 'fallen' women in response to concerns over the moral health of the country – epitomizes that theoretical gulf in a too sadly tangible way.[29] Amanda Coogan confronts this problematic positioning of the female body in Irish culture by staging hers as a locus for the exploration of these overlapping tensions.

Coogan's women: challenging patriarchal imagery

In the performances of the *Madonna* series, including *Madonna in Blue*, *Madonna III*, and *The Sacred Heart*, Coogan performs a sophisticated critical questioning of the virgin–mother identification on the one hand, and the virgin/whore dichotomy on the other. Grosz suggests that the conflict between the two terms of the virgin/whore dichotomy does not admit any mediation because patriarchy, in its attempt 'to preserve the contradictory role of the mother (as pure and seducer),' consciously removes this contradiction by projecting its features onto two different types of women: 'either virgin or whore, subject or object, asexual or only sexual, with no possible mediation.'[30]

In the *Madonna* series, Coogan critically displays the mother/Madonna/whore dichotomy, where, as Freud says, 'the sphere of love remains divided in the two directions personified in art as sacred [Madonna] and profane (or animal) [whore] love.'[31] Throughout these performances Coogan offers her body as the privileged site for these two types of 'woman' to coexist in a symbolic balance in what can be considered the uncomfortable paradox embodied by the Virgin Mary who, simultaneously virgin and mother, literally embodies the antithetical paradigm of renunciation and celebration of motherhood.

In *Madonna in Blue* Coogan wears a partially unbuttoned blue silk shirt and, as she cups her exposed right breast, her gaze avoids the encounter with the audience, making her appear absent and yet inviting – virgin *and* whore. As Coogan describes it, *Madonna in Blue* is 'the first photograph in the *Madonna* series – a domestic-sized image that could be put in a purse along with one's prayer cards.'[32] Coogan explains the dichotomous message of this image:

> the core image of this piece is on the one hand the physical reproduction of a sacred painting exhibited in the National Gallery of Ireland, and on the other hand one of the many nameless girls

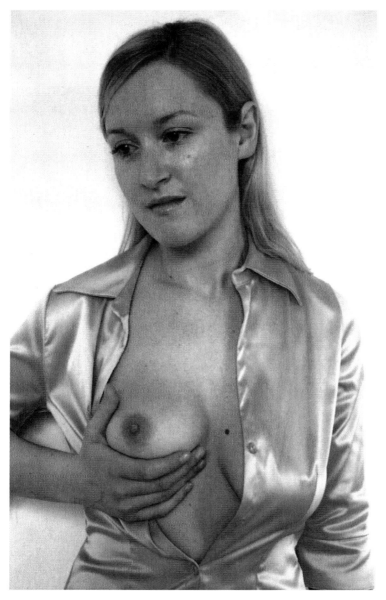

Figure 5   Madonna in Blue 2001. A photograph from the *Madonna* series. A religious/ iconic image, domestic that could be put in a purse along with one's prayer cards. This image blurs the line between religious prayer cards and sex-line advertisements. Photo by Jimmy Fay.

who advertise their body for sex through their pictures in telephone booths and magazines.[33]

The photograph of *Madonna in Blue* was presented to Irish audiences from 2003 to 2005 as part of the solo exhibition *Amanda Coogan: A Brick in the Handbag*. The figurative image of *Madonna in Blue*, the photograph became a 'living installation' in the companion piece *Madonna III*. Coogan first presented this durational performance at Dublin's Irish Museum of Modern Art (IMMA) in 2001, where she stood perfectly still 'for up to two hours'[34] holding her right breast. This time wearing a white suit and tennis shoes with the jacket unbuttoned to expose her breast, she stood on a mantelpiece with her back to a mirror, 'as in a church or an outside grotto,'[35] offering herself to the viewer's gaze as a living sculpture, resembling the human sculptures of Gilbert & George. Coogan also showed the piece in 2004 as part of *Performance Loop* at the PS1 Contemporary Art Center in New York, this time wearing a black suit. The chromatic choice was made to contrast with the whiteness of the gallery walls and, as Amanda Coogan highlights, 'to focus the audience's attention on the female body confined within the male uniform of the black suit.'[36]

In the performance *Sacred Heart*, presented in 2003 at the Padiglione d'Arte Contemporanea (PAC) in Milan, and at the Royal Hibernian Academy (RHA) in Dublin, Coogan went even further in her feminist critique of Irish patriarchy, moving from the embodiment of the sacred female, the Virgin Mary, to the embodiment of the sacred male, Jesus Christ. In this piece she stands on a stool, wearing a long skirt, which, touching the ground, elongates her stature, and a mauve jacket appositely designed by her father to remain perfectly open on her bare chest where, over a 45-minute period, a red heart-shaped stain materializes. This seemingly mystical apparition of the Sacred Heart, as the title of the piece suggests, is the only 'action' that happens. However, no miracle is taking place; the stain is achieved through a chemical reaction produced by a hair dye that the performer has applied. In this piece Coogan takes probably the most sacred image of international Catholicism and fundamentally inverts it. By reversing this image, synecdoche of the Catholic institution in Ireland, Coogan blatantly and shockingly draws attention to the fact that the Sacred Heart is institutionally gendered and has always been exclusively the heart of Jesus, the sacred male. More so than the two previous *Madonnas*, this performance thus symbolically interrogates the systematization of the patriarchal order from within.

From an Irish perspective the devotion to the Sacred Heart, prominent since the mid-nineteenth century,[37] became part of the religious shared iconography of the nation, through the presence of its image hung on the walls of Irish households. Coogan recalls that on the kitchen wall of her family home there was an image of the Sacred Heart of Jesus. She remembers her early fascination with that icon of Jesus, 'so beautiful and colourful,'[38] who was there to protect and judge: Law of the Father *par excellence*.

Although positively associated with the domestic space, the Sacred Heart bears another, insidious connotation in recent Irish history, as its name is also linked with the institutions of the Magdalene Laundries. The religious order of the Sacred Heart, in fact, was one of the orders of nuns running the Asylums in Ireland. In the *Inferno*-like[39] realm of the Magdalene Asylums, women were forced under a vow of silence to work in laundries attached to the institutions, unpaid and generally addressed as 'sinners,'[40] a term used in a very loose way to include women who were considered by the community to be in danger of sin.

> The sins varied from being unmarried mothers to being too ugly, too simple minded, too clever, or a victim of rape who talked about it; or, if an orphaned teenage girl, they could be incarcerated as a precautionary move if they were thought to be too attractive.[41]

The Sacred Heart on Coogan's chest is a dark red stain which could serve as a metaphor of the 'stain of sin' that the penitents were forced to symbolically cleanse by their work in the laundries. By staining her body with the imagery of the Sacred Heart, Coogan challenges the nationally shared iconography of this image, turning her body into what Grosz calls a 'cultural product.'[42] In Coogan's performative context the Sacred Heart loses its religious connotation, becoming a scar on the skin. The connection with the Magdalene Laundries elicits an expansion of this metaphor, where the scar is the one that the Magdalene Asylums have left on the 'skin-ego' of the Irish Catholic inheritance, to borrow Didier Anzieu's term.[43] According to this interpretation, what the *Sacred Heart* performance points to is the patriarchal nature of Catholic Ireland, while suggesting through its connection to the Laundries the unspeakable nature of female sexuality in Ireland, at least in the recent past. Tom Inglis, however, points out that, even in contemporary Ireland, 'sex and sexuality are still seen as problems rather than pleasures' and that 'there is still a double standard in Ireland,' arguing that 'sexually transgressive women are more likely to be pilloried and demonised then men who violate accepted norms.' [44]

An example of such transgression appears in Coogan's *The Fountain*.[45] Performed in 2001 at the Hebbel Theatre in Berlin and subsequently at IMMA in Dublin, Coogan's *Fountain* moves beyond the sacred/profane dichotomy in relation to the female body and draws the audience into the realm of the abject. During this performance Coogan, wearing only a black wraparound dress, walks barefoot in silence onto an unlit stage, then squats on the floor against the wall exposing her genitalia illuminated by a spotlight, as in a gynecological examination. She holds that image for few seconds and then urinates in front of the audience. By this act of urinating under the viewer's gaze while holding her genitalia, Coogan plays with notions of abjection – that which one cannot bear to look at, one cannot engage with. According to Julia Kristeva, bodily waste is one of the manifestations of the abject, of that psychical process that 'draws me toward the place where meaning collapses.'[46] The experience of the abject, then, does not produce any understanding, but resembles an abrupt encounter with something that, resisting signification, throws the individual into a wordless state of disgust and horror:

> A wound with blood and pus, or the sickly, acrid smell of sweat, of decay, does not *signify* death. ... No, as in true theatre, without makeup or masks, refuse and corpses *show me* what I permanently thrust aside in order to live. These body fluids, this defilement, this shit are what life withstands, hardly and with difficulty, on the part of death. There, I am at the border of my condition as a living being.[47]

Coogan's public urination incarnates the real physicality of the female body, opposing it to the metaphysical depiction of woman as the paradoxical asexual blurring of virgin and mother. A performance that openly displays bodily waste and female genitalia, this piece addresses the very nature of the feminine abject, which is seen as a threat to patriarchy, in its dimension of collapse of meaning, since the process of naming and symbolizing is inherently patriarchal.[48] Coogan explains that this piece was influenced both by the image of a woman pissing up against the doorway of her studio in Dublin and by the story of Ann Lovett,[49] a 15 year old who had secretly given birth to a baby boy and was found in a grotto lying at the feet of a statue of the Virgin Mary just outside the town of Granard, County Longford, on

31 January 1984. Within a few hours of the discovery, both Ann and her baby died. Kathryn Conrad relates Lovett to the larger debate around abortion, observing that these discussions 'were linked with a number of controversial cases including ... Ann Lovett's death,' and stressing that 'all of the cases concerned the tension between the private and the public and the silencing of women's voices in the discussion of women's agencies over their bodies.'[50] The connection to the Irish anti-abortion legislation reveals another scar on the 'skin-ego' of the Irish Catholic inheritance. Coogan explains:

> When I made both *The Fountain* and the *Madonna* series, it was Ann Lovett giving birth and the Virgin statue looking down upon her, witnessing it. I've never shown them together but they were conceived as companion pieces.[51]

The image of the Virgin Mother – the epitome of motherhood without sin – who witnesses the hidden pain and death of a mother and her child conceived in sin (outside wedlock) is one of the powerful metaphors at the core of Coogan's piece. It appears clear, therefore, how in *The Fountain* Coogan integrates in one action some of the legal implications and religious significations of Irish womanhood, combining them under the cipher of the abject.

Coogan further explains that another inspiration for *The Fountain* was the image of the many Sheela-na-Gig figures found in Ireland on both secular and religious buildings. 'First brought to scientific attention in the 1840s by antiquarians,' these figures are seen 'by some ... as a symbol of Irishness and by others, particularly Irish feminists'; for others 'they are a symbol of active female power.'[52] The distinctive features of Sheela-na-Gig carvings are widespread legs with hands between them, which emphasize the already enlarged genitalia. Initially 'related to the church's teaching that sinners were punished in Hell through the bodily organs by which they have offended,' these images later appeared also 'on town walls and on tower-houses ... [where] they seem to have functioned as protective carvings,' producing, therefore, an interesting shift in meaning 'from figure of lust to protective icon.'[53] Coogan's connection of *The Fountain* with Sheela-na-Gig addresses, once again, the troubling dichotomy that Freud identified in the Madonna/whore opposition. The Sheela-na-Gig in its various interpretations represents simultaneously the safeguarding Madonna and the carnal sinner.

Conclusion: an alternative image of womanhood

One of Coogan's more controversial pieces, *The Fountain* has inspired a variety of critical readings thus far. Apinian Poshyananda cites voyeurism as its core feature: 'the blue-eyed blond [Coogan] in doll-like pose releases the acidy ochre fluids from her body' as if the audience were in 'the game of water sports' where 'the girl displays the fountain of urine for the excited customers.'[54] For Kerstin Mey, *The Fountain* displays a commentary 'on (young) Irish people's "out-of-control" excessive and transgressive behaviour when out and about in the urban pub/dance/night club scene.'[55]

What the *Madonna* series and *The Fountain* embody far exceeds these simplified analyses. Identifying the voyeur as the only addressee of these performances imprisons us again within the cage of heterosexist patriarchy, where voyeurism, always gendered, is by default male. What is at stake in the performances not only involves Coogan's personal feminist critique of Irish icons and beliefs about womanhood, but also Pat O'Connor's claim that 'issues surrounding sexuality, especially abortion, are [still] highly emotive.'[56] By displaying the co-existence of the virgin/whore dichotomy on the one hand, and the uncanny performance of the feminine abject on the other, Coogan explicitly challenges patriarchal symbolization, thereby proposing a new image of womanhood. In her most recent work, the durational performance *Yellow* (2008), Coogan returns to the Magdalene Laundries for inspiration, offering an alternative, critical construction of womanhood. In this performance she straddles a galvanized bin full of soapy water, dressed in a long yellow gown.[57] She plunges the fabric between her legs into the water creating, while scrubbing, an ejaculatorily cleansing foam. By appropriating the quintessential male act – ejaculation – she cleanses the 'sins' incurred by the Magdalenes through this foam. *Yellow* exemplifies fertility with this symbol of semen cleansed of sin to foster an image that should provoke a questioning of both womanhood and manhood in contemporary Ireland.

Notes

1 Michel Foucault, *The Will to Knowledge, The History of Sexuality*, Vol. 1 (London: Penguin, 1998), 121.
2 Amanda Coogan, lecture for undergraduate drama studies students, Trinity College, Dublin, 12 February 2008.
3 Elizabeth Grosz, *Volatile Bodies: Toward a Corporeal Feminism* (Bloomington: Indiana University Press, 1994), xiii, 19.

4 *Ibid.*, 18.
5 Rebecca Schneider has coined the expression the 'explicit body' 'as a means of addressing the ways' feminist performance art 'aims to explicate bodies in social relation,' explaining that 'the words "explicit" and "explicate" stem from the Latin *explicare*, which means to "unfold."' Rebecca Schneider, *The Explicit Body in Performance* (London; New York: Routledge, 1997), 2.
6 Tom Inglis has written widely on Irish society and the problematic socio-logical and cultural nuances of Irish identity and sexuality. In 'Origins and Legacies of Irish Prudery: Sexuality and Social Control in Modern Ireland,' *Éire-Ireland: A Journal of Irish Studies*, 40 (3/4) (Fall–Winter 2005): 9–37, Inglis points out that 'the history of Irish sexuality remains a relatively hidden, secretive area' (9) and that 'the lack of research into the history of Irish sexuality ... corresponds to a general lack of interest in sexuality in Irish academia' (10).
7 According to the Organization for Economic Co-operation and Development, *Economic Surveys: Ireland*, 3 (2006), 'the gender pay gap is very wide in high status occupations: women managers and senior officials are, on average, paid 28% less than their male colleagues. The difference is also large at the other end of the spectrum in elementary occupations, where women's hourly earn-ings are 25% below men's' (113).
8 Mark Cassidy, Eric Strobl, and Robert Thornton, 'Gender Pay Differentials and Equality Legislation in the Republic of Ireland,' *Canadian Public Policy / Analyse de Politiques*, 28, Supplement 'Occupational Gender Segregation: Public Policies and Economic Forces' (May 2002), S149–59, S150.
9 *Ibid.*, S151.
10 Pat O'Connor, *Emerging Voices: Women in Contemporary Irish Society* (Dublin: Institute of Public Administration, 1998), 51.
11 *Ibid.*
12 In the Republic of Ireland abortion was declared illegal by the 1861 Offences Against the Person Act. For an engaging postcolonial reading of the legal and political aspects and consequences of the abortion debate in Ireland, see Ruth Fletcher, 'Post-colonial Fragments: Representations of Abortion in Irish Law and Politics,' *Journal of Law and Society*, 28 (4) (December 2001): 568–89.
13 The 1983 referendum brought about the 8th Amendment to the Irish Con-stitution (Article 40.3.3), which reads: 'The State acknowledges the right to life of the unborn and, with due regard to the equal right to life of the mother, guarantees to respect, and as far as practicable, by its laws to vin-dicate that right.' For an in-depth analysis of the 1983 abortion referendum, see Ursula Barry, 'Abortion in the Republic of Ireland,' *Feminist Review*, 29 (Summer 1998): 57–63. Barry notes that the 8th Amendment 'puts the right to life of a pregnant woman on equal terms with the foetus she is carrying,' adding that 'without a doubt, this is a radical redefinition of woman under the law: Irish women have been recategorised to be equal to that which is *not yet born*' (59). The 1992 referendum granted Irish women the right to travel to other countries in order to have an abortion and also allowed them access to information on abortion (13th and 14th Amendments). This referendum was a direct consequence of the so-called 'X Case' concerning a 14-year-old rape victim who was prevented by a High Court injunction from leaving Ireland to obtain an abortion in England. After an appeal to

the Supreme Court, she was permitted to travel to England and terminate her pregnancy. See Ailbhe Smyth, 'The "X" Case: Women and Abortion in the Republic of Ireland, 1992,' *Feminist Legal Studies*, 1 (2) (1993): 163–77. In 1995 the Regulation of Information (Services outside the State for Termination of Pregnancies) Act 'regulated the conditions in which it was permissible to provide abortion information' (Fletcher, 2001, 583). Finally, the 2002 referendum sought to prohibit abortion even when suicide is a health risk for the mother. This referendum was defeated.

The abortion debate in Ireland is a deeply complex matter, which has divided the country into two factions: pro-life and pro-choice; and has forced thousands of women to travel abroad each year for an abortion. For further reading about the abortion debate and issues, see *Green Paper on Abortion* (Dublin: Stationery Office, 1999); Ailbhe Smyth, ed., *The Abortion Papers* (Dublin: Attic Press, 1992); Andrew Rynne, *Abortion–The Irish Question* (Ward River Press, 1982); Michael Solomons, *Pro-life? The Irish Question* (Dublin: Lilliput Press 1992); Ruth Fletcher, 'Reproducing Irishness: Race, Gender and Abortion Law,' *Canadian Journal of Women and the Law*, 17 (2) (2005): 365–404; Siobhán Mullally, 'Debating Reproductive Rights in Ireland,' *Human Rights Quarterly*, 27 (1) (2005): 78–104.

14 O'Connor, 1998, 51.

15 Fletcher (2001), 574.

16 *Ibid.*, 573.

17 Tom Inglis, *Moral Monopoly: The Catholic Church in Modern Irish Society* (Dublin: Gill & Macmillan, 1987), 187–214, quoted in Martin McLoone, *Irish Film: The Emergence of a Contemporary Cinema* (London: British Film Institute, 2000), 22.

18 Barry Collins and Patrick Hanafin, 'Mothers, Maidens and the Myth of Origins in the Irish Constitution,' *Law and Critique* 12 (2001): 53–73, 58–9.

19 Department of the Taoiseach, *Bunreacht na hÉireann/Constitution of Ireland*, http://www.taoiseach.gov.ie/index.asp?docID=243 (accessed 23 June 2008).

20 Patrick Hanafin, 'Defying the Female: the Irish Constitutional Text as Phallocentric Manifesto,' *Textual Practice*, 11 (2) (1997): 249–73. Hanafin attempts 'to explain the conditions which favoured the adoption of a patri-archal model of motherhood in the constitutional text' (249), concluding that 'even within a changing social climate, the dominant discourse in Irish law continues to be patriarchal' (267).

21 Collins and Hanafin, 2001, 54.

22 *Ibid.*, 63.

23 Declan Kiberd, *Inventing Ireland: The Literature of the Modern Nation* (London: Jonathan Cape, 1995), 362.

24 Inglis 2005, 28. In 1990 Mary Robinson was elected President of the Republic of Ireland. The first female President in the history of the Republic, she became to a certain extent the spokeswoman of a new Irish womanhood. Molly O'Hagan Hardy argues that, although it is true that 'Article 13 of Bunreacht na hÉireann, the Irish Constitution (1937) essentially limits the function of the president to that of a figurehead or symbol,' Robinson none-theless fought to decriminalize contraception, to reform the abortion law, and to remove the constitutional prohibition on divorce. See Molly O'Hagan Hardy, 'Symbolic Power: Mary Robinson's Presidency and Eavan Boland's

Poetry,' *New Hibernia Review*, 12 (3) (Autumn 2008): 47–65, particularly 57–60.

25 Inglis, 2005, 29. Inglis refers to women such as Annie Murphy, Ann Lovett, Eileen Flynn, and Joanne Hayes. Annie Murphy was an American who had an affair with the Bishop of Galway, Eamon Casey, and had a baby boy with him. Ann Lovett was a 14-year-old girl who became pregnant and died in childbirth. Eileen Flynn lost her job as a school teacher after having an affair and a child with a married man. Joanne Hayes had an affair with a married man and was involved in 'the case of the Kerry babies.' See also Tom Inglis, 'Sexual Transgression and Scapegoats: A Case Study from Modern Ireland,' in *Sexualities*, 5 (1) (2002): 5–24.

26 Sigmund Freud, 'On the Universal Tendency to Debasement in the Sphere of Love (Contributions to the Psychology of Love II),' in *The Standard Edition of the Complete Psychological Works of Sigmund Freud*, Volume XI (London: Vintage, 2001 [1912]), 179–90, 183.

27 *Ibid.* (emphasis in original).

28 See, for example, Richard Kearney, *Postnationalist Ireland: Politics, Literature, Philosophy* (London: Routledge, 1997); Liam O'Dowd, 'Church, State and Women: The Aftermath of Partition,' in *Gender in Irish Society*, eds. Chris Curtin, Pauline Jackson, and Barbara O'Connor (Galway: Galway University Press, 1987), 3–36; Gerardine Meaney, *Sex and Nation: Women in Irish Culture and Politics* (Dublin: Attic Press, 1991); Siobhán Kilfeather, 'Irish Feminism,' in *The Cambridge Companion to Modern Irish Culture*, eds. Joe Cleary and Clair Connolly (Cambridge: Cambridge University Press, 2005), 96–116.

29 Founded at the beginning of the eighteenth century, the Magdalene Laundries, also called Magdalene Asylums, were opened in response to increasing worries regarding prostitution, venereal diseases, and the moral health of the country. See Frances Finnegan, *Do Penance or Perish: Magdalene Asylums in Ireland* (Oxford: Oxford University Press, 2001); Leanne McCormick, 'Sinister Sisters? The Portrayal of Ireland's Magdalene Asylums in Popular Culture,' *Cultural and Social History* 3 (3) (2005): 373–9; Dympna McLoughlin, 'Women and Sexuality in Nineteenth-Century Ireland,' *Irish Journal of Psychology*, 15 (2) (1994): 266–75; Eric Trudgill, *Madonna and Magdalens: the Origins and Development of Victorian Sexual Attitudes* (New York: Holmes & Meier, 1976); James M. Smith, *Ireland's Magdalen Laundries and the Nation's Architecture of Containment* (Manchester: Manchester University Press, 2008). It is believed that the last Magdalene Laundry was closed in October 1996. See Gary Culliton, 'Last Days of a Laundry,' *Irish Times*, 25 September 1996, http://www.ireland.com/newspaper/features/1996/0925/96092500093.html (accessed 23 June 2008).

30 Elizabeth Grosz, *Jacques Lacan: A Feminist Introduction* (London: Routledge, 1990), 129.

31 Freud, 2001, 183.

32 Amanda Coogan, 'Madonna in Blue 2001,' http://www.amandacoogan.com/IMAGES/2002/ webpg_02/Madonna_inBlue.htm (accessed 23 June 2008).

33 Amanda Coogan, lecture, 12 February 2008.

34 Amanda Coogan interviewed by Mike Fitzpatrick, 'Through My Eyes and My Body,' in *Amanda Coogan: Profile 21*, ed. John O'Regan (Limerick: Gandon Editions, 2005), 15–19, 18.

35 Coogan quoted in *ibid.*, 18.

36 Amanda Coogan, interview with author, Dublin, March 2008.

37 For details about the religious state of Ireland in the eighteenth and nineteenth centuries and the first Irish convent of Sacred Heart nuns, see Nigel Yates, *The Religious Condition of Ireland, 1770–1850* (Oxford: Oxford University Press, 2006).

38 Amanda Coogan, interview with author.

39 Reminiscences of Dante Alighieri's *The Divine Comedy* spontaneously arise. In the Magdalene Asylums Dante's principle of the 'law of retaliation' (*la legge del contrappasso*) is actualized according to which in hell and purgatory the penance is analogous and antithetical to the committed sin. As the women in the Magdalene Asylums were marked by the stain of supposed carnal sins, they were forced by the nuns to clean stained bed-linen in the Laundries for the rest of their lives.

40 Kathie O'Beirne survived her imprisonment in the Magdalene asylums. In her biography she recalls that 'the nuns considered the Maggies, as the girls were known, to be literally the scum of the earth, sinners who would never earn redemption.' Kathy O'Beirne, *Kathy's Story: A Childhood Hell Inside the Magdalen Laundries* (Edinburgh: Mainstream, 2005), 116.

41 Stewart R. Clegg, David Courpasson, and Nelson Phillips, *Power and Organizations* (London: Sage, 2006), 167. See also the documentary *Sex in a Cold Climate* (1998) by the English filmmaker Steve Humphries, which inspired the award-winning Peter Mullan's film *The Magdalene Sisters* (2002).

42 Grosz, 1990, 24.

43 See Didier Anzieu, *The Skin Ego* (New Haven, CT: Yale University Press, 1989).

44 Inglis, 2005, 33.

45 Artistic sources for *The Fountain*, apart from Marcel Duchamp's *Fountain* (1917), include Andy Warhol's *Piss Painting* (1961), Bruce Nauman's *Fountain* (1965), Robert Mapplethorpe's *Jim and Tom, Sausalito* (1977), Andy Warhol's *Oxidation Painting* (1977), Pierre et Gilles' *Le Petite Jardinier* (1980s), Andres Serrano's *Piss Christ* (1987), Gilbert & George's *Urinight* (1987) and *Friendship Pissing* (1989), Larry Clark's *Untitled* (1992), and Tony Tasset's *I Peed in My Pants* (1994).

46 Julia Kristeva, *Powers of Horror* (New York: Columbia University Press, 1982), 2.

47 *Ibid.*, 3 (emphasis in original).

48 'It is in the *name of the father* that we must recognise the support of the symbolic function which, from the dawn of history, has identified his person with the figure of the law' (Jacques Lacan, *Écrits: A Selection* [London and New York: Routledge, 2001], 74, emphasis in original).

49 Coogan, quoted in Fitzpatrick, 2005, 17.

50 Kathryn Conrad, 'Fetal Ireland: National Bodies and Political Agencies,' in *Éire-Ireland: a Journal of Irish Studies* (Fall–Winter 2001): 153–73, 162. For further reading on Ann Lovett's case, see Nell McCafferty, 'The Death of Ann Lovett,' in *The Abortion Papers, Ireland*, ed. Ailbhe Smyth (Dublin: Attic Press, 1992), 99–106; Moira J. Maguire, 'The Changing Face of Catholic Ireland: Conservatism and Liberalism in the Ann Lovett and Kerry Babies Scandals,' *Feminist Studies*, 27, 2 (Summer 2001): 335–58.

51 Coogan, quoted in Fitzpatrick, 2005, 17–18.
52 Eamonn P. Kelly, *Sheela-na-Gigs. Origins and Functions* (Dublin: Country House and The National Museum of Ireland, 1996), 5.
53 Brian Lalor, *The Encyclopaedia of Ireland* (Dublin: Gill & Macmillan, 2003), 984–5.
54 Apinan Poshyananda, 'The Celtic Slant,' in *Amanda Coogan. Profile 21*, ed. John O'Regan (Limerick: Gandon Editions, 2005), 11–13, 12.
55 Kerstin Mey, *Art and Obscenity* (London: I.B. Tauris, 2007), 32.
56 O'Connor, 1987, 1.
57 Yellow is the colour of the mimosa, the flower that symbolizes Women's Day.

15
Homelysexuality and the 'Beauty' Pageant

Fintan Walsh

> By choosing an individual whose deportment, appearance, and style embodies the values and goals of a nation, locality, or group, beauty contests expose these same values and goals to interpretation and challenge.[1]

The beauty pageant typically rewards females for a public expression of gender and sexuality, and for this reason it must always be understood as a performance. Rooted in the ritualistic presentation of girls to society, the pageant has appeared in a variety of modes and milieus throughout its history. Given its particular cultural function, it is no surprise that the form has consistently divided opinion. Heightened competitiveness has split critics into those who champion its celebration of embodied femininity and those who denounce its objectification of women. Viewed suspiciously from this latter perspective, there is little room for originality, individuality, or any kind of subjective agency where participants must ultimately operate as local, national, and global currencies of exchange.

In recent years the increasingly mediatized pageant has courted international controversy. While the two most famous competitions, *Miss World* and *Miss Universe*, have continued seemingly to automatize their entrants into fantasy sex objects who love children and want to save the world, the murder of child beauty queen JonBenét Ramsey in 1996 confirmed widespread fears that pageants dangerously promote the sexualization of young girls. Ever since 2002, however, when riots broke out at *Miss World* in Nigeria following a newspaper's suggestion that the Prophet Muhammad, were he still alive, would likely take a contestant as his wife, the political dimension to these performances could no longer be ignored.[2] Beauty pageants have since emerged as highly contentious cultural phenomena where social norms are produced, challenged, and reified – events through which lives are lived and lost.

It should come as no surprise to those familiar with postcolonial patterns of representation that public figurations of women might be especially divisive. In the context of Irish culture, the category 'woman' has long constituted a charged locus of political struggle. Less familiar, perhaps, is the unwritten account of how the ever-mutative Cathleen Ni Houlihan became an actual beauty queen. This article considers this symbolic shift by assessing the role played by popular pageants such as *The Rose of Tralee*, *The Calor Housewife of the Year*, and *Miss Ireland* in the contestation, reification, and commodification of these standards at local, global, and diasporic levels. In particular, it analyzes how these pageants have participated in the production of what I refer to as 'homelysexuality': a domesticated, marketable, and commercially profitable sexual accent, paradoxically devoid of eroticism, but integral to the brand concept 'Irishness.' In contrast to these establishment events, this chapter considers how the emergence of queer pageants, such as *The Alternative Miss Ireland* and *Mr Gay Ireland*, work to debilitate heteronormative constructions of femininity and masculinity by subverting, disidentifying with, and pornographically imploding idealized prescriptions of gender and sexuality in a manner that challenges traditionally appropriated versions of Irish identity, including the representational schema through which those identities are produced and regulated.

Sexuality and the public domain

While concerns over embodied sexuality are not exclusive to Irish culture, the uniquely powerful presence of nationalism and Catholicism throughout the twentieth century heightened tensions surrounding public expressions of gender and sexuality, giving rise to what Cheryl Herr has referred to as the stilled, desomatized 'erotics of Irishness.'[3] While Irish manhood may have been cursed by impotency within a colonial imaginary, Irish womanhood was shaped by restrictive norms measured against the Virgin Mary, Mother Ireland, and Eamon de Valera's fantasy of happy maidens.[4] Within this climate of libidinal redirection, sexuality was inadvertently deemed to be a highly political affair. But even as these sublimated drives mobilized local and national affairs, sexuality's uninhibited bodily celebration was largely considered to be in breach of the social, political, and moral conventions that – ever since W. B. Yeats's heroic hallucinations – presumed the Irish to be a prized race of exceptionally high values.

It was not until Ireland opened its borders to international invest-
ment, the free market, and economic expansion that personal identity
politics received any detailed consideration within wider cultural debates.
The abandonment of protectionist policies under the First Programme
of Economic Expansion (1958–63) inevitably required a rethinking of
nationalism's homogenizing tendency and a revaluation of the individual's relationship to the material market, and not just the symbolic
nation. While civil liberties were not quite prioritized, the possibility of
an individual occupying numerous subject positions presented great
economic potential which allowed for the cultivation of Irish identity
in more commercially profitable ways. For the most part, it fell to
'woman' to stand in as a symbol of the capitalizing nation in an international context and enact identity as an economy of exchange.[5]
While Beverly Stoeltje has argued that the beauty pageant typically
replicates a ritual form that creates the context for the formal introduction of young women to their community, state, or nation,'[6] in
Ireland it became a powerful medium through which notions of
national identity were played out, and womanhood negotiated a life
outside introspective republican rhetoric through cultivating diasporic
connections, nurturing a nascent tourist industry, and gestating profitable Irishness.

Picking roses, cultivating homelysexuality

It is against this commercializing backdrop that Ireland's most famous
pageant, the *Rose of Tralee* (1959–), developed. The competition began
when a group of Tralee businessmen met to consider ways of promoting tourism in the area. Under the guidance of Dan Nolan, then managing director of the *Kerryman* newspaper, the *Rose of Tralee* was born.
While the first event cost only IR £750 to produce, and was open
to young, unmarried, childless women native to Tralee, it fulfilled its
commercial objective by hosting contestants and their families from
places such as Dublin, London, Birmingham, and New York. By 1965,
the budget had risen to IR £10,000, and the organizers soon realized
that opening the competition to women of 'Irish birth and ancestry'
would set the growing event in a more lucrative direction. In 1970, as
the country celebrated Dana's victory at the *Eurovision Song Contest*, the
Rose of Tralee began marketing itself as the *Rose of Tralee International
Festival*.

  Since its inception, and throughout its rapid festivalization and
internationalization, the *Rose of Tralee* has resisted associations with

other beauty pageant formats. Organized around regional and national heats, it is expressly committed to celebrating 'Irishness,' and the genetically suggestive 'inner' beauty of its national and diasporic entrants: 'The *Rose of Tralee International Festival* celebrates modern young women in terms of their aspirations, ambitions, intellect, social responsibility, and Irish heritage.'[7] The competition derives this guiding criterion from a song by William Mulchinock, a wealthy nineteenth-century Protestant merchant said to have penned 'The Rose of Tralee' to describe his love for an impoverished Catholic girl who died of tuberculosis. The influential refrain runs:

Though lovely and fair as the Rose of the summer,
Yet 'twas not her beauty alone that won me;
Oh no, 'twas the truth in her eyes ever dawning
That made me love Mary, the Rose of Tralee.

That Irish culture would take a story that reeks of Ascendancy fetishism and spin it to its own advantage is not an entirely new concept. The drama of Dion Boucicault, for example, is replete with similar invention. That the fetish would be turned into a highly marketable brand of colleenism is a more recent phenomenon, which originally found much of its impetus in the depiction of Mary Kate Danaher in *The Quiet Man* (1952),[8] and has since been supported by a wider system of representation and production. As Ireland's expansion continued through the Celtic Tiger years, that the truth in Mary's eyes had possibly more to do with hunger, disease, or incipient death than unrequited love or Celtic purity became increasingly irrelevant to the festival's more pressing economic agenda.

When truth resides in the eyes, there is no need for daywear, eveningwear, or swimwear sections. Instead, the *Rose of Tralee* values attributes such as a socially committed job, the gift of the gab, and a talent for Irish dancing, traditional music, or poetry. In contrast to the dominant pageant format that champions an overt sexual display, the *Rose of Tralee* honors the ability to conceal and temper sexuality in the hope that the winner will be a fitting ambassador for Ireland as she travels around the world fulfilling various duties during her tenure. Under the international spotlight and the inevitable pressures of liberalization, the *Rose of Tralee* responded to the cultural contradiction of sexualized Irish womanhood by domesticating it.

In 'Unhomley Stages: Women Taking (a) Place in Irish Theatre,' Anna McMullan observes how women have often been associated with the concept of home in Irish culture, whether linked to Mother Ireland or to the family sphere. However, with reference to theater in particular, she emphasizes that home never seems to be a place, but 'a past memory or a future possibility.'[9] I suggest that in the *Rose of Tralee* these anxieties of displacement are engaged through the performative production of homelysexuality: not a place, or even a stable subject position, but rather the default aestheticization of female sexuality designed to match nostalgic perceptions of Irish cultural experience. For Irish womanhood to take on the new role of figuring the nation toward commercial success, albeit in the name of some sense of diasporic celebration, it was important to perpetuate the myth of premodern innocence by appearing utterly homelysexual: safe as houses, functional, and ultimately lucrative.

While the *Rose of Tralee* remains committed to the validation and production of female homelysexuality, between 2002 and 2004 the festival was hampered by poor finance and, more seriously, an identity crisis. This problem did not just concern the avuncular shift (replacing long-standing hosts Gay Byrne, Derek Davis, and Marty Whelan with the younger Ryan Tubridy and Ray D'Arcy); the venue (attaching the iconic Dome marquee to the back of the Brandon Hotel to save on security, catering, and bar expenditure); or the festival's general organization (downscaling the Rose committee of 56 volunteers upon the appointment of Anthony O'Gara as managing director in 2003). Rather, these concerns can be seen as symptomatic of what was a larger problem intimately tied to its conception of Irish womanhood against the backdrop of an economic boom.

In 2002 the *Rose of Tralee* had its first major brush with 'the real' of contemporary women's experiences. In December of that year, reigning Sligo-born, Italian Rose Tamara Gervasoni was arrested for shoplifting in Longford. Soon after, Gervasoni admitted that she suffered from anorexia and bulimia, and did not know what she was doing at the time. While the incident attracted an abundance of media attention and threatened to sully the festival's image for good, Gervasoni's commitment to seek professional help kept sensationalism at bay, while simultaneously inviting national debate about the impact of certain representations of females in the public sphere.

In *Beauty Queens on the Global Stage*, Colleen Ballerino Cohen and Richard Wilk impress that 'The idealized femininity put on stage in beauty contests is often closely associated with broader concepts such as morality, or with larger social entities such as the "nation."'[10] These connections resonate strongly in the development of the Gervasoni incident. In an effort to resolve the case, the festival's executive direc-tor Siobhán Hanley announced: 'The Rose of Tralee is not a beauty contest. Tamara won for her personality and her Irishness, and we feel she is a great ambassador for the festival and for Ireland.'[11] While this comment seemingly absolved Gervasoni, it also compounded the fest-ival's homelysexualization of female identity. The organization's pos-ition reflected a refusal to consider the impact of the idealization of certain forms of femininity on real lives, while distancing itself from the hint of female hysteria by desexualizing and disembodying its contestants, emphasizing the Rose's primary symbolic function as a figurehead of Irishness. This resolution received official backing when President McAleese stepped forward to assert that the festival was unlike others around the world which, 'despite growing international distaste, exploit rather than celebrate femininity.'[12]

Domesticating wives and mothers

While the *Rose of Tralee* was seminal in parading domicile femininity, its spirit has found fullest expression in *Calor Housewife of the Year*. From 1968 through the mid-1990s, Irish housewives competed in this pageant on the basis of their cookery, nurturing, and general house-hold management skills. For the final event, televised by RTÉ, con-testants were shadowed by a camera crew in their homes as they performed housework and prepared family meals. While the demo-graphic of entrants did not match a typical beauty pageant profile, and was largely considered by the nation to be a '*Rose of Tralee* for Mammies,'[13] the event drew on this format by assessing contestants on particular skills as well as personal attributes.

Formal beauty pageant or not, the *Housewife of the Year* also parti-cipated in the production and celebration of containable sexuality. In the spirit of de Valera's constitutional rhetoric, the competition rein-forced the relationship between woman, mother, and home, giving credence to the culturally embedded notion that there was, in fact, something special about the Irish Mammy. While the event publicly acknowledged the long-undervalued work of women, the pitting of so-called 'housewives' against each other in public and on national television must also be understood in light of the rigorous disciplining of female gender and sexuality. Everything about the contest – from the sponsorship, to the entry requirements, to the tasks and prize (a home-heating system) – cultivated as it awarded the homely-sexuality of the Irish female. That Gay Byrne, the *Rose of Tralee*'s front man, hosted the event only affirmed its position within this particular genealogy.

When questions arose over the political correctness of competition, the *Housewife of the Year* was to be renamed *Homemaker of the Year*. While this was determined to reflect the fact that Irish women were no longer 'only' housewives, but increasingly worked inside and outside the home, the event never managed to bridge the twenty-first century. While the international scope and financial backing of the *Rose of Tralee* has enabled the festival to manage identity crises such as the Gervasoni incident, the *Housewife of the Year*'s focus on any kind of homemaking enterprise was severely challenged in the 1990s when the country was awash with broken marriages, single mothers, and growing support for divorce and abortion legalization. Of course, the inability of the competition to adapt is only a measure of the degree to which it idealized Irish womanhood.

Sex, scandal, and commercialism

While the *Rose of Tralee* and the *Calor Housewife of the Year* deserve special consideration for their pioneering work in fashioning oven-baked fantasies of woman into a commercially profitable concept, other pageants have performed Irishness through the matrix of gender and sexual performativity in much more fluid terms. Of those considered here, *Miss Ireland* is the longest-running, beginning in Belfast in 1949. Eric Morely, an Englishman, first organized the event with the intention of improving the declining standards of dress in local dancehalls. By the time Morley established *Miss World* in 1951, under the auspices of Mecca entertainment group, the event had become a major corporate enterprise.

Funded by an entertainment entrepreneur with vested interests in dancing and gambling, *Miss Ireland*, and the *Miss World* of which it was a subsidiary of sorts, has always been a much more glamorous affair than other pageants, drawing contestants who typically move in modeling, fashion, and socialite circles. This trend was initially influenced by its relationship to British culture, and it was not until 1980 that the competition interwove with the new energy of the modernizing Republic. It was in that year that South African Krish Naidoo took charge of the *Miss Ireland* pageant as a marketing extension to his nightclub Rumours at the Gresham Hotel, Dublin. Under Naidoo's direction, the first winner of the competition was Michelle Rocca (*Miss Ireland* 1980) who became one of the country's first famous international models and media personalities.

Although Rocca's high visibility in the late 1980s was not exceptional, it can be readily understood within the context of a general
erosion of public/private divides and moral and political liberalization.
For many, the model – and the social milieu of which she was seen to
be a part – signified the vulgar anglicization and tabloidization of Irish
culture. With its international focus (different from the *Rose of Tralee*
in so far as contestants hoped to advance to *Miss World*), *Miss Ireland*
always aspired to a more cosmopolitan than local appeal, and the
tempering of sexuality was neither fostered nor especially valued.
Miss Ireland has always been less committed to domestic affairs *per se*,
in respect of home, nation, and sexual accent, although this status has
not developed without complication.

This uneasy relationship became particularly evident in the 1990s
when Rocca took her husband Cathal Ryan (co-founder of Ryanair) to
court for domestic violence. He was eventually found guilty of beating
Rocca, after she discovered him having an affair, but not before issues
surrounding female propriety were aired in court and in the press.
Much of Ryan's personal defense centered on his assertion that the
woman he was having an affair with was a 'lady,' unlike Rocca, who
attacked him when she found out and wore, according to her husband,
'provocative clothes.' He appealed to the jury and country that Rocca
was effectively an unhomely woman who could not be successfully
contained. The suggestion was not lost on the judge, who advised the
jury that if they believed Rocca to be 'the authoress of her own mis-
fortune,' they should reduce Ryan's damages. In so doing, the judge
gave substance to the media's coinage 'The Rocca Trial,' by suggesting
that Rocca was somehow to blame.

The *Irish Times* went so far as to compare the couple to Ireland's
version of British aristocracy, wryly proffering: 'Our gentry are cele-
brities … former Miss Irelands and high flying businessmen.'[14] Noting
the event to be significant for the public circulation of issues surrounding gender and sexuality, the *Irish Times* reported the trial to be 'A
morality tale for our times. A case study of male violence and society's
responses to it. A media blitz.'[15] Further, it suggested that the real
battles were being fought 'in the bedrooms of the nation,'[16] in a discursive move that marked the case as a turning point in the demo-
cratization of Irish society in terms of its public treatment of gender,
sexuality, and power.

Since then, the association between *Miss Ireland* contestants and
an overtly performed sexuality has strengthened. In addition to Rocca,
contestants Siobhán McClafferty (*Miss World* runner-up 1990), Amanda

Brunker (*Miss Ireland* 1991), Pamela Flood (*Miss Ireland* 1993), and Andrea Roche (1997) went on to establish successful modeling careers and with high media profiles. It was not until 2003, however, when the franchise was taken over by Mags Humphries of Assets Model Agency and Andrea Roche that *Miss Ireland* concretized its relationship to the growing modeling and media industries in Ireland. In the same year, Rosanna Davidson (daughter of singer Chris de Burg) won *Miss World* and, from then on, winners would all be associated with the Assets franchise and Ireland's new, seemingly wealthy, social elites.

From homely to homo: the *unheimlich* shift

In contrast to the established forms discussed, the *Alternative Miss Ireland* is a queer beauty pageant which radically disidentifies with prevailing homelysexual and commodified figurations of woman as part of a wider disarticulation of normative gender and sexuality. It invites us to think not only about homelysexuality but its recalcitrant, *unheimlich* relative, homosexuality.[17] Emerging at the intersection of local and global gay culture, the pageant was initially inspired by Andrew Logan's *Alternative Miss World* and first produced by Frank Stanley, Ross Elliot Tallon, and Niall Sweeney in Sides nightclub, Dublin in 1987. After the first year, it did not take place again until 1996 (three years after homosexuality was decriminalized), when it moved to the Olympia Theatre to raise much needed finance for AIDS charities.

In its 15-year run the *Alternative Miss Ireland* has emerged as one of the largest events in Ireland's queer calendar. In addition to raising money, the pageant's cultural objective is to disturb the homogeneity of international beauty pageants, especially Ireland's *Rose of Tralee* and *Miss Ireland* competitions by 'Transgressing Beauty and Inventing New Desires.'[18] Men and women of all sexualities may compete; the only requirement is that performances must be fueled by a queer energy. Accordingly, the title 'Queen of Ireland' – bestowed with the placing of 'The Medusa Crown of Shamrocks' on the winner's head – shapes the event with an anti-masculinist spirit while perverting deep-rooted traditions that served different types of 'Queens,' including Our Lady and Cathleen. Routinely taking place on the Sunday before St Patrick's Day, the pageant firmly positions itself in a subversive relationship to all things considered normatively 'Irish.'[19] Many of the competition's winners, such as Shirley Temple Bar (1997), Veda Beaux Rêves (1999), and Heidi Konnt (2005), have subsequently led careers as established queer performers. In recent years, the pageant has developed a more international profile, spawning the *Alternative Miss Philippines* (2002), a feeder competition for the show.

Despite the event's radical agenda, one of the factors crucial to success is its ability to key into the homelysexual code of other pageants. If Gay Byrne set the avuncular tone for the *Rose of Tralee* and the *Calor Housewife of the Year*, long-time host and producer Panti (Rory O'Neill) sets the maternal tone for *Alternative Miss Ireland*. A mainstay of the Irish queer performance scene, the persona of the cross-dressed, self-styled 'gender illusionist' is modeled on a mid-Atlantic aunt that reminds us of the Irish immigrant returned home, and the varied diasporic networks from which she fictively came. But those familiar with Panti's earlier career also know about the controversial clubs she ran in the 1990s, such as GAG and Powder Bubble, which regularly featured obscene dialogue, pornographic displays, and live sex acts. Ultimately, the success and power of Panti and *Alternative Miss Ireland* stem from the work described by Eve Kosofsky Sedgwick as periperformative critique and affective reparation: not only does Panti enact a tempered femininity (unusual given drag's hyperbolic

Figure 6   Miss Panti with competitors at the Alternative Miss Ireland, Olympia Theatre, Dublin, 2007. Courtesy Fintan Walsh.

tendency) that indexes homelysexuality, she shatters that self-same system of construction through ribald camp and pornographic terrorism.[20] Panti hystericizes the maternal fantasy to deprive it of its more insidious agency.

In recent years this queer initiative has found extension in the *Mr Gay Ireland* competition. Organized by the Dublin International Gay Theatre Festival since 2003, the contest selects one winner to possibly enter the *Mister Gay* World competition, while raising money for designated AIDS charities. While we might map the interest in Irish male sexuality from the 1960s onwards along coordinates that include show bands (Dickie Rock, Joe Dolan), boy bands (Boyzone, Westlife), and Hollywood film stars (Colin Farrell and Jonathan Rhys Myers), *Mister Gay Ireland* is the first public event of its kind to celebrate gay sexuality through the pageant form. While the contest might generate good feeling among the gay community and go some way through its own recusant carnality to eroticize sexuality more generally (through dialoguing with female beauty pageants, if not actually representing females), it always runs the risk of commodifying homosexuality or playing it as cosmopolitan affect. This became most apparent in 2007–8 when the event attracted significant media attention after it was won by a member of the Irish Gay Rugby Team, the Emerald Warriors, during the year Dublin was hosting the Bingham Cup (Gay Rugby World Cup) for the first time; the apparent contradiction was too sensational to ignore. In 2009, *Mr Gay World* was won for the first time by the Irish entrant, Max Krzyzanowski.

The queen is dead, long live the queer

While the beauty pageant developed from the induction of females to social life, since the 1960s Irish pageants have been motivated by the more ambitious desire to launch Ireland onto the international economic stage. Interrogating the popular notion that pageants openly stage sexuality, this chapter has considered how the Irish pageant has regulated the production of a female sexual accent in particular, emptied of depth, eroticism, or even what might be understood as subjectivity. While I have focused on the most significant and successful competitions invested in the reification and contestation of homelysexuality, it is worth noting how other pageants for women (*Mary from Dungloe International Festival*; *Miss Macra*) and men (*Ballybunion International Bachelor Festival*; *The Mullingar Guinness International Bachelor*

Contest) continue to appropriate gender and sexuality through the festivalization of the forms in commercially profitable ways. In 2007 the
Association of Irish Festival Events reported that these festivals combined
would generate €300 million for the economy in that year, and were
critical to sustaining the Irish cultural tourism product.[21]

Interestingly, following accusations of prejudice and claims that the
event was outdated, the 49-year-old *Rose of Tralee* announced in 2008
that mothers would be allowed to enter the competition for the first
time, while still maintaining the ban on married women and women
over 28 years of age. Further, the country's first *Miss University Competition* (also organized by Assets, who award the winner with a modeling contract and a pass to *Miss Ireland*) was launched to controversial
reception. Much of this response centered on protests to the *Miss UCD*
heat on the institution's Belfield campus, where staff and students
objected to the competition's ban on mothers, wives, the disabled, and
entrants under 5 ft 4 in. Professor of Equality Studies Kathleen Lynch
spoke out: 'It is not the job of a university to promote an event like
this ... I feel it is bringing us back to the 1950s where women are evaluated on the basis of appearance.'[22] What both these instances expose
is an unrelenting tension in contemporary Ireland between the desire
to harness the commercial value of 'woman' as signifier on the international stage and the need to guard the domestic worth of that same
figure. While studies of gender and sexuality in Irish culture have typically involved the intersection of postcolonial theory and Irish literature,
the appropriation of gender, and especially sexuality, for economic gain
within the beauty pageant form invites further consideration of the manifold ways in which Irish culture, past and present, does not simply
repress sexuality as dominant critical narratives maintain, but willfully
harnesses, manipulates, and exploits it to perform itself and its others.

Notes

1 Colleen Ballerino Cohen, and Richard Wilk, with Beverly Stoeltje, 'Introduction: Beauty Queens on the Global Stage,' in *Beauty Queens on the Global
   Stage: Gender, Contests, and Power*, eds. Colleen Ballerino Cohen, Richard Wilk,
   and Beverly Stoeltje (London: Routledge, 1996), 1–12, 2.
2 See 'Nigeria Riots Spread to Capital,' BBC News online, http://news.bbc.co.uk/
   2/ hi/africa/2501893.stm (accessed 27 June 2008).
3 Cheryl Herr, 'The Erotics of Irishness,' *Critical Inquiry* 17 (1) (Autumn 1990):
   1–34.
4 Eamon de Valera's speech of 1943 imagines 'happy maidens' in his vision
   of Ireland. See RTÉ Libraries and Archives at http://www.rte.ie/laweb/ll/
   ll_t09b.html (accessed 7 July 2008).

5 It is important to note that women were not entirely banished from the public sphere prior to this period. Melissa Sihra's *Women in Irish Drama: A Century of Authorship and Representation* (Basingstoke: Palgrave Macmillan, 2007) uncovers the vast contributions of women throughout the twentieth century, while Paige Reynolds's *Modernism, Drama, and the Audience of Irish Spectacle* (Cambridge: Cambridge University Press, 2007) explores how suffragette pageantry and consumer culture afforded women access to more fluid subject positions (90).

6 Beverly Stoeltje, 'The Snake Charmer: Ritual, Competition, and Signification in American Festival,' in Colleen Ballerino Cohen, Richard Wilk, and Beverly Stoeltje, eds., 1996, 13–30, 26.

7 'How to Become a Rose,' Rose of Tralee International Festival website, http://www.roseoftralee.ie/catalog/roses.php/cPath/1_76 (accessed 9 July 2008).

8 *The Quiet Man*, dir. John Ford, produced by Argosy Pictures, 1952.

9 Anna McMullan, 'Unhomely Stages: Women Taking (a) Place in Irish Theatre,' in *Druids, Dudes and Beauty Queens*, ed. Dermot Bolger (Dublin: New Island, 2001), 72–90, 73.

10 Ballerino Cohen and Wilk, 1996, 3.

11 Quoted in Róisín Ingle, 'Rose Resumes Engagements after Battle with Bulimia,' *Irish Times*, 13 March 2003.

12 Róisín Ingle, 'Thorny Year,' *Irish Times*, 14 August 2004.

13 Mary Cummins, 'The Changing Face of Gay,' *Irish Times*, 6 April 1995.

14 Áine McCarthy, 'Rocca Trial Had More to Do with Power than Gossip,' *Irish Times*, 15 February 1997.

15 *Ibid.*

16 *Ibid.*

17 Freud describes the uncanny as the familiar turned strange. He builds his argument by discussing encounters with the homely (*heimlich*) and the unhomely (*unheimlich*). In the present context I suggest that homosexuality might be imagined as the uncanny double of the dominant homelysexuality: 'familiar' in etymology and tendency toward 'sameness'; 'strange' in symbolic significance. See Sigmund Freud, 'The Uncanny,' in *Studies in Parapsychology*, trans. Alix Strachey (New York: Macmillan, 1963), 19–60.

18 *Alternative Miss Ireland*, http://www.alternativemissireland.com (accessed 7 July 2008).

19 This conflict between Irishness and homosexuality came to the fore in 1992 when the Irish Lesbian and Gay Organization was banned from participating in the New York City Patrick's Day Parade by the Ancient Order of Hibernians. New York City's Commission on Human Rights upheld the ban, claiming sponsors had a First Amendment right to discriminate because of the parade's 'Irish and Roman Catholic' nature.

20 Eve Kosofsky Sedgwick, 'Paranoid Reading and Reparative Reading. Or, You're So Paranoid, You Probably Think this Essay Is about You,' in *Touching Feeling: Affect, Pedagogy, Performativity* (Durham, NC: Duke University Press, 2003), 123–51. I would also like to acknowledge Anne Mulhall's discussion of the Alternative Miss Ireland in her analysis of 'camp' and 'kitch' in Irish culture in 'Camping up the Emerald Aisle: Queerness in Irish Popular Culture,' in *Irish*

Postmodernisms and Popular Culture, eds. Wanda Balzano, Anne Mulhall, and Moynagh Sullivan (Basingstoke: Palgrave Macmillan, 2007).

21　In the *Irish Times* (5 April 2007) journalist Fiona Gartland reported on the Association of Irish Festival Events announcement that festivals around country were expected to earn €300 million for economy in the coming year.

22　Quoted in Genevieve Carbery, 'Protest at UCD Beauty Competition,' *Irish Times,* 16 April 2008.

Part V

Diaspora, Migration, and Globalization

16
Taking Northern Irish Identity on the Road: The Smithsonian Folklife Festival of 2007

E. Moore Quinn

A people who have known resistance as well as dissent, rebellion, dispute, religious enthusiasm in the midst of rural and urban deprivation, have an interesting story to tell of themselves – one of essential homelessness, dependency, anxiety, obdurate fantasizing, sacrifices in the name of liberty, villainous political opportunism, moments of idealistic aspiration. And in the telling of it, they may come to realize at least where they are most at home and with whom they share that home.[1]

Introduction

In the two weeks surrounding the July 4th holiday, the Smithsonian Folklife Festival is held annually on the National Mall in Washington, DC. Organized as an exhibition to increase and diffuse knowledge about grassroots culture, the event attracts considerable media attention. Focusing on 'living cultural heritage from across the United States and around the world,' it works to energize the 'efforts of featured tradition bearers and organizations to continue their own research, education, cultural conservation and advocacy' in their locales.[2] With motivations like these, it is clear that the Smithsonian sees culture as vibrant and viable, full of the 'pushes and pulls' that enable it to exist with richness and color. However, other agendas come into play in the actual 'performance' of culture, and those enacting it on the international stage may have particular reasons for representing it through lenses that do not necessarily tell 'the whole story.'

A case in point was the Smithsonian's 41st anniversary of its Folklife Festival in 2007 when the distinctive culture of Northern Ireland was presented via exhibits, lectures, ballad performances, food and crafts displays, concerts, lectures, and other events.[3] Performers included musicians, storytellers, and Northern Irish craftswomen and men gathered to display and discuss their trades and ways of life. The ostensible purposes of presenting Northern Ireland were informative, entertaining, and educational; organizers sought to resolve for the general public some of the mysteries and apprehensions surrounding it. To those ends, and to encourage the many tourist efforts currently underway in Northern Ireland,[4] promotional brochures and other paraphernalia were distributed free of charge; CDs extolling Northern Ireland's landscape and heritage were also available at many public venues.

This chapter has a number of aims. First, it utilizes Arnold van Gennep's theory of the liminal to explore current expressions of ambivalent selfhood in Northern Ireland that have resulted from rapid economic, political, and social change. Second, it argues that the bulk of festival events obviated this ambivalence by presenting both Northern Ireland and its artists as functioning within a 'timeless present.' Collectively, performers went to great lengths to train their creative energies on non-confrontational epochs and events and to avoid any reference to sectarian partisanship. The third section of the chapter argues that these performances, events, and repertoires enabled the enactment of what is known in linguistic anthropology as entextualization, the discursive process of freeing traditional materials from customary interpretations and reconfiguring them for others. In this process, narrators with a stake in the 'master narrative' of Northern Ireland found a suitable venue within which to rehearse and perform a new identity.

Northern Ireland's identity in flux

Ireland has undergone strong economic performance since the mid-1990s. The Celtic Tiger's economic boom began then, exhibiting 'growth rates well above the European average, little inflation, growth of exports and a firm exchange rate.'[5] Other expansive factors included strong purchasing power, low death rates for young mothers and children, high levels of food consumption, and increased home ownership. By 2001, economic realities in the Republic of Ireland appeared vital enough to motivate a redefinition of Irish selfhood in terms of language revitalization and instruction.[6]

The same process seems to be at work in Northern Ireland, for recent political, economic, and historical processes have resulted in what the former Taoiseach Bertie Ahern recently labeled 'Ireland at peace.'[7]

The process has been engendered by a series of historical events and landmark decisions. These include the Anglo-Irish Agreement of 1985, the Downing Street Declaration of 1993, the St Andrew's Agreement of 2006, and the Belfast/Good Friday Agreement of 1998. The tenth anniversary of the Good Friday Agreement was marked by a number of important events, conferences, and position papers.[8] Although these economic and political initiatives continue to evolve, the fact that they are viewed as a *fait accompli* has produced a fair share of anxiety in Northern Ireland. As one Belfast native revealed to me in an informal conversation in March 2008, people 'don't know where they stand any more. At least before, we knew where we stood.'

'Ambivalent selfhood' is an anthropological concept which describes the simultaneous existence within a person of conflicting desires not comfortably synthesized into a stable identity.[9] Dovetailing with it is the 'liminal state,' a threshold period in which former paradigms no longer 'make sense' and new ones have yet to adhere. During this time when formerly integrated statuses and roles fluctuate, opportunities emerge for the reshaping of narratives so that aspects of identity heretofore overlooked, unheeded, or unrecognized can be emphasized. Ideological language often aids ambivalent subjects by providing opportunities to communicate intentions denied or rendered meaningless in other contexts; it also permits the expression of forbidden desires.[10] In particular, ideological language stated in narrative fills the liminal gap, especially if fresh opportunities become available to communicate a reconstructed 'sense of self.' Successful navigation of liminality and resolution of ambivalence are able to produce intact 'selves' equipped with an arsenal of new linguistic symbols to actualize identity. As we shall see, the Smithsonian Folklife Festival accommodated and facilitated this process well.

Anchoring in the tradition

Many sites at the Smithsonian featured *de rigueur* topics that attend many Irish festivals, like whiskey distilling, Gaelic games, and pottery, linen, and lacemaking. Some venues encouraged interaction from festival goers; for instance, a 'hands-on' mural emerged and a basketry tent reproduced masks and costumes of strawmen performing mumming traditions. Genealogical information, food culture, and various other exhibitions completed the Smithsonian's offerings. Local residents, folk *aficionados*, international tourists, and interested others meandered, stopping to enjoy the celebration of folk culture.

An eel fisherman working for 70 years on the border between Armagh and Tyrone detailed the history and logistics of a tradition that purportedly dates to the fifth century CE. Audiences were presented with a Northern Ireland connected, not to twenty-first-century modernity, but to reputedly ancient waterways. Recollections were both intimate and personal as the fisherman and his son answered questions about the seasonality of their labor and their emotional response to their trade. The elder's melodeon-playing underlined that music-making is integral to the heritage of craftworkers in Northern Ireland.

The importance of their sense of place was corroborated when singers from Counties Down, Armagh, and Antrim explained the townlands from which they hailed. One extolled the features of his family tree. Both women and men balladeers, many among them well-known artists who had performed in the US on numerous occasion, swapped songs, providing gender balance and broad repertoires.

Categories of Ulster song and story included universal subjects such as work and play, childhood and folly, love and romance; their longevity was emphasized repeatedly. For example, 'The Armagh Volunteer' was presented as a Napoleonic song. The collecting process itself, including the fact that older tradition-bearers had shared their sources and materials, was stressed in terms of the salience of tradition. As a way to claim both the local and the global and to inform folk music *aficionados* of his knowledge of the 'big ballad' tradition, one singer referred to the 'Armagh version' of Child Ballad No. 279.

Ireland's history provided the backdrop to the song 'Whiskey in Me Tae.' The balladeer noted that 'those "dealing men" knew every trick in the book for getting a good animal and giving little or no money for it.' Others, referring to obscure subjects like hiring fairs, commanded audience respect for their knowledge as well as for the importance of the Irish past. They reproduced classics like 'The Rocks of Bawn,' about the hard life of laborers, 'The Flower of Sweet Strabane,' about the 'lovely Martha,' and 'Bonny Kells Water,' about the charms of Irish life. 'The Apprentice Boy' with its 'wait for me' plot, 'The Bonny Laboring Boy,' with its motif of following the lad who eventually succeeds, and 'The Boys of Mullabawn,' with its focus on transportation, engendered a strong sense of authenticity. Although a few scatological stories lent comic relief, the mood was respectful informality; audiences, eager to hear what was being sung or discussed, felt they were being made privy to 'the real Ireland.'

These small and intimate performances were both balanced and offset by performances designed for showmanship and crowd-pleasing.

On the main stages, a drummer and his pupil tried to outdo one other; a 'world champion' piped his way to the stage and an award-winning Irish-American fiddler and her virtuoso guitarist performed 'crossover' energies. These 'anchor' concerts attracted much larger audiences.

The performance of a costumed group of rhymers in elaborately con-structed straw masks constituted one of the most spectacular visual performances. Attracting family-oriented and interactive audiences, the program opened in a tableau with an ancestral voice relating the story of Ireland. Later, the singing of 'Oró sé do bheatha abhaile,' an Irish language piece welcoming home soldiers from overseas wars, intensified perceptions that authentic linguistic traditions were being preserved.

The rhymers' outfits reflected mumming traditions once celebrated in many regions of Ulster at Christmastime. The ten-minute tableau appeared to be designed for visual consumption; it involved formulaic characters re-enacting a 'mock-battle' in which St Patrick was slain by St George and a magico-physician was hired to revive him. Although the classic 'Captain Mummer' appeared, the entire plot was not repli-cated; rather, a masked 'donkey' sought children to dance and sing. When the masks were removed, numbers like 'The Wee Falorie man' and 'I'll Tell Me Ma' were sung, along with 'St Patrick was a Gentle-man.' The latter's lyrics argue that the illustrious saint 'came from decent people'; its chorus revisits the famous legend that St Patrick drove the snakes from Ireland.

In the context of the summer festival on the Washington Mall, the reiteration of the comfortable and familiar was at work; many of these musical pieces served as reminders of melodies that entered the American audioscape via parades and military marches. The subtle implication of security permeated the atmosphere, enticing those who might have previously been disinclined to go to Northern Ireland to consider a visit.

Collectively, the many ballad sessions, workshops, and spectacle per-formances functioned as the crux of the festival and presented an enduring past not about to be eschewed or discarded. Eric Hobsbawm argues that events such as these 'shed light on the human relation to the past ... for all invented traditions use history as a legitimator of action and [a] cement of group cohesion.'[11] Liminality in terms of political, economic, and social conditions and ambivalence regarding selfhood went unrecognized. An 'emergent,' developing, and unfolding Northern Irish culture, still adversarial, was for all intents and purposes denied, in favor of the presentation of a fixed and harmonious reality. Of course, by virtue of its past and its rapidly transforming present,

Northern Ireland possesses fractious identities and divergent points of view.

Audiences, seeking entertainment rather than enlightenment, were not prepared to tease out difference; they embraced with alacrity the sounds, sights, tastes, and smells of Ireland 'as a whole.' Festival attendees became imbued with the belief that Northern Ireland's ways of life and musical 'texts,' ranging from love stories to fast-paced dances, proceeded according to traditions that endure throughout the island.

Events and players were oriented toward attracting visitors to Northern Ireland and creating a broad sense of Irish culture. At the level of exchange, or, in anthropological parlance, reciprocity, to emphasize upheaval or disjunction might have been seen as a form of ingratitude, especially in light of the fact that the powers of the White House had, in effect, 'gifted' Ireland with energetic efforts toward reconciliation.[12] One might suggest that Northern Ireland's artists and craftworkers became effective pawns in the hands of policy-makers: by performing a 'traditional' Ireland, stable and 'at peace,' they served as visible and public expressions of Northern Ireland's gratitude.[13] In doing so, however, they blunted a number of narratives and repertoires that would have – and could have – expressed a different version of its cultural and folkloric heritage.

Entextualization

On other stages evocative of nineteenth-century parlors, however, another dimension of Northern Ireland's history was unfolding. In these settings, mostly Protestant leaders introduced the background of the 'border Scots,' those who had occupied lands that lay between Scotland and England in the late 1500s and early 1600s. Not only was their independence stressed, so too was their 'outlaw' nature. They were 'reivers'[14] – thieves, so to speak. When the larder was empty, the crowd was told, spurs were placed on a covered dish; when the lid was removed, the sign was obvious: it was time to 'reive,' or raid for food.

In an anthropological context, the entextualization process is an attempt to manipulate, fix, and/or restore cultural and ideological meaning by imbuing putative 'ancient lore' with authority.[15] Taking into consideration the fact that a preacher from County Down, a leader of the Ulster Scots Agency, a self-proclaimed 'cultural ambassador,' and a representative of the Orange Order were performing their identities for US audiences in particular, we are in a position to examine emergent discursive strategies of identity: in short, 'identity in the making.'

Perhaps unconsciously, these speakers were providing as well as performing[16] an 'alternative vision' for Loyalism and Unionism, something that certain writers have been seeking for a number of years.[17] What cannot be questioned, however, is the fact that these people were marketing and managing heritage, presenting it in terms of 'longevity, brilliance, perseverance, and power.'[18]

In the narrative practices under discussion, many threads of the new narrative were woven. These speakers introduced a new set of origin myths: King William and the Battle of the Boyne were not alluded to; rather, the year 1690 claimed the day, as did 'the Glorious Revolution and John Locke.' Echoing the Declaration of Independence and the belief that government could be overthrown if it failed to execute the principles upon which the consent of the governed had been granted, one narrator told of a captain who had 'raised his voice' to his militia and 'his men all left.' The speaker explained, 'They had given the captain the power to govern them and they could just as easily take it away.' Such action resonated well with audiences in Washington, DC.

Allegedly, the reivers (also known as the 'steel bonnets') were in the habit of reversing the spelling of the surname Graham to 'Maharg' to disguise and protect their families from legal reprisals. Although the Grahams were characterized as 'really bad actors,' they shared that notoriety with others. A visitor to the border, for example, was reported to have asked, 'Are there any Christians here?' 'No,' came the reply, 'only Humes and Armstrongs.' The audience was then informed that Grahams, Humes, and Armstrongs were among those who emigrated to Ulster.

What they did when they arrived there was ignored, however. Rather, the next wave of migration to America – from 1717 to 1776 – continued the narrative, as did the role that Ulster Scots, now labeled 'Scots-Irish,' played in North America. Of major importance was the 'mostly Presbyterian' faith structure of these 'ancestors.' Presbyterians were not Anglican (Episcopalian in American parlance); their rejection of a state-imposed religion was presented as an index of autonomy.

Building the image of feisty freethinkers demanding the right to worship as they pleased, the speakers turned to the issue of the ancestral 'language' of Ulster Scots. The writings of James Orr, a Weaver Poet who hailed from Northern Ireland and wrote in Ulster Scots, were utilized to validate the claim that Orr's contemporaries – the grandfathers and grandmothers of the people on the stage – were speaking the same language as Orr and were therefore ancestral forebears of the 'mother tongue.' One man said, 'Some say James Orr is the Robbie Burns of

Ulster but we say that Robbie Burns is the James Orr of the Scots'[19] language.' Another drew on 'expert testimony' by citing Michael Montgomery, author of *From Ulster to America: The Scotch-Irish Heritage in American English*. The audience was informed that Montgomery traced Scots-Irish expressions like 'a bra' wee,' which means 'a whole lot,' and 'feart,' which appears in American English as 'a-feared.' Montgomery also noted that the English word 'bereaved' derived from 'reivers' and initially meant 'blackmail.' Not surprisingly, the audience took great delight in these revelations.[20]

Other terms mentioned included 'the devil's buttermilk' for whiskey, and 'the devil's box' for the fiddle. Attention was drawn to the fact that the Presbyterian clergy disapproved of drinking, dancing, and musical entertainment. They, like so many of their flock, were described as 'thran,' that is to say, parsimonious, austere, strict, straitlaced, stubborn. Thran was characterized by the expression, 'We breathe in but we don't breathe out.' Qualifying the label, one of the speakers joked, 'but we're loving in our "thran."' Clearly, 'a bra' wee' of self-definition accompanied this claim.

Speakers spoke of becoming personally excited that etymological scholarship was resolving some of the mysteries behind lost words and expressions. One man spoke of his grandmother's use of the term 'squaws,' meaning 'a place to stay away from.' Learning that putting the letter 's' in front of a word was a common feature of Ulster Scots, he located in his research the Ulster-Scots word 'quaw,' meaning 'a wet damp area.'[21] This discovery, he informed the audience, provided a personal sense of satisfaction, in that another lost word from his childhood had been rediscovered and 'reclaimed for the tradition.'

The search for lost roots was another key aspect of the speakers' narratives, which emphasized connections to the US, especially to the American South. To a question about whether the Scots Irish settled in Appalachia, one speaker replied, 'hundreds of thousands.' He added, 'one quarter million [Scots Irish] emigrated to North America, and some historians argue that this number may be too low.' To encourage new scholarship, the fact that 'Many family networks have not been fully explored' was stressed. Possibly distancing some emigrants from their reiver past, speakers noted that Andrew Jackson's mother was buried in a cemetery where Ulster surnames can be found on headstones. In terms of connecting an American president with Northern Irish heritage, James Frazer's concept of sympathetic magic[22] is instructive here; perhaps the 'good' of Jackson's name could offset the 'bad' one of the 'mahargs.'

One of the speakers, reciting a poem with a repetitious final line, urged that Ulstermen be remembered for their roles in establishing a successful America:

Hi! Uncle Sam!
Virginia sent her brave men,
The North paraded grave men,
That they might not be slavemen,
But ponder with this calm:
The first to face the Tory
And the first to lift Old Glory
Made your war an Ulster story:
Think it over, Uncle Sam![23]

Another commentator immediately paraphrased George Washington's assertion that, were he to be defeated everywhere else, he would stand with the Scots Irish of his native Virginia. The speaker glossed Washington's meaning: 'In other words, he would fight to the death with these brave Ulster men.'

Additional sound-bites difficult to abjure, such as 'we were the people of the borders,' 'we have a strong concept of "hame" [home],' and 'we desired to live our lives according to the Bible rather than to state religion,' enriched the storytellers' anecdotes and left audiences convinced of the authenticity of their rhetoric.

Conclusion

Due to the fact that rapid social change is underway, Northern Irish caught in its throes are best described as occupying an ambivalent state of selfhood within what anthropologists refer to as a 'threshold' or liminal period, wherein processual narratives of identity continue to unfold. Both ambivalent selfhood and the liminal serve as complementary heuristics by which to understand how some culture-brokers with a stake in reconfiguring narratives of identity in Northern Ireland made use of the Smithsonian Institution's Folklife Festival of 2007 to re-narrate their ancestral past. These discourses, and indeed the festival itself, must be seen against the backdrop of ongoing peacemaking efforts and strong economic growth in Ireland.

Grassroots crafts, trades, and oral and musical traditions provided anchors to tradition so that alternative rhetorical strategies and a fresh set of linguistic ideologies could be introduced imperceptibly.

The latter may be capable of transforming ambivalent selves into more secure ones.[24] In entextualizing, or reframing, or even re-inventing Northern Irish identity, storytellers posited two relatively new origin myths: 'ancestral' life in Scotland on the one hand, and still to be discovered 'ancestral' life in colonial America on the other. Faith structure, language revitalization and reclamation, and identification with the pioneering Scots-Irish stock who migrated to the US prior to the American Revolution served as building blocks on which the entextualizing process of identity could be constructed. Not unlike that advanced by the 'Scots-Irish' in eighteenth-century America,[25] the claim to identity was connected to admirable values like independence, thrift, and forthrightness. Perhaps unwittingly, the suggestion made in the epigraph was taken to heart: via entextualizing narratives of identity, liminal figures in liminal times and places could use the notion of ancestral 'people of the borders' – ironically, people who could be considered liminal themselves – and in the process became cognizant of other places where they could feel 'at home.'

Notes

1   Terence Brown, *The Whole Protestant Community: The Making of a Historical Myth* (Derry: Field Day, 1985), 85.
2   Richard Kurin, in *Smithsonian Folklife Festival: Culture Of, By, and For the People* (Washington, DC: Smithsonian Institution, 1998), 6–8 *passim*.
3   Richard Kurin, in *2007 Smithsonian Folklife Festival* program (Washington, DC: Smithsonian Institution, 2007), 8–11, 8, explained the Smithsonian's choice of Northern Ireland in the Festival program: 'The Festival program comes at a very important time in the history of the island region. In just the last few months, leaders of the two major parties, Unionist (Protestant) and Republican (Catholic) have agreed to form a self-government to help surmount "The troubles" that plagued the region. Music, crafts, occupational traditions, and culinary arts are flourishing. Cultural expressions, often a means of resistance and conflict, increasingly foster understanding, reconciliation, and the economy.'
4   Tourism is currently one of the healthiest industries in Northern Ireland, with numerous pilot projects underway to encourage community infrastructure and training. The Renewing Communities Visitor Servicing Project of the Shankill Road and North Belfast is one of the latest pilot projects to have proved very successful in raising awareness of the benefits of community tourism (Jayne O'Neile, Project Officer, personal communication, 28 May 2008).
5   Denis O'Hearn, *Inside the Celtic Tiger: The Irish Economy and the Asian Model* (London: Pluto Press, 1998), 1. Northern Ireland's stabilization contributed greatly to the Republic's overall health; this in turn motivated an increase in cross-border initiatives.

6 Eileen Moore Quinn, 'Entextualizing Famine, Reconstituting Self: Testimonial Narratives From Ireland,' *Anthropological Quarterly* 74 (2) (2001), 72–88, 82.

7 Ahern used this term when he visited the White House in May 2008.

8 See, for example, the *Irish Times* series of March and April 2008 in which the key players of the Good Friday/Belfast Agreement presented major statements.

9 Peter Stromberg, 'Ideological Language in the Transformation of Identity,' *American Anthropologist* 92 (1990): 42–56.

10 *Ibid.*, 52.

11 Eric Hobsbawm, 'Introduction: Inventing Traditions,' in *The Invention of Tradition*, eds. Eric Hobsbawm and Terence Ranger (New York: Cambridge University Press, 1983), 1–14, 11.

12 This was especially the case in 1998 with the political brokering of Senator George Mitchell and President Bill Clinton.

13 I thank the co-editor of this volume, Fintan Walsh, for this suggestion.

14 The word does not appear in most English dictionaries. Alexander Worrack, compiler of *The Concise Scots Dictionary*, describes the word 'reaver' as a noun meaning 'a thief, a freebooter, a plunderer.' As a verb, 'to reave' means 'to take away by force' (New York: Crown Publishers, 1989 [1911]), 447.

15 Joel Kuipers, *Power in Performance* (Philadelphia: University of Pennsylvania Press, 1990); Gloria G. Raheja, 'Caste, Colonialism and the Speech of the Colonized: Entextualization and Disciplinary Control in India,' *American Ethnologist* 12 (3) (1996): 494–513; Quinn, 'Entextualizing Famine,' 72–88.

16 I use the term performance in the sense of '[s]ocial and dramatic actors, in and out of the theatre [who] give performances scripted to alter or confirm their particular definition of political reality,' John P. Harrington and Elizabeth J. Mitchell, 'Introduction,' in *Politics and Performance in Contemporary Northern Ireland*, eds. John P. Harrington and Elizabeth J. Mitchell (Amherst: University of Massachusetts Press, 1999), 1–6, 1.

17 In *The Whole Protestant Community* (1985), Terence Brown called for Unionists to recognize that they have a fascinating narrative to reveal; likewise Norman Porter, in *Rethinking Unionism: An Alternative Vision of Northern Ireland* (Belfast: Blackstaff, 1996), introduced the concept of 'civic unionism' for acknowledging the many historical components of Unionist identity.

18 Kelli Ann Costa, 'Conflating Past and Present: Marketing Archaeological Heritage Sites in Ireland,' in *Marketing Heritage: Archaeology and the Consumption of the Past*, eds. Yorke Rowan and Uzi Baram (New York: Altamira Press, 2004), 69–91.

19 The claim to pride and identity through language is not unlike the reclamation of Gullah-Geechee and Ebonics in the US. It might also be compared successfully with the growth of the Irish language in Northern Ireland. The latter subject arose briefly at the workshops, but was not elaborated to any great extent.

20 Montgomery's embeddedness in the Ulster-Scots 'language debate' is worthy of note. His book was published by the Ulster Historical Foundation (Belfast, 2006), and he serves as honorary president of the Ulster-Scots Language Society.

21 Perhaps we would refer to such a place as a bog or a swamp.

22　Sir James George Frazer (1854–1941) divided sympathetic magic, the idea that 'things act on each other at a distance through a secret sympathy,' into two types: 1) homeopathic, or imitative magic, is based on the belief that 'like produces like' or 'like cures like'; and 2) the 'law of contagion,' which is based on the idea of contiguity, or 'the part for the whole.' In other words, once something has come into contact with a person or thing, it continues to contain and emit that person's or thing's substance in spite of physical separation. See James G. Frazer, *The Golden Bough: A Study in Magic and Religion* (New York: Macmillan, 1963 [1922]), sympathetic magic: 12–55; 233; 234; 246; 255; 271; 276; 448; 467; 617; contagious magic: 12–13; 45–52; 267–72; 273.

23　William F. Marshall, *Ulster Sails West: The Story of the Great Emigration from Ulster* (Belfast: The Ulster Scots Society of America, 1950 [1943]), 5.

24　See Stromberg, 1990.

25　Eileen Moore Quinn, 'Toasters and Boasters: John D. Crimmins' *St. Patrick's Day* (1902),' *New Hibernia Review* 8, 3 (2004): 18–30.

17
Who's Laughing Now? Comic Currents for a New Irish Audience

Eric Weitz

The theatrical humor dynamic has undergone interesting experiment-ation in an Irish context over the past few years by virtue of a suc-cession of productions mounted by the Dublin-based theater company Arambe Productions. Arambe, since its inception in 2003, has pro-duced devised pieces as well as existing dramatic texts by African and Irish playwrights. Two productions in particular, *The Kings of the Kilburn High Road* (2006) and *The Dilemma of a Ghost* (2007), created distinctive twists on the humor transaction initiated by playwright and actualized in subsequent performance for a multicultural audience.

Arambe was founded by Bisi Adigun, a Nigerian-born theater practi-tioner, to provide a performing platform for fellow transplanted Africans. The company has sought to cultivate a widest possible audience, so as to entertain and enlighten across the boundaries of cultural inscription. Adigun, who moved to Ireland in 1993, directed both *Kings* and *Dilemma*. He chose these texts as potent vehicles for the illumination of immigrant experiences, with an awareness of Ireland's own cultural memories of mass relocation.

The social phenomenologist Alfred Schutz supplies a way of looking at the immigrant's entry into another culture, with helpful implications for study of the humor transaction in a multicultural theater context. His take on cultural inscription includes 'systems of knowledge' acquired through one's 'cultural community,' which become self-evident matrices of interpretive apparatus. Beholden to these structures, any given person's 'biographically determined situation' implies a 'stock of knowledge,'[1] continually accessed and updated through experience – which, incident-ally, provides the reservoir of material humor attempts to exploit.

The French philosopher Henri Bergson famously observed that 'laugh-ter is always the laughter of a group,' and that it 'always implies a kind of secret freemasonry, or even complicity, with other laughers.'² Relating this to Schutz's terminology, a joke separates its audience into an 'in-group' for which it is aimed (those who possess the stock of knowledge and cultural dispositions it seeks to validate) and an 'out-group' (those who do not). We carry a basic element of joking success in our bodies, through our sociocultural inscriptions and acquired attitudes. It has everything to do with Norman Holland's observation that, '[i]n laughing, we suddenly and playfully recreate our identities,'³ which are made up not only of what we think, but how we feel about things, and, indeed, the entirety of our worldview.

Schutz goes on to discuss the Stranger in the Community, 'who has to place in question nearly everything that seems to be unquestionable to the members of the approached group.'⁴ Both Arambe plays center on the ambiguous position occupied by the Stranger in the Community, with humor a mode of discourse which, in predicating itself on in-groups and out-groups, places some interesting spins on the tides of audience engagement. Ireland's recent immigrant populations have begun a process of 'learning' the host culture they have entered, while, of course, remaining irrevocably tethered to their own. Meanwhile, the collective Irish consciousness harbors a memory or two about the travails of emigration.

I should pause to acknowledge my bracketing of entirely relevant issues, notably the deep-seated differences in cultural performance palettes. Patrice Pavis reminds us, 'Actors simultaneously reveal the culture of the community where they have trained and where they live, and the bodily technique they have acquired.'⁵ Nonetheless, I would contend that the productions assumed the fact that African and Irish/Western theatergoers should be capable of accommodating differences to process the play at a competent level. Along these lines, I should announce my own cultural moorings (for the inscribed dispositions they imply), as a white male of middle-class US enculturation, who has lived in Ireland for more than 14 years, making me somewhat familiar with an immigrant experience.

The Arambe production of Jimmy Murphy's *Kings of the Kilburn High Road* overlays the immigrant experience of the Irish past with that of the African present. The play, originally mounted in 2000 by Red Kettle Theatre Company at the Garter Lane Arts Centre in Waterford, assembles in the backroom of a London social club five Irish-born men who left their homeland years earlier for the economic promise of the English labor market. The play builds to a series of emotional flashpoints in which the men are forced to confront the punctured illusions and failures of character that have made their immigrant experience much less than once they had envisaged. There is also a strong sense of their Irish roots having withered, even while the men harbor a resentment of things English, thereby stranding them in a no-man's land of cultural identity.

Although the play would not formally be considered a comedy, humorous potential resides in the dramatic text through a certain Irish strain of laddish banter, itself pointing to the grinding plates beneath encrusted social patterns. It is clear, for example, that abstention from alcohol contravenes some sort of code within the group. Maurteen, who we learn has beaten his wife when drunk, chooses lemonade for his first drink of the day, prompting playful yet pointed disapproval from Jap, the putative leader of the group:

> JAP: Lemonade, jaysus, Mary an' Joseph. Lemonade, I ask yeh.
> MAURTEEN: You'd swear it never passed your lips before.
> JAP: You'll be pissin' all day with that Maurteen, pissin' all day,
> tell him Shay.
> SHAY: Run the guts out 'a yeh that will.[6]

The sequence applies an inverted conversational framing to Maurteen's forbearance, as if lemonade is potentially a more harmful drink than the options sanctioned by the group. Although playfully couched, it

Figure 7   The Kings of the Kilburn High Road by Jimmy Murphy. Directed by Bisi Adigun of Arambe Productions. Photo by John Nelson.

remains a recognizable coercive strategy, intended to apply social pressure through backhanded ridicule.

This is as good a place as any from which to peer into the gap opened by Arambe's casting of five black men in their 2006 Fringe Festival production at the Teacher's Club in Dublin. Despite – or perhaps because of – the use of a cast noticeably younger than the men 'in their late forties' described by the original text, the production insinuated an ironic consideration of the African immigrant experience on the back of the so-called Celtic Tiger.

Linda Hutcheon attributes to ironic meaning a 'rubbing together' of the explicit and implicit. She also proposes that it has a defining 'edge,' an affective disposition, observing more closely:

> In interpreting irony, we can and do oscillate very rapidly between the said and the unsaid ... But – and here the visual analogy needs adapting – it is not the two 'poles' themselves that are important; it is the idea of a kind of rapid perceptual or hermeneutic *movement* *between* them that makes this image a possibly suggestive and productive one for thinking about irony.[7]

Remarkably, there are passages of text from *Kings* which played like an up-to-the-minute cautionary tale for African-born spectators who have emigrated to Ireland for economic betterment. Preparing to launch into a self-mythologizing vision of his triumphant return 'home,' Jap says, 'Save for about three months, plenty of overtime, cut down a bit on the drink. Scrimp an' save till I've about a grand in the bank. I puts me good suit on, draws the grand out an' next thing yeh know I'm Lord Muck, King of the Irish sea.'[8] The corrosive effects of an uphill struggle in a less than hospitable society suffuses the text, as does the inevitable toll of resorting to alcohol-based balms for the spirit. Speaking through the mouth of Irish characters, there were many poignant opportunities for the Arambe actors – all but one of whom were born in Nigeria and spoke in their own accents – to give voice to yearnings and disappointments concerning the concept of 'home.' The spectacle of five young black men caught in similar circumstances and enacting the potentially destructive social rites of their adopted country implies a hard glance in the rearview mirror at a wave of Irish emigration, even as it looks forward to our African-born immigrants. The oscillation between them evoked lament and warning simultaneously, though surely in different measure for the two main groups of spectators.

In so ironizing the entire stage world, Arambe's *Kings* generated some interesting dynamics for humorous moments. At the start of the play, Jap is grooming himself in the mirror and cannot suppress a burst of self-admiration: 'If there's one thing that can be said about yeh Jap Kavanagh, yeh never lost it boy. Yeh never lost it!'[9] In the Arambe production, the actor playing Jap, Yare Jegbefume, was born in Dublin of Nigerian parents. His authentic Dublin accent no doubt contributed to the huge laugh he received routinely in response to this opening line. African-born and Irish-born spectators could find amusement in the mingling of black man and Dublin argot, though, of course, from different angles. Humor loves a stripping of pretence, and the character's excess of self-approval disarmingly slices across the grain of fitting modesty in either culture's eyes. In this case the ironic doubled the charge of the humorous, perhaps through recognition of a self-styled 'character' destined to become more familiar in years to come.

Another character, Shay (played by Gabriel Akujobi), then enters, tossing off a comment on the selection emanating from the jukebox: 'Daniel O'Donnell, jays, if there's one thing I can't stand, it's that Donegal bastard.'[10] This citation of popular cultural experience and attitude – private joking for a local theater audience – would have most resonance for spectators who have heard O'Donnell's music, know his reputation, and, importantly, have formed an unfavorable opinion of it. The utterance also invokes a common Irish pride in one's home county, the basis for a sliding scale of tribal aggression from good-natured one-upmanship to uncharitable stereotyping. The remark's magic circle would court joking recognition for many an Irish-born spectator, less so for newer arrivals.

In the above moment, though, actor Gabriel Akujobi's race and accent again injected humor with irony: For many of us, black and white spectators alike, it would be impossible to disengage Shay's off-handed disparagement from the routine racist sentiment we know Africans and other immigrants face. In fact, a later passage from the original text suggests that Jap has a black girlfriend, whom he cannot quite bring himself to think of in committed terms. Jap says, 'Ain't no racist, me but ... yeh know ... yeh know, want me kids to look like me.'[11] Irony 'happens,' as Hutcheon likes to phrase it. Humor happens too, sometimes, at the expense of an unsuspecting text, as the Arambe casting generated an unforeseen Brechtian reversal in the gap between original text and New Irish character.[12] The line fails to qualify as a scripted joke amid the tautening mood of the scene, but in production became worthy of a few wry chuckles by virtue of the obvious irony of racial juxtaposition.

Humor is accommodated primarily within the bounds of *Kings'* stage world, but it almost always supplies a troubling undertow and disappears entirely as the tensions mount. *The Dilemma of a Ghost* is built more like a comedy, and therefore plants the seeds for joking in its structure. It was written by Ghanaian playwright Ama Ata Aidoo in 1964, at a time when the civil rights movement was gathering force in the US and many black Americans were taking newfound pride in their African ancestry. The play's narrative depicts the return of a young Ghanaian man named Ato to his home, following completion of his university education in the US. He arrives with Eulalie, his African-American wife, who is apprehensive about meeting her husband's family, but also thrilled about the opportunity to experience her heritage at its source. African and American cultures clash, as Ato straddles the divide between his family's strong sense of communal custom and his wife's unmindful persistence in line with her own cultural inscription.

The plot might be seen to approximate a comedy of manners familiar to Western audiences, in which a character enters a society with highly codified and quite different behavioral expectations, thereby priming the stage world for misunderstandings and frame-breaks. In this case, Eulalie unwittingly contravenes values and codes taken as self-evident by Ato's clan; the transgressions are underscored comically by the family's sheer incomprehension of her ways.

Such a comic construction usually relies on an acknowledged in-group as the target audience – a sociocultural orientation from which the thrust of humorous intent emanates. The play premiered for an in-group audience at the University of Ghana in 1964. It received a UK production in 2007 in a joint venture featuring Ghanaian and British performers, which, like Arambe's, was intended in part to mark the 50th anniversary of Ghanaian independence. Over and above the dominant angle of the play's humorous attack there lies an undeniable spirit of even-handedness to Aidoo's treatment of the opposing cultural forces, anchored in the characters of two unnamed village women who supply choral reflection on the unfolding situation. The play's aesthetic motion of laying out a question or issue worthy of debate locates itself within a particular African storytelling tradition called the 'dilemma tale.' In contextualizing Aidoo's work, Lloyd W. Brown explains, 'The dilemma tale usually poses difficult questions of moral or legal significance. These questions are usually debated both by the narrator and the audience – and on this basis the dilemma is a good example of the highly functional nature of oral art in traditional Africa.'[13] Brown observes that the form prioritizes discussion over resolution, thereby seeking to instill in the audience a constructive dialogic mechanism for the weighing of everyday issues.

The comic construction familiar to Western audiences and the dilemma tale of African oral tradition intersect in the character of Ato. Aidoo expresses the young man's ambivalence toward bridging the cultural gap between wife and clan through a dream sequence with two children playing a game and singing about a 'wretched ghost' who cannot decide which of two roads to take. Ato's indecision, however, could be seen from a Western genre perspective as a strain of comic cowardice.

The humor foreseen by Aidoo's text was, of course, aimed in the first instance at the life-worlds of a Ghanaian audience at a precise historical moment. At the Project Arts Centre in 2007, the angles of comic reflection altered for an opening-night audience which seemed a fairly equal mix of black and white theater-goers. African-born spectators still occupied a position of privilege with regard to the text's joking intentions, but half the audience represented a surrounding Western context more aligned to Eulalie's sociocultural presumptions than those of the play's Odumna clan. Western-born spectators would identify more readily with Eulalie's culturally enshrined sense of individualism – and would possess little or no awareness of the text's assumptions rooted in African custom (nor possess a generic template for interpretation of the dilemma tale). On the other hand, the joking positions of the African audience would surely have been tempered by a 'lived' familiarity with the worldview manifested by Eulalie. The play still presumes a certain cultural competence, placing African spectators as a 'home group,' innately aware of Eulalie's code breaches.

In most cases humorous intent could easily be apprehended by the audience as a whole, even if the breakdown of the joking action would be less straightforward for all involved. One of Ato's uncles, in anticipation of his nephew's arrival, says, 'But where is our master, the white man himself?'[14] The character's skin color and his uncle's facetious rebranding throw up an obvious absurdity. The joking material, of course, draws on knowledge of Ato's stint in the US and his potential re-inscription in a land where Caucasians dominate. What amounts to a validation of African-born perspective on the culture beneath the skin might also spark a minor revelation for Irish and Western-born Caucasians about their own racial perceptions.

This fault-line is plumbed further throughout the aforementioned scene. The family members in *Dilemma* do not even seem to be aware that Ato has taken a wife. The Arambe production emphasizes Ato's unease, with actor Gabriel Akujobi (who played Shay in *Kings*) shifting uneasily and loosening his tie in a recognizable comic outlining of discomfort. His relatives' responses are also crafted for humorous effect, sudden, full-blooded, and simultaneous, manifesting the awesome force of family opinion.

Family members mispronounce Eulalie's name ('Hurere!'), a common form of humorous ridicule, meant to emphasize the visitor's alien nature to the home group, as well as to gain some comic mileage from the degree of 'unwitting' phonetic distortion. They then discover Eulalie does not have a tribe. Nana, the grandmother, says, 'Since I was born, I have not heard of a human being born out of the womb of a woman who has no tribe. Are there trees which never have any roots?'[15] Westerners may have found Nana's sudden resort to metaphor an amusing switch of framing, but were unlikely to perceive the full value of the utterance as a proverb, a form of discourse far more endemic to African culture. African-born spectators would have occupied an interesting comic vantage point, able to appreciate Nana's incomprehension and expression internally while recognizing the Westerner's completely other orientation toward the concept.

Ato then explains that his wife comes from America, which further cranks up the comic consternation for the family. Utterances erupt from all sides about the implications of their young clan member marrying a woman they assume to be white: 'Will not people laugh at us?' The barrage culminates with Ato finally getting out the words, 'I say my wife is as black as we all are,'[16] whereupon the collective sigh of relief onstage elicited a huge laughter response from the Project audience. This is an interesting joke for a multicultural Dublin audience, recalling the utterance described above from *Kings* in which Jap says he wants his 'kids to look like me.' This time, however, it was couched in a sequence rigged for comic recognition of such family scenes, and, perhaps, of tribal prejudices prone to surface in them.

The sequence marked itself for humorous intent, embodied by the Arambe company as a sudden emotional release, comically enhanced by the intensity and simultaneity with which the collective sigh was orchestrated. The line would seem to divide the audience according to race, but it is the response (the sigh) that got the laugh. This might suggest recognition of a strip of domestic experience rather than a straightforward response to racial ring-fencing. Most of us have experience of class and religion (not to mention factors like country, county, town, and even neighborhood) leading to this kind of domestic interrogation. I believe there is one further factor in play, and that is the audience's awareness of its own multicultural makeup. The mutually acknowledged presence of black and white spectators in the theater transaction, the occasion to laugh 'together' despite the divisive nature of the joke's setup, exert a defamiliarizing effect with implications for the increasingly multiracial Irish society here and now.

The Arambe portrayal of Eulalie by Merrina Millsapp includes just that bit of swagger in body and voice to mark the character as a sociocultural stereotype of American Other for both African- *and* Irish-born spectators. By way of settling into her accommodation, the Arambe production has her produce photographs of Muhammad Ali and the Statue of Liberty to hang outside her living space. She then goes on to settle into her new surroundings by unselfconsciously producing a cigarette. This brought a sharp burst of laughter from the African audience. Sociologist Chris Powell asserts 'that an anomalous, strange or untoward event, idea or cultural expression is often initially defined as "funny." The converse of this is that a "humor response" is likely when a social role of some kind is perceived as having been infracted.'[17] In the wake of the in-group response, the out-group suddenly discovered the extent to which smoking by a woman – here undertaken so blithely – is strictly circumscribed by codes of comportment for the in-group of the stage world.

Ato's relatives come to assume that he and Eulalie have been thus far unable to have children. They are not to know that the subject has become a point of discussion for the couple and that they have thus far chosen to delay starting a family. Concerned, Ato's relatives come to the couple's quarters to perform a fertility ritual. Eulalie leaves, unaware of what was meant to transpire and unenlightened by her husband. The relatives are astounded, culminating in an uncle's concerned query: 'And if she leaves now, whose stomach shall we wash with this medicine?'[18]

The uncle's question, delivered in earnest, received a peak laugh from the Project audience. On the surface the humor attempt trades on the false possibility that there might be an alternative candidate, which is laughably beside the point. In context of the Project performance, though, it is the inference of direct treatment by family members to Eulalie's stomach and, perhaps, a mental image of what her reaction might be, that triggers amusement. African-born spectators might be familiar with such rites, but they and everyone else in the theater would recognize the extent to which Western social codes and medical practices would render such an image incongruous. The audience also knows that Eulalie remains unaware of the family's misconception about her reproductive viability. We can only imagine how she would respond to the news *and* the treatment.

Eventually, Esi Kom confronts her son about the pregnancy issue, voicing her inescapable conclusion that Eulalie's 'womb has receded':

> ATO: But her womb has not receded!
> ESI: What are you telling me?
> ATO: If we wanted children, she would have given birth to some.
> ESI: *Ei*, everyone should come and listen to this. I have not heard anything like it before ... Human beings deciding when they must have children? Meanwhile, where is God?'[19]

It should be apparent in this instance that contemporary Western thinking would be more likely to allow that two humans are entitled to plan and control reproduction, or to decline childbearing altogether. The utter dismissal of such a possibility from Esi Kom's grounding throws up a double-sided defamiliarization, bluntly articulated from one side and revelatory from the other.

Most Western-born spectators do not have an intellectual awareness – let alone a lived awareness – of the cultural codes whose contravention is intended to cause amusement. Umberto Eco observes that, like tragedy, comedy cannot help but root itself in the rules of social and cultural behavior in force at a given time and place. Conflict usually arises from some violation of those rules. The difference, Eco indicates, is that in comedy, 'the broken frame must be *presupposed* but *never spelled out.*'[20] This is why comedy can be difficult to process for someone outside the text's presumed home-group: The cultural practices and social codes are taken for granted by the stage world. Given the African orientation of *Dilemma*, an out-group spectator – an Irish person or any other Westerner – would stand to learn something about those codes directly from the stage world. Perhaps more importantly, the depth of African laughter attests to a hard-wired resonance in the in-group's bodied circuitry. It might be suggested that there was a similar sense of reciprocal discovery due to comic ironizing in *Kings* in which African spectators might have felt the rumblings of some striking defamiliarizations about the Irish audience's past and present.

The theater audience is a most complex being, with a collective relationship to the phenomenal activities transpiring on the stage. We in the audience are not a collection of hermetically-sealed consciousnesses, nor do we break down so neatly into in-groups and out-groups as I may have suggested. Herbert Blau considers an audience 'not so much a mere con-gregation of people as a body of thought and desire.'[21] It may seem that the vectors of thought and desire circulating in the room of Arambe's productions have forced me to observe so generally and disclaim so stren-uously as to leave precious little by way of meaningful conclusion. It is, alas, the nature of theater and of humor.

What is interesting about these productions, however, is their exposure of sedimentations in humorous resonance for a home audience in a new home, and for the host audience around them. When existing texts are actualized for a body of bodies like Dublin's multicultural audience, the two dominant cultures in the room may well learn something about themselves. More importantly, they have recourse to learn more about one another. What Eco infers without actually observing, is that by watching a comedy on stage *and attending to the audience laughter* the culturally uninitiated can learn quite a lot about another in-group. We may also find that our respective in-groups discover areas of overlapping experience, and that there is no better basis on which to build a new, embracing sense of cultural identity than by laughing together.

Notes

1 Alfred Schutz, *On Phenomenology and Social Relations*, ed. Helmut R. Wagner (Chicago: University of Chicago, 1970), 73–5.

2 Henri Bergson, 'Laughter,' in *Comedy*, ed. by Wylie Sypher (Baltimore, MD: Johns Hopkins University, 1980 [1900]), 59–190, 64.

3 Norman Holland, *Laughing: A Psychology of Humor* (Ithaca, NY: Cornell University, 1982), 198.

4 Schutz, 1970, 87.

5 Patrice Pavis, 'Introduction: Towards a Theory of Interculturalism in Theatre?' in *The Intercultural Performance Reader*, ed. Patrice Pavis (London: Routledge, 1996), 1–21, 3.

6 Jimmy Murphy, *The Kings of the Kilburn High Road*, in *Two Plays* (London: Oberon, 2001), 7–66, 12.

7 Linda Hutcheon, *Irony's Edge: The Theory and Politics of Irony* (London: Routledge, 1994), 60 (emphasis in original).

8 Murphy, 2001, 17.

9 *Ibid.*, 11.

10 *Ibid.*

11 *Ibid.*, 21.

12 'New Irish' has been applied journalistically to immigrant populations from Africa, Asia, and Eastern Europe.

13 Lloyd W. Brown, *Women Writers in Black Africa* (Westport, CT: Greenwood Press, 1981), 85.

14 Ama Ata Aidoo, *The Dilemma of a Ghost*, in *The Dilemma of a Ghost and Anowa* (Harlow: Longman, 1987), 1–53, 14.

15 *Ibid.*, 17.

16 *Ibid.*

17 Chris Powell, 'A Phenomenological Analysis of Humour in Society,' in *Humour in Society: Resistance and Control*, eds. Chris Powell and George E. C. Paton (Basingstoke: Macmillan, 1988), 86–105, 88.

18 Aidoo, 1987, 43.

19 *Ibid.*, 51.

20 Umberto Eco, 'Frames of Comic Freedom,' in *Carnival!*, ed. Thomas Sebeok (Berlin: Mouton, 1984), 1–9, 4 (emphasis in original).

21 Herbert Blau, *The Audience* (Baltimore, MD: Johns Hopkins University, 1990), 25.

18
Parading Multicultural Ireland: Identity Politics and National Agendas in the 2007 St Patrick's Festival

Holly Maples

The Dublin St Patrick's Day Festival Parade conjures in the popular imagination images of green-clad participants, groups of Irish dancers, and marching bands giving a performance of imagined Irishness. In 2007, however, along with the usual Irish school children, tidy town pageants, and Irish American marching bands which have dominated the parade since its inception in 1996,[1] 650,000 spectators came out to see Brazilian samba bands, African drummers, and a host of Irish and immigrant community groups. The Dublin City Council and St Patrick's Festival City Fusion 2007 pageant, Citychange, addressed 'the challenges faced and contributions made by the new citizens from all corners of the globe to the city.'[2] The cultural diversity amongst participants was evidence of the Festival organizers' aim to increase the presence of the 'New Ireland' in its parade.

The St Patrick's Festival is a performance of contradictions. Both professional and amateur, the Festival is funded by the Dublin City Council as a highly visible public relations project to celebrate the city for tourist and local audiences; however, it is also a community-based project devised in collaboration with local groups. In 2007, I worked as a performance facilitator and costume coordinator for City Fusion. Working with fellow artists and immigrant community groups, we attempted to devise a performative representation of our participative *fusion* of cultures, and represent the New Dublin through iconic images of a city undergoing widespread social change. This chapter examines the transformation of contemporary Irish cultural identity as enacted through the collaboration of local Irish and immigrant community participants in the 2007 Festival. Though the City Fusion pageant was granted the 2007 Chairman's Award for its interpretation of a modern, multicultural Ireland, the combination of professional artists and community groups remained fraught with tension over how Citychange presented the many cultures represented. While Dublin City Council and City Fusion concentrated on the merging of cultures reflecting the 'New Irish identity' of Dublin in the 2000s, many of the communities themselves were more concerned with presenting their own distinct national heritage to the public. By documenting the creative process behind the City Fusion pageant, the following analysis considers the politics behind City Fusion's parading of an evolving Ireland.

St Patrick's Day: A festival of 'malleability'

Parades in honor of St Patrick began not in Ireland, but in North America in the late eighteenth century as a public platform for both the establishment of, and resistance to, civic allegiances for Irish American community groups.[3] Since the formation of the Irish Free State in the 1920s, the national holiday has been celebrated through small-scale events, while the parades in Dublin were made up primarily of school groups and marching bands. Despite complaints in the 1980s and early 1990s that the Irish parades did not engage with the local community, Frank Magee of the Dublin Tourism organization defended the event in 1993 by proclaiming: 'Our function is to promote Dublin as a tourist destination, not necessarily to entertain the people of Dublin.'[4] In November 1995, however, the Irish government decided to change the country's traditional celebrations of St Patrick's Day as a part of a double effort to create a new initiative revitalizing the increasingly competitive tourist industry and promote participation from the local community. Orchestrated by the newly appointed artistic director Rupert Murray, the St Patrick's Festival premiered as a four-day event celebrating Irish culture and identity, culminating in a large-scale parade through Dublin city center. The Department of Arts, Sport, and Tourism argued that the event was 'designed to evoke celebration and pride among our people and extend a genuine Irish welcome to our visitors.'[5] The government also hired a designer to create a unified artistic aesthetic for the parade pageants and other Festival performance events.

Adaptation becomes tradition

Early domestic response to the parade was mixed. Many criticized it as the 'Americanization' of Ireland's national day, while others argued that it catered to tourist audiences, especially those from North America, and therefore lacked a local community presence.[6] Public skepticism became caught up in contemporary Irish debates over the increasing con-sumer culture of Celtic Tiger Ireland as well as the manufacturing of Irishness for an overseas market. However, in the years since the parade began, local community response has evolved. What was first seen as an international event created specifically to target international rather than national audiences has, in recent years, been increasingly embraced by the Irish public, including the previously scorned public displays of Irishness by the tourist community. As Miriam Lord acknowledged in 2007:

> For years, they came searching for that authentic Irish experience, decked from head to toe in green tat, ready to blend in with the natives – just as the man from the tourist board had promised. Whereupon the locals enjoyed a good sneer at their expense. ... The only surprise on Saturday was that the Taoiseach didn't arrive at the GPO grandstand wearing a 'Kiss me, I'm Irish and Running for Election' hat.[7]

Despite the supposed 'Americanization' of St Patrick's Day, the reappropriation of the St Patrick's Festival in Dublin has included changes to the style of the parade itself. Ever a site of transformation and hybridity, the parade in Dublin has become more adaptive and performative than its American counterpart. The large-scale New York City St Patrick's Day parade is a formal affair, as John T. Ridge describes, where 'the horse-mounted police come clattering along followed by the unmistakable sound of the brass band with the 69th Regiment.'[8] The solemnity and military style of the parading (mostly) Irish American members of the police force and well-known figures of the Ancient Order of Hibernians in New York City has been reappropriated in Ireland to reflect the changes to the country. A mixture of carnival, pageants, and parade events from a variety of other traditions, including Caribbean, Brazilian, and African, have added new life to the marching figures found in the US holiday.

  Like other outdoor Irish spectacles, such as Macnas's Galway Arts Festival parade, the expanding St Patrick's Festival incorporates street performance, clowning, puppeteering, carnival, and other performances of cultural hybridity. Subverting any solemnity found in the parade, the 2007 City Fusion pageant included a large-scale dance choreographed by Nigerian-born entertainer Dr Rhumba, performed by all 250 participants at strategic points throughout the parade. Another headline event during the 2007 Festival was Barabbas theatre company's *40 Songs of Green*, which was a tongue-in-cheek, self-reflexive 'musical celebration of "Irishness" played by 200 singers and five Barabbas actors/clowns.'[9] The Festival negotiated the slippery domain of public displays of Irishness, strongly located in St Patrick's Day imaginings, by presenting more abstract images of the nation in the Festival Pageant, allowing performances to acknowledge and subvert notions of 'Staged Irishry' during the event. In this way, though influenced by North American culture, the Dublin St Patrick's Day parade has been subsumed by the changes to Dublin and reflects on the hybrid exchange of cultures affecting the modern Irish landscape.

Immigration and the new Ireland

The 1990s brought drastic socioeconomic change to Ireland with the establishment of the European Union in 1993 and the 'Celtic Tiger' boom, beginning in the mid-1990s.[10] Ireland's population began to grow for the first time in decades through immigration and a decline in emigration. The 2006 Census estimated that over 420,000 non-Irish nationals were living in Ireland – a nearly 100 per cent increase from 224,000 in 2002.[11] The resulting changes to the social fabric of Irish life have given rise to a number of debates over social inclusion, multiculturalism, and globalization.[12]

Ireland's changing social topography has provided a theme for recent national events, festivals, and public performances. Though some critics balked at the seeming incongruity of celebrating the new immigrant cultures on a day traditionally devoted to the celebration of Irish heritage, the St Patrick's Day Parade – both in Ireland and abroad – has traditionally offered a public site for the performance of communal understandings of identity. Joseph Roach asserts that public performances such as parades provide valuable sites for the establishment and revision of collective identity.[13] Roach develops Benedict Anderson's notion of the nation as an 'imagined community,' a symbolic space formed by its members through public imaginings of identity. As Anderson states, 'all communities larger than primordial villages of face-to-face contact (and perhaps even these) are imagined.'[14] Public performances such as festivals and parades aid in the construction of national identity. Through such community-building devices, national images take form and spread, giving the wider community collective understandings of the nation.

Parades have been used by immigrant communities for generations to symbolically fuse new cultures to those of the status quo, as well as to subvert the hegemonic culture through highly visible performances of difference. Joanne Schneider argues that 'parade commentators stress unity and community self-identification,'[15] while collective civic performances continue to provide public platforms to display and celebrate communal identity for a society. Ireland has an established tradition of using parades as sites for the community to negotiate issues of identity politics and societal change. Christie Fox argues that Irish parades use entertainment and often abstract methods to explore relevant issues. 'Grounded in local, topical themes, the parades can provide the audience with alternative means to interact with current societal problems.'[16] Social and economic change has greatly influenced the Irish community's reflections on the nation, turning cultural presentations of Irishness into contested sites of performance. Thus, since 1996, the Dublin St Patrick's Festival has become a *locus operandi* for manifestations of communal anxiety from a society undergoing rapid social change.

City Fusion

City Fusion 2007 explored issues of identity and multiculturalism in a general way through the thematic structures of the pageant and on a more specific level with community-led workshops. Though the entire Dublin St Patrick's Day Parade had in the past included performance groups from other countries and cultures, City Fusion, the pageant commissioned by the Festival and the Dublin City Council, incorporated professional designers and performance facilitators to work exclusively with Dublin school groups to create the pageant. After the tenth anniversary of the St Patrick's Festival Parade in 2006, City Fusion decided to change their pageant to include adult immigrant community groups and celebrate the 'New Dublin' in the 'official' pageant. The impetus behind the project was to investigate the impact immigration has on the Irish community and examine how diverse cultures can coexist, without destroying individual cultures. In a documentary about City Fusion, Laura Garbataviciute Down, a member of the Lithuanian Association, narrates the aims of the project:

> Ireland is a country, someone said, small enough to see its own borders ... When those borders opened up, and the faces, customs and languages of the small island multiplied rapidly, some wondered if this country was perhaps too small to meet the needs of so many.[17]

City Fusion created a participatory pageant involving 16 immigrant and Irish community groups charged with designing a story of the

'New Dublin' through an examination of the question: 'How [can] a country of this size absorb so many influences yet maintain its own identity?'[18] By combining different community groups in a single pageant, the Festival aimed to celebrate difference but also create unity within the St Patrick's Day parade.

Designed to complement the Parade's overall theme of 'Legendary,' City Fusion's 2007 pageant, Citychange,[19] created a utopian legend of the New Dublin. The pageant involved thematic sections indicating a new immigrant's journey from being a 'stranger' to the city and its culture, to a final integration into the community. Designed through a storyboard by the pageant's artistic director, Kareen Pennyfather, different community groups helped design and construct individual sections. At its opening, the audience was invited to think of themselves as strangers in a city: upon arrival, the invisible immigrants have to negotiate the dragons of bureaucracy (red tape, visas, immigration, etc.), after which they find themselves caught in the rhythm of a city they do not understand. As the strangers navigate through the pulse of the people, they come face to face with the powerful towers of the city itself. Slowly, the immigrants begin to understand the city's rhythm and adapt to life in their new environment. The pageant ends with the successful integration of the stranger into society, celebrated with a dance led by the Carnival Queen (Eloho Eqwuterai from the Sporasi Asylum Seekers Organization) and the Chameleons (performed by two other Sporasi members), representing a constantly evolving city. Eqwuterai was presented as the focal point of the final 'celebration' section of the pageant, while the Chameleons danced samba with large, green 'backpacks' and costumes symbolizing the 'hybridity' of Dublin. Each community group's contribution created a whole of woven performances.

As the first year of a project intended to continue annually, organizers of City Fusion encountered different challenges working with adult community groups from those encountered with school groups. The mixture of professional and amateur participants raised many ethical questions over issues of representation and authenticity. Though the groups performed in the parade themselves, their input and cultural contributions were interpreted and adapted by the professional designers working on the project. Despite the encouragement by the organizers of group participation in the creative process, designing the large-scale, high-profile parade event mainly fell to project designer Vanessa Daws, artistic director Kareen Pennyfather, and their team of facilitators. This formula worked well with school children, who were used to following the advice of their leaders, but the complex issues of identity politics and community allegiance found within the immigrant groups raised concerns previously unknown by the Festival staff. Except for the Polish community organization, Arts Polonia, which relies on amateur artistic creations to promote Polish culture in Ireland, and the Igbo Association, which, though made up of nonprofessional amateurs, perform the Igbo ritual of the 'Masquerade' with dances, drumming, and costumes from their native Nigeria, most participants were new to artistic design and performance. Despite the contribution of amateur groups in weekly facilitated workshops, most of the costumes, puppets, hats, and backpacks were completed by professional artists.

Working as a performance facilitator for City Fusion in 2007, I had several concerns over the conflicting agendas between the professional artists (including myself) and some of the participating immigrant community groups. Painfully aware of the stereotyping of Irishness associated with St Patrick's Day, and reluctant to advertise corporate sponsorship, Dublin City Council refused to allow logos of any kind in the parade itself, including banners, signs, national colors, or obvious signifiers from the various cultures involved.[20] The multicultural concept behind the City Fusion project highlighted the mix of cultures involved without offering any distinction among the cultures themselves. As a result, the Festival presented abstract images of cultures through an artistic aesthetic largely based on notions of interculturalism which directly contradicted the primary motivation of many of the immigrant community groups, who desired to highlight the uniqueness of their culture rather than fuse with others in an amalgamated whole.

Despite the focus on a fusion of cultures by the Festival organizers, some of the community groups found ways to subvert the overall theme of merging cultures in their participation in the parade. The Arts Polonia group had a strong sense of collective identity within their organization and wanted to highlight their participation in the parade with the specificity of their membership in the Polish community in Ireland. The group had their own photographer and press consultant to advertise their experience to the Dublin Irish and Polish communities, and constantly vocalized, through their leader Monica Sapielak, their concerns with City Fusion. The group's role was to represent the new globalized 'fusion' cities in the Pageant, with the women wearing elaborate hats representing famous buildings such as the Eiffel Tower, the Sydney Opera House, and other signature buildings. However, members of the

Polish group were concerned over the cultural ambiguity of their costumes. The predominantly female group was dressed as 'Welcoming
Women,' in costumes inspired by Spanish flamenco dancers. The
group insisted that the dresses be made of colors evoking Polish traditions and that the men portray traditional horse-mounted knights,
known as the Lajkonik, a powerful image of the Polish city of Krakow.
Due to the abstract nature of their alterations to the parade figures, the
professional designers found themselves able to allow for these 'Polish'
additions to the pageant because the largely non-Polish audience
would not necessarily associate figures on horseback or red costumes
with Poland. For Arts Polonia, however, the integration of these symbols into the pageant was designed to signify to the parade's Polish
audience the group's nationality, thus communicating different codified
meanings to an audience in the know: a subtle presentation of national
identity in the parade for a specific national community.

Members of the Lithuanian Association were also determined to display
their identity through subtle subversions throughout the construction
and performance process. Inspired by a choral section of the musical
Oliver, Kareen Pennyfather wished to create a choreographed celebration
of diversity in the urban landscape through the performance. Originally
paired up with another group from the Warrenmount School in Dublin,
the Association adamantly desired to be on their own, maintaining a
strong sense of collective identity in the pageant.[21] Tasked with performing the rhythm of urban life by portraying workers in the city, they
refused to depict blue-collar workers such as maids, construction workers,
or waiters in the pageant as they did not want to be stereotyped as
unskilled laborers. Eventually the facilitators decided, with the group's
approval, to include characters from their actual trades and professions
– a chemist and two office workers, as well as bakers, post office workers,
and mothers with babies. The carnivalesque style of the parade exaggerated these characters' features to perform the bustle of city life. Characters burlesqued Dublin society through their portrayal of the corporate
world with overworked computer personnel and 'PR ladies' with over-
sized mobile phones.

Female shoppers and 'Yummy Mummies' (wealthy, celebrity women
whose babies are seen as accessories) represented the consumer-oriented
culture. The parade's social commentary on Dublin culture, though
embraced by the group, created some concern that their section of the
pageant was not 'Lithuanian' enough. The group wanted to include a
national food, *cepelinai*,[22] for the bakers to carry, as well as Lithuanian
signs advertising their own cultural association to audience members.

Figure 8   Members of the Lithuanian Association perform the rhythm of urban life in the 2007 St Patrick's Festival, Dublin. Courtesy St Patrick's Festival.

Extreme consternation occurred when the cepelinai – which had been painstakingly painted the *right* shade of grey by the group – were repainted a bright yellow by the City Fusion designer, who felt that the pastries did not look 'carnival' enough. The anger expressed by the group over this seemingly minor issue illustrates the importance for many of the immigrant communities of performing a preferred, visible heritage. In addition, despite being told they were not allowed to wear Lithuanian flags, or banners, scarves, and t-shirts displaying the country's national colors, in the parade, some of the participants rebelled against this dictum by wrapping Lithuanian scarves around their necks, allowing them to peek out of their elaborate 'city worker' costumes. This understated rebellion against Festival rules emphasizes the loyalty of Lithuanian Association members to the Lithuanian parade audience members through the signification of markers of origin and belonging, which remained largely unnoticed by non-Lithuanian viewers.

Despite these tensions, many participants were not concerned over issues of representation. The smaller community groups, such as the Indonesian Association (five participants) and the Nigerian Association (two participants) were able to enjoy all aspects of the process without misgivings over representation in the parade. These reactions indicate that concern with cultural visibility in the parade came more from larger, established organizations with strong notions of identity distinct from the St Patrick's Festival.

For some of the new immigrants, the project also provided a space to get to know others from their own country. The Polish section of the *Evening Herald*'s coverage of the 2007 Festival describes why a new member of the Arts Polonia group joined the Parade:

> It's Michał's first time here. He only came here, hasn't even started a job yet. He found out about the project, also that a Polish group will be participating, and that this is where Poles meet.[23]

The aims of the participants are not only to provide the 'first step in bringing together some of the new and established communities of Dublin'[24] as the St Patrick's Festival states in its official documentary of the project, but for Michał and others like him, it also provides opportunities to foster support networks in home communities that can help immigrants adapt to their new country.

For the multinational asylum seekers' organization Sporasi, the project also brought together people from different communities and helped them find ways to meet members of the larger Dublin community. Sporasi participant Eloho Egwuterai describes the difficulties inherent in the asylum seeker's experience and how important projects like the St Patrick's Festival remain to her and her peers:

> As a new person in the country, you can't work, you can't do anything, you just get yourself involved with things like this because at the end of the day you get papers or your permit to stay and work and you'll be like a fish out of water. I had my fears about integrating with white people because you share different cultures, you feel you're so different, but ... [when you do] projects with them like this, you realize you share a lot of things in common.[25]

The project aimed to foster exchanges between cultures, and many of the participants found that they were able not only to participate in the St Patrick's Festival, but to also find other arts-based projects to get involved in after the Festival ended. Of the 16 organizations involved in the 2007 parade, many of the groups participated again in 2008, making the City Fusion community project a long-term event that can continue to forge connections among the different community groups in the years to come.

While the St Patrick's Festival organizers desired to create a pageant celebrating the fusion of cultures in a ubiquitous multicultural whole, many of the groups themselves desired to strengthen ties to their own community as well as assert individual cultural heritage through public display. The tension between universal signs of post-national society favored by the artists and the need for iconic displays of national identity by the community groups provided an arena for the creation and loss of identity inherent in the performance of multiculturalism. That this occurred during a parade in honor of St Patrick's Day, a holiday traditionally intended for a specific national community, illustrates widespread anxiety in Ireland around issues of cultural identity, nationalism, immigration, globalization, and the performance of Irishness on the Irish social stage. Cultural signifiers, no matter how subtle, indicating unique cultural heritages were consistently sought by the Polish, Lithuanian, Igbo Associations, and others to celebrate not a *fusion* of cultures, but particular contributions to the Festival. For the Lithuanians and the St Patrick's Festival staff, the rushed repainting of the *cepelinai* to their appropriate color exemplifies the constant negotiation needed for the representation of collective identity among communities in the performance of multicultural Ireland in the St Patrick's Festival.

Notes

1 The Dublin City Council created the St Patrick's Day Festival in November 1995, with the first parade occurring on St Patrick's Day 1996.
2 St Patrick's Festival, 'St Patrick's Festival and Dublin City Council Launch City Fusion,' press release, March 2007.
3 Jane Gladden Kelton, 'The New York St Patrick's Day Parade: Invention of Contention and Consensus,' *The Drama Review* 29 (3) (1985): 93–105.
4 Frank Magee, quoted in Kathy Sheridan, 'Don't Hail, St Patrick, on Our Glorious £500,000 Parade,' *Irish Times*, 15 March 1996, http://www.ireland.com/ newspaper/ ireland/1996/0316/96031600066.html (accessed 3 March 2008).
5 'Speech by John O'Donoghue, T.D., Minister for Arts, Sport and Tourism, at the launch of the St Patrick's Festival 2007 in Royal Hibernian Academy, Ely Place, Dublin 2 on Wednesday 14th February at 6.00 pm,' Department of Arts, Sport and Tourism Press Release, 14 February 2007, http://www.arts-sport-tourism.gov.ie/publications/release.asp?ID=1873 (accessed 2 March 2008).
6 Kevin Myers, 'An Irishman's Diary,' *Irish Times,* 15 March 1996, http:// www.ireland.com/newspaper/opinion/1996/0315/96031500103.html (accessed 3 March 2008).
7 Miriam Lord, 'Natives Join New Irish in Jamboree of Silly Hats,' *Irish Times*, 19 March 2007, http://www.ireland.com/newspaper/ireland/2007/0319/ 1173880550031. html (accessed 29 March 2007).
8 John T. Ridge, *The St Patrick's Day Parade in New York* (New York: St Patrick's Day Parade Committee, 1988), 172–3.

9   St Patrick's Festival Press Release 2008.

10 The Irish economy transformed from being ranked 22nd per capita among the world's industrial nations in 1993 to 8th in 1999. See Patrick Honohan and Brendan Walsh, 'Catching up with the Leaders: The Irish Hare,' *Brookings Papers on Economic Activity*, 1 (2002), 1–77.

11 The 2006 Census reported population growth of 8.1 percent since the 2002 Census, the highest increase on record. The fastest-growing category was non-Irish/UK EU nationals, along with Africans and Asians. Polish nationals numbered 63,300 while the number of Lithuanian nationals was 24,600. Overall, non-Irish made up 10 per cent of the usual resident population indicating a nationality in 2006. See Central Statistics Office, 'Census 2006: Central Demographic Results' (Dublin: Stationery Office, 2007), 25.

12 Despite the politics of inclusion promoted by the Fianna Fáil government since 1995, the integration of recent immigrants has fostered uneasy relations between diverse social groups. The increasing numbers of asylum seekers and migrant workers in Ireland during the early 2000s caused a change of senti-ment toward immigration in the Republic. See Department of Justice, Equality and Law Reform, *Strategy Statements: 2003-2005* (Dublin: Stationery Office, 2003), 60–5.

13 Joseph Roach, *Cities of the Dead: Circum-Atlantic Performance* (New York: Columbia University Press, 1996).

14 Benedict Anderson, *Imagined Communities: Reflections on the Origin and Spread of Nationalism* (London: Verso, 1983), 5–7.

15 Joanne Schneider, 'Defining Boundaries, Creating Contacts: Puerto Rico and Polish Presentations of Group Identity Through Ethnic Parades,' *The Journal of Ethnic Studies*, 18, 1 (Spring 1990): 33–57, 36.

16 Christie Fox, 'Creating Community: Macnas' Galway Arts Festival Parade, 2000,' *New Hibernia Review* 7 (2) (Summer 2003): 19–37, 20.

17 Laura Garbataviciute Down, quoted in *Future Legend: The Story of City Fusion an Intercultural Initiative for St Patrick's Festival 2007*, dir. Raven. 2007. DVD. Producer: St Patrick's Festival and Dublin City Council, Ireland.

18 *Ibid.*

19 The St Patrick's Festival Pageant is known as City Fusion. Each year, a subtitle reflects the overall Dublin St Patrick Parade's theme. In 2007, this subtitle was Citychange.

20 Due to complaints from all of the community groups requesting a public display of their participation in the parade, eventually the City Fusion facil-itators successfully negotiated with the St Patrick's Festival and the Dublin City Council the creation of a banner that appeared at the beginning of the Fusion pageant naming all of the participating organizations.

21 The school group, which eventually thinned to just three participants, per-formed directly in front of the Lithuanian Association.

22 *Cepelinai* are a kind of potato cake served at festivals and on national holidays.

23 Trans. Maria O'Reilly, 'Narodowe Święto, Topienie Tęsknoty Za Krajem I Dzban Patryka,' *Evening Herald*, 16 March 2007, http://www.artpolonia.org/press/16HN057.pdf (accessed 3 March 2008).

24 Laura Garbataviciute Down, quoted in *Future Legend*.

25 Eloho Eqwuterai, quoted in *Future Legend*.

Index

249

Printed and bound by CPI Group (UK) Ltd, Croydon, CR0 4YY